Women in Developing

Making Visible the Invisible

Women in Developing Economies:

Making Visible the Invisible

Berg/UNESCO

First published in 1993 by

Berg Publishers, Inc.

Editorial offices:
221 Waterman Street, Providence, RI 02906, U.S.A.
150 Cowley Road, Oxford, OX4 1JJ, UK

in co-operation with

**the United Nations Educational, Scientific and Cultural
Organization**
7 Place de Fontenoy
75700 Paris, France

© UNESCO 1993

The authors are responsible for the choice and the presentation of
the facts contained in this book and for the opinions expressed therein,
which are not necessarily those of UNESCO and do not commit the
Organization.

Library of Congress Cataloging-in-Publication Data
  Women in developing economies : making visible the invisible
     p. cm.
     Edited by Joycelin Massiah
     Includes bibliographical references and index.
     ISBN 0–85496–345–6 (cloth),—ISBN 0–85496–346–4 (paper).—
  ISBN 92–3–102807–3 (Unesco)
     1. Women in development—Developing countries. 2. Informal
  sector (Economics)—Developing countries. I. Massiah, Joycelin.
  HQ1240.5.D44W662 1993   92-24168
  305.42'09172'4—dc20   CIP

British Library Cataloguing in Publication Data
A CIP catalogue record for this book is available from the British Library.

Printed in the United States by E. B. Edwards Brothers, Ann Arbor, MI.

Table of contents

Mrs. Joycelin Massiah is a sociologist and the Director of the Institute of Social and Economic Research (Eastern Caribbean) of the University of the West Indies in Bridgetown (Barbados). She specializes in population, fertility, women and development. With UNESCO she has published articles, a book, and participated in many meetings.

El Amouri Institute, located in Tunis (Tunisia), is a Center of Applied Psychology specializing in population and fertility problems, women and development.

Mrs. Vicky Okine is a sociologist working at the National Council on Women and Development in Ghana.

Marie-Dominique De Suremain is an urbanist and the Head of ENDA (Environmental Development in the Third World) Latin America located in Bogota (Columbia).

Singamma Sreenivasan Foundation, Bangalore (India). This Foundation has always taken a keen interest in the welfare of women. The main interests of this Foundation are women and development, strategies of the poor, traditional wisdom, environment and development.

Preface

This publication is a selection of studies and articles aimed to sensitize planners and decision-makers to the invisible socio-economic and cultural contribution of women in developing countries. Even after twenty years of debates about the invisible work of women, very little has been done to collect information, analyse its contribution to national economies, not to mention to give women adequate financial support or training. Women's productivity remains therefore at a very low level.

The need is obvious to gather information to make women's work visible and to train planners to become familiar with women's issues and develop measures to include such information in national plans. If we now find some changes in the attitudes of planner and decision-makers concerning the impact of women's contribution to development, it is because they are beginning to understand that the informal sector — and women's work — is the motor of national economies especially in the developing world.

Due to difficulties encountered in development policies, the role played by the informal sector[1] — also called unstructured sector, unorganized or traditional sector — in food self-security, in commerce and in services is being rediscovered. In fact, 'observations show that these rapidly expanding activities contribute in Africa to the majority of urban jobs, provide goods and services essential to actor's way of life, distribute incomes that are higher than those of the rural areas, are often comparable to those of the modern sector and meet the needs of the masses for food, clothing, transport and leisure'.[2] Even if it does not constitute an alternative development model, 'yet it does reveal potentials and dynamisms that make it an essential element in a resumption of growth and the formation of a basic social, technical and economic fabric'.[3] In the present economic recession which in the developing world is instead a crisis situation, it would be wise to utilize better the circuit of production, accumulation and distribution of the informal sector.

Various studies also show that it plays a strategic role between urban and rural areas and between agricultural and industrial systems. One can consider it as the necessary step for transition from the traditional to the modern world; a period that economists wrongly thought brief but which now is recognized to be of much longer duration.

The informal sector and the role of women therein has thus to be taken into account in national policies and in development planning. It is urgent to respond to what can be done at macro and micro levels to let this sector survive and even be strengthened. New quantitative data as well as a good knowledge of the social milieu and networks is necessary. Obstacles which reduce the productivity of this sector as access to training, to credit, to inputs, to information, etc. should be identified and overcome. The concerns of the 'silent women', the majority of the poor and the rural population, have to be highlighted and analysed. Some excellent methodological suggestions are given in Chapter I on the priorities of women in Caribbean development.

But rural and urban women work in the informal sector, and today, none should under-evaluate their role in survival strategies. Chapter III gives a good example of this for Ghana as does Chapter II for Tunisia.

After years of debate, many economists now admit that women are the basis of the subsistence economy. Their productive role inside the family is no longer questioned, thus making obsolete the economic theories of the beginning of the century which considered women as a consumer only. Thanks to the contribution of women of the developing countries in reducing the effects of hunger and the economic crisis, recognition is coming that women who are not working in the formal economy are participating fully towards development. This recognition also helps women in the North who work either at home or informally to be recognized as valuable contributors to the family's economy.

The production and distribution of goods by small urban units with low capital using rudimentary techniques and poorly qualified manpower create jobs, even if at low salaries, and produce goods and services at low costs which they make available to local populations. This sector, by escaping from social and legal restrictions, provides also one of the few opportunities for the poorest women and minorities to make money rapidly from only a small investment. Women working in this sector also lessen the negative effects of the economic crisis and manage to surmount the deficiencies in state services whether it be access to water, garbage collection, sewage facilities, etc. Chapter IV illustrates such remarkable work by poor women in towns in Latin America.

If we can begin to evaluate more easily the invisible work of women in

There, women's informal work in the subsistence economy and in cash crop production is little studied — an important lacuna because, as a result of debt, national food security is becoming more and more precarious as countries are obliged to reduce their imports. For many countries, therefore, serious efforts have to be made in order to achieve basic food needs based on a policy using local human resources and local agricultural production. Women's food production needs to be supported by increasing its productivity and facilitating the transportation of food surpluses to towns. Neither the food economy nor the material situation of women in rural areas can improve until women are given national production quotas and sufficient channels to sell their products at prices which will not suffer high variations. The improvement of the road network, the transportation price of goods, price and market regulation, are all key elements to be taken into account.

In order to attain sustainable development, the often forgotten social and cultural dimensions have to be systematically integrated into development planning. Tradition and modernity are not conflicting concepts. Several good examples of utilizing traditional wisdom for modernization are given for India in Chapter V. New types of actions which will use existing informational networks, and not destroy them, must be elaborated by planners in close co-operation with social scientists. In fact, such integrated methods cannot be conceived without a concrete perception of the social and cultural milieu.

How can we make the contribution of women visible and more productive? How can we better utilize human resources that are often illiterate? How can we build on traditional wisdom in order to modernize? How can we reduce poverty? How can we prevent women from being excluded from the more lucrative activities of the informal sector? These are questions that planners and decision-makers will have to face over the short term and to which much thought will be given. UNESCO hopes that this publication will somehow further the debate.

Notes

1. The informal sector can be defined statistically as the set of activities that falls outside empirical means of investigation: it consists of producers working without a fixed location, who do not pay licences or taxes, are excluded from social regulations and/or keep no accounts. (Hugon): Women and development planning in Africa: the role of the informal sector, UNESCO SHS/SDV FEM 3.
2. Women and development planning in Africa: the role of the informal sector, UNESCO SHS/SDV FEM 3.
3. Idem.

Chapter I

Indicators for planning for women in Caribbean development

Joycelin Massiah

Introduction

The objective of this in-depth study is the better understanding of the socio-economic situation of women in the Commonwealth Caribbean and the identification of basic indicators for equipping planners to take appropriate measures to improve their quality of life.

The specific aims are to:

(i) review and analyse the latest national development plans and the programmes or actions therein for improving the quality of women's life in urban and rural areas;

(ii) synthesize women's problems and concerns as noted in various studies and surveys undertaken in the Caribbean territories chosen over the last five years in order to identify indicators; and to

(iii) analyse the informal networks created by women in order to identify measures that could be taken to reinforce and develop such networks.

To accomplish this, the study relies on available material from official and survey sources. No primary data collection was undertaken. Rather the methodology consisted essentially of a review of statistical and documentary literature, reflection on the wide range of seminars/discussions/workshops in which the author has participated over the years, and consultation with key women in the region and government officials in the base territory, Barbados.

Preparing this study provided an opportunity to reflect on the question 'Why are we, in 1989, still asking the same questions we asked in

1975 at the beginning of the UN Decade for Women?' The past two decades have witnessed a tremendous surge of activity in research, documentation, action programmes, organizational development, yet women in the Caribbean remain invisible in national development plans. Women in development is now firmly entrenched on the agenda of international donor agencies, even to the extent, in some cases, of rejecting proposals unable to identify significant benefits for women in target communities. Yet, in the Caribbean, planning authorities are still reluctant to accept gender as a development planning issue. Why has this attitude persisted?

The answers have been many, varied and by no means definitive. One set of answers revolves around the disjuncture between traditional planning processes and techniques, which focus on macro-economic issues, and gender planning, which seeks to ally different planning interventions to different gender needs. Until planners become alert to the differing roles of men and women in society and, consequently, to their differing needs, they will continue to assume that the 'trickle-down' approach they adopt will benefit all persons equally.

It is by now well documented that women around the world have not benefited from development efforts to the same extent as men. In many cases, their economic and social position has deteriorated markedly through poor planning and ill-conceived development projects. The Caribbean is no exception. On the contrary, recent trends in the international and regional economies have exacerbated the disadvantaged situation of Caribbean women. During the decade of the 1980s Caribbean economies have been characterized by falling export earnings, rising prices of imports, unstable exchange rates, increasing inflation, rapidly escalating public debt and increasing flight of capital. The real costs of these strains have fallen on the poorest sections of the population in the form of falling real wages, growing unemployment and higher costs of basic needs. Efforts to address these have taken the form of structural adjustment measures based on a development philosophy which advocates export-led growth. The particular package of measures adopted in the region has included reduction of public expenditure, movement from direct to indirect taxation, investment promotion, trade liberalization and privatization.

Available evidence suggests that Caribbean women bore the brunt of the economic crisis and suffered most severely from the structural adjustment measures introduced (Antrobus, 1989; Rivera, 1989). Because they have primary responsibility for the care of children, men, the sick and the elderly, women were the first line of defence as the men faced growing unemployment and the cost of living escalated. Household survival came to rely on women's productive labour, their earnings, and their domestic management skills to a greater extent than before. The price women paid in terms of their mental and physical health also became higher than it ever was.

Little, if any, of these matters can be found in national development plans in the region. Rather, women's issues continue to be interpreted as infant, childhood and maternal mortality and as social welfare programmes. For these some provision is included in the relevant sector of the plans. Anything else which may relate to women is considered the concern of the women's bureaux, for which minimal provision is made. But in neither case is there any effort to link women's issues to the wider economy, thus to the plans proposed to stimulate that economy.

Further, even though Caribbean territories actively supported and participated in the events of the UN Decade for Women, nothing in the planning documents reflects the many conceptual and methodological insights offered in the research produced. Of particular relevance was the realization that women are not only beneficiaries but also participants in development; that women's productive and reproductive work are integrally connected; and that women's issues require a multidisciplinary analytic and planning approach. Because planners have failed to acknowledge this and because they continue to rely on the terminology and methodology of economics, they continue to equate women's issues solely with welfare issues. That this should be continuing after two decades of knowledge accumulation and sharing reflects more than the influence of traditional methods of training, planning techniques and processes to which planners are accustomed. It reflects the perpetuation of a gender ideology which subordinates women's interests to those of men, which marginalizes women's activities and which fails to acknowledge the pivotal role played by women in the development and maintenance of society.

This raises the question of precisely what are these women's interests which should be reflected in development plans. This notion implies a certain communality of interest showed by women simply by virtue of their gender. But research repeatedly points to the differences between women in respect of age, socio-economic circumstances, ethnicity and so on. These differences necessarily shape the definition, articulation and policy responses to 'women's interests'. Recent work distinguishing between 'gender interests' and 'women's interests' and between 'practical gender interests' and 'strategic gender interests' provides an important conceptual tool for identifying the interest and needs of women generally and of particular groups of women (Molyneux, 1985; Moser, 1989; Young, 1988).[1]

Clarifying the variety of 'women's interests', however, assumes that the parameters of different groups of women are known. This brings us to the question of identifying 'silent' or invisible women whose concerns the study was asked to highlight. Who are these invisible women and what determines their invisibility? It is clear from the literature that the issue of women's invisibility has been discussed primarily in the context of the statistical invisibility of women's economic activity. The literature is equally clear on the point that economic activity represents but one as-

13

pect of the lives of women and one of the numerous characteristics by which women are differentiated. Identifying invisibility, therefore, like identifying women's interests, must recognize both the similarity and differences between women.

Invisibility may refer to women, their concerns or both. Its various forms may be recognized by women themselves, by external observers or both. Strategies to reduce invisibility (or increase visibility) vary across time, and between groups, both of which are affected by the prevailing socio-economic, cultural and political environment. Much depends on women's recognition of their own invisibility and their perception of the relative advantage to be gained from attaining high levels of visibility.

This raises the final question of the extent to which women perceive national development planning as a useful vehicle for meeting their practical needs and increasing their visibility. Related to that is the question of the extent to which women are prepared to unite around the common theme of gender interests in order to influence the national planning process. Whilst the issue really fell outside the scope of this study, closer collaboration of women's groups for this purpose is advocated as a strategy for the future.

Underlying each of these issues is the rapidly changing socio-economic environment of the region during the 1970s and 1980s. Changes have been initiated by both external and internal forces, sometimes by women themselves, more often not. These have inevitably affected women's circumstances and people's perceptions of and responses to those circumstances. Responses, whether at the individual, group or institutional level, have triggered direct or indirect effects which, in turn, have generated further change. The identification of 'women's problems and concerns' therefore needs to be placed in the context of this continually changing environment in which change occurs not in unilateral progression but in a continual process of ebb and flow, of challenge and response.

It is against this background that the present study argues that some of the momentum gained by research and action strategies of women has been lost by the inaction of planning authorities. However, creative use of information, communication and collaboration can serve to develop new approaches to planning which can serve to maintain and sustain further development which truly benefits women.

Recent studies on women in the Caribbean

Up until the late 1970s it would have been true to say that little research existed on women beyond that which focused on family structure and fertility patterns. Useful as these studies were, they did little to enhance our knowledge of the problems and concerns of women and the strategies they adopted to confront these concerns. The decade of the 1980s however, has witnessed a considerable change under the impetus of a number of regional institutions.

At the governmental level, the regional CARICOM Secretariat, in response to initiatives from CARIWA and recommendations of a Regional Plan of Action for women in the English-speaking Caribbean, established in 1978 the post of Nutritionist/Women's Affairs Officer in 1978.[2] Two years later, the post of Women's Affairs Officer was fully established, with the main objective of promoting the integration of women in Caribbean development. Since then the Women's Affairs Desk has been involved in an active regional programme based on five priority areas identified by national governments. Included amongst these areas are data collection, information dissemination and public education. In that connection, the CARICOM Women's Desk has promoted and supported research activities in a wide range of areas in consultation with relevant national, regional and international agencies.

At the non-governmental level, the CARIWA Regional Plan of Action had also called for the establishment, within the regional UWI, of a unit concerned with promoting women's issues. This unit — the Women and Development Unit (WAND) — came into being in 1976 as a unit within the Department of Extra Mural Studies to monitor the plan of action for the integration of women in the social and economic development of the Caribbean and to assist in programmes designed for its implementation.[3] WAND's initial concern with integrating women into development entailed the provision of short-term technical assistance, the development of pilot projects, consciousness raising and the promotion of collaboration between relevant groups and agencies (Yudelman, 1987). WAND has now shifted its focus towards a more activist stance in a search for alternative modes of development. Despite this shift, however, WAND has continued to pin its strategies for action on the basis of participatory research at the community level.

Also within the UWI, the Institute of Social and Economic Research (ISER) developed and implemented the first comprehensive project on Women in the Caribbean over the period 1979–82, marking the entry of women's issues into the academic programme of that University. One of the major follow-up activities to that project was the establishment of an inter-disciplinary programme of Women and Development Studies linking teaching, research and outreach in a modular system of teacher training, undergraduate and graduate teaching and outreach activity.

Another regional development, this time with an international dimension, has been the establishment in 1979/80 of the post of Women's Affairs Officer at the headquarters of UNECLAC in Trinidad and Tobago. This officer is responsible for ensuring the inclusion of women's issues in the sub-regional programmes of Headquarters by liaising with relevant regional and national programmes.

Finally, the year 1985 witnessed the creation of an independent association of feminist researchers and activists (CAFRA) 'committed to understanding the relationship between the oppression of women and other forms of exploitation in society — and working actively for change' (CAFRA, brochure). The major aim of CAFRA is to promote inter-relationship between research and action and to develop the feminist movement in the region by analysing women's problems from the perspective of race, class and sex and by analysing relations between men and women in non-capitalist and socialist societies. Unlike the CARICOM and UWI units, which are restricted to the Commonwealth Caribbean, CAFRA's activities embrace the Dutch, English, French and Spanish-speaking Caribbean.

Working together, separately or in collaboration with other agencies, the CARICOM and UWI units have been largely responsible for bringing women on to the development agenda of national governments, regional development agencies and the curricula of regional tertiary level academic institutions. They have adopted a range of strategies including formal and informal research, workshops, seminars, conferences, technical assistance to government and non-government agencies, all designed to ventilate the concerns of women and to develop programmes aimed at alleviating those problems. UNECLAC and CAFRA have been engaged in a number of research undertakings, the former on women traders, the latter on women in agriculture, and women's history. The studies undertaken by these four regional agencies have provided, and continue to provide, a wealth of information which has widened the knowledge base about women's participation in the development of the region.[4] Perhaps more importantly, the information they have uncovered has clearly demonstrated that alleviating the problems of women necessarily improves the situation of all persons in the community.

To illustrate the range of issues in the research of the 1980s, the following section focuses on three regional studies which demonstrate the progression in research as the examination of issues concerning women widened and deepened from micro to macro level in the search for a model linking the two levels. The Women in the Caribbean Project (WICP) was concerned with the search for theoretical and methodological strategies to reflect the micro-level reality of the lives of Caribbean women and to use results to develop guidelines for defining social policy towards women. The WAND/Population Council project was concerned with assessing the impact of rural development schemes on low-income households and the role of women. The PACCA project was concerned with the impact of international economic policies in the Caribbean and Central America and identifying an alternative development strategy, in the light of recent structural adjustment measures in the 1980s which have had most deleterious effects on women, especially poor women.

Women in the Caribbean project

This multidisciplinary study was conducted in 1979–82 under the auspices of the Institute of Social and Economic Research (Eastern Caribbean) (ISER(EC)) by a team of researchers from the UWI and the University of Guyana and covered the disciplines anthropology, demography, sociology, social psychology and political science (Massiah, 1986*a* and *b*). Data were collected in two phases — a documentary phase at regional level and an empirical phase at the national level. The former phase consisted of a literature review of the situation of women in the five areas of law, education, the family, politics, work and development. A study of perceptions of women gleaned from newspapers in Jamaica, Barbados, Trinidad and Tobago between 1838 and 1970 was also part of this first phase. The second consisted of a multi-level interviewing process involving a questionnaire survey of 1,600 women aged 20–64 in Barbados, Antigua and St. Vincent; life history interviews of a sub-sample of 38 women from the original sample; and sector studies exploring specific issues in Barbados, Guyana, Jamaica and the Eastern Caribbean. The various levels of interviewing produced a mix of quantitative and qualitative data linked by three themes — sources of livelihood, emotional support and power and authority.

The questionnaire survey concentrated initially on developing a socio-economic profile of respondents and locating them in their household contexts. Next, it focused on four major areas: education, family and kin, work, participation in group activities. In each case, the intent was not only to seek an indication of women's activity or experience but also to obtain their assessment of that experience. It was anticipated that the data generated could assist WID practitioners in the government and non-government sectors, planning units, statistical agencies and future researchers. To assist in the latter, the project developed a multi-media dissemination programme aimed at directing different aspects of the findings to different audiences. The target groups included planners, policy-makers, administrators of women's programmes, researchers, university students and the general public. The package included community and national workshops, a regional conference, a video tape recording, a synchro-slide production, published papers and reports.

Findings were reported and recommendations offered in a number of areas. In the area of education, data on levels of educational attainment, performance rates and extent of specialization suggest that Caribbean women have been proceeding through the educational system without much hindrance (McKenzie, 1986). However, it is equally clear that many women harbour unfulfilled aspirations especially in terms of their ability to transform their educational experience into significant and satisfying economic opportunities. They cherish ambitions for their children to achieve better education and better earning capacity than themselves, while at the same time accepting the limited options available to themselves. The project provided a number of recommendations relating to the formal school system, to vocational training, continuing education programmes, and public awareness programmes about women.

In the area of family and kin, a major finding is the high (about 40 per cent) proportion of households headed by women, the persistence of the idea of marriage as the ideal family form, the high value placed on motherhood, and the importance of kinship and friendship networks as a means of enabling the woman to fulfil her family responsibilities (Powell, 1986). Recommendations in this area focused on programmes of family life education and the provision of day care services. Research studies were advocated on adolescent pregnancy, female household headship, household decision-making and male/female relationships.

Alternative employment status categories adopted by WICP suggest that conventional statistical systems adequately report the situation of women in the formal sector of the economy (Massiah, 1986c). The pattern remains one of high levels of participation in traditionally female areas (teaching, nursing, clerical and sales), low levels in manufacturing and low and declining levels in agriculture. However, in the informal sector there still persist difficulties in identification of what may be called the invisible informal sector, of differentiation between self-employed (own account) and women in home-production and home services. These difficulties were, in turn, subsumed under the general problem of defining the informal sector which was not the primary focus of the Project.

Of more direct concern was identification of women's perception of what constitutes women's work. Here, the major finding was that women in the project consider work to be any activity which is functionally necessary to maintain themselves and their households. The criteria they used were time, physical or mental energy, income-earning potential and necessity. Paid employment, and self-employment, the two activities which provide a direct earned income, represent only two activities on a continuum of work activities along which women shift according to their situation and needs at different points in their life cycle. Other work activities include household chores, unpaid productive work in family business enterprises and home-based production for both household consumption and sale. Further, income need not be the only product of this range of work activities. Goods, services and information, singly or in combination are also produced from a variety of sources including kin and friendship networks, institutional mechanisms, mating partner relationships and organization and group membership. The management of this range of resources and activities is what constitutes work and what shapes the working lives of Caribbean women. The goal of the entire process is to maintain her economic independence, provide for the welfare of her children and contribute to maintenance of the household.

The recommendations from this sector of the study included suggestions for statistical measurement, infrastructural improvements of training programmes and public education campaigns. Several recommendations were offered for the improvement of facilities for women in agriculture and for research studies about women in a number of non-agricultural occupations.

The final area considered, organization and group membership, revealed that although women strongly favoured group membership as a means of self-education, few actually belonged to any formal group (Clarke, 1986). Those who did were to be found mostly in church groups where older women figured prominently. Involvement in group activities ranged from participation at the highest levels of decision-making to involvement in routine activities. The women in the study exhibited limited knowledge of projects/programmes offered by organizations specifically for the benefit of women. But they did provide clear ideas on what such projects should be doing.

Recommendations arising from this sector focused on the need to establish and/or improve national machinery for women, the need for improving organizational activity of non-government organizations and for greater collaboration between them, the need for involving NGOs in development programmes and the need for greater public awareness campaigns.

Apart from recommendations to government and NGOs, the WICP also offered recommendations to researchers for further study in the various sectors covered by WICP. Of specific interest to the present study was a proposal for 'separate studies designed to obtain a profile of the following groups of women:

• women in manufacturing industries, including those in industries operated by multi-national corporations;
• women in agriculture, particularly in the smaller territories;
• women in domestic service;
• women traders, particularly those operating in territories in which the economic system appears to have broken down;
• women in professions.' (Massiah, 1983)

WAND/Population Council project

This project, a joint venture between WAND and the Population Council, was conducted in 1982–83 in co-operation with the CARICOM Secretariat and the governments of Dominica, St. Lucia and Jamaica (UWI, WAND, 1983; Ellis, 1986a). The project was designed to develop links between various government ministries and agencies, to encourage a participatory approach to problem-solving and to strengthen research and development networks between countries and agencies.

Each of the countries selected for analysis a rural development project which had been in operation for more than five years. Selected projects had each been originally envisaged as a possible model for replication, had experienced problems in achieving goals and had been exposed to minimal social analysis.[5] Each territory put together a research team consisting of a social science researcher, and one representative each from the Planning Agency, the Ministry of Agriculture, the National Machinery for Women and the administrative staff of the development project itself. Consultative groups representing a wide cross-section of interests provided support and advice as the project progressed. The research team worked together to develop an appropriate methodology, design survey instruments, implement the field work, analyse the material and present the findings to national workshops and a regional workshop.

The three projects chosen included a multi-million dollar integrated rural development project covering 20,000 persons in Jamaica; a micro project involving 11 households engaged in vegetable production in St. Lucia; and a co-operative project in eight small villages in northwestern Dominica. The projects differed in several respects. The Jamaica and Dominica projects were integrated rural development projects while the St. Lucia project was sector specific. The Jamaica and St. Lucia projects were initiated by government, i.e. top down, while the Dominica project originated from within the community, i.e. bottom up. The Dominica project included extensive participation of women in decision-making at the initial stages, but that petered out. The Jamaica project had limited but direct involvement of women in decision-making through membership of farmer committees and women's groups. The St. Lucia project provided only indirect participation for women since the farmer advisory structure was very weak. One final area of differentiation lay in the degree of sensitivity exhibited to women's issues and reflected in the extent to which project design included needs of women. The St. Lucia project was initially designed without reference to the needs of women; the Jamaica project introduced a women's component half-way through; and the Dominica project did so from the start but did not follow through by involving women in the decision-making process.

Despite the differences in organizational structure and focus, these three projects demonstrated several important lessons, among which may be included the following, which are of particular relevance to the present exercise.

1. The need to involve the community from the planning and design stage of the project.

• Few participants in the Jamaica project knew about the project before it came on stream. One result of this was that the project ended up creating serious divisions between itself and the farmers who it was intended to be helping.

• The St. Lucia project failed to consult with local farmers about the selection of the site for the project. Advice from farmers familiar with the shortcomings of the site was ignored. The project failed.

2. The need for basic data about the farm families/households in the project community to be reliable and to be reflected in the project design.

• The St. Lucia project underestimated the structure and size of farm households and based its design on the assumption of a family size of four, whereas the actual family size was much larger.

• The St. Lucia project recognized a high average age of farmers, a wide age-span of family members and considerable geographic scatter of children. Yet the design was based on the expectation of high input from family labour.

3. The need to assess the environmental context in order to anticipate possible problems.

• One of the activities of the Dominica project — the Boxing Plant — was undertaken with no study of the production potential of the area, the flow of produce to market and the costs of operating the plant at different levels of utilization. It turned out that production levels were inadequate to start with and did not increase significantly due to inadequate supply of fertilizer and no changes in patterns of land use. The plant was eventually closed.

4. The need to include women and women's issues in the planning, design, implementation and evaluation stages of the project.

• Pre-project survey data for the Jamaica project indicated that over half the total target population consisted of women as farmers in their own right or as joint farm managers. Yet a project design was developed as if male farmers were the sole clientele. When this gap was recognized, a WID component was tacked on to the project to provide women with vegetable gardening skills and nutrition education. But even though this was perceived as beneficial by women, men and project officials, nothing was done to extend the component to build on those skills. Thus the opportunity was lost to assist women to contribute to the economic sector of their country by e.g. providing skills in processing and marketing of the food crops grown.

5. The need to include women in the decision-making levels of the project.

• The Dominica Cooperative consisted of 250 members, 90 or 36 per cent of whom were women. There was one woman on the initial steering committee and there continues to be one woman on the Board of 11. Despite general recognition of her contribution, the powerful male Board is strongly resistant to increasing the number of women on the Board. The single woman Board member reportedly felt 'overpowered' by the majority of men. Without a strong presence on the Board to represent their interests, women as a social group, have failed to break the power structure in the Cooperative, to hold leadership positions or to influence critical decisions in the Cooperative. Thus, for example, despite overwhelming support from women members of the Cooperative for a woman to be offered a management position for which she was trained, and in which she had already given considerable voluntary assistance, this was summarily rejected by the Board.

In conclusion, it may be stated that this project clearly demonstrated the pitfalls in the way of development projects which fail to address, satisfactorily, or at all, the social and cultural environment in which potential beneficiaries reside. It demonstrated the need for planners to be involved not only at the planning stage of a project but at the implementation, monitoring and input assessment stages. Of special significance was the model the project developed for conducting policy-oriented research on women and development.

The policy alternatives for the Caribbean and Central America (PACCA) project: alternative visions of development

The PACCA project was executed by a team of seven, including two Caribbean-based women researchers, one of whom was the Coordinator of WAND, two American-based women Caribbeanists, one of whom was associated with WICP, two male economists, one of whom was Caribbean and the overall co-ordinator, a woman economist.[6] The project, conducted in 1987-89, was concerned with assessing US–Caribbean relations, locating the issue of gender in the design, execution and impact of those relations and devising a framework for alternative development strategies within the Caribbean and alternative US policy towards the region.[7] To achieve this, the project deliberately adopted a feminist stance and was accordingly structured to include the following:

(i)   a feminist analysis of the crisis in the Caribbean and its social consequences;

(ii)   an analysis of the new social movements in the Caribbean and of the relative visions of development emerging from them;

(iii) an assessment of US policy towards the region;

(iv)   the promotion of an alternative development strategy based on promoting self-reliance and democratic development; and

(v)   the production of an alternative US policy towards the region.

Heavy reliance was thus placed on macro-economic data and secondary data about women in the region. No survey field work was conducted.

The project was organized as a team effort in which individual members contributed papers towards the preparation of a book, the structure and format of which was determined in a series of meetings. The first draft of the book was submitted for comment to a Board of Advisors since which time it has been undergoing revision for publication (PACCA, 1989). It is proposed to produce a series of popular education materials for use by NGOs and other development groups in both the Caribbean and the US.

The genesis of the book is in the economic crisis in the Caribbean in the 1980s. Originating in the recession in advanced industrial economies and the ensuing collapse of institutionalized structures of capital accumulation within and outside the region, the crisis exhibited three facets: a balance of payments crisis, a fiscal crisis and a debt crisis. These, in turn, are reflected in declining foreign investment and unprecedented and rising levels of unemployment. Caribbean governments have responded with a package of structural adjustment programmes consisting of stabilization measures intended to reduce the balance of payments deficit and export diversification intended to increase economic growth. The project argues that by focusing largely on trade, the proposals fail to address the fundamental structural problem of Caribbean economies, i.e. the structure of production and the distribution of assets. Further, the proposals fail to address the potential and actual impact on the majority of the population and in particular of the most vulnerable sections among which women feature prominently.

Using data from Jamaica and the Dominican Republic, the study has demonstrated that as a result of the economic crisis and structural adjustment measures, Caribbean women are experiencing higher rates of unemployment and lower wages. Cuts in the provision of government social services have meant an increasing cost of social reproduction. Reductions in public expenditure have also resulted in cutbacks in employment in the public service which has traditionally employed large numbers of women. Thus a major source of wages has been removed from women.

Because they have primary responsibility for the care of children, the sick and the elderly, women, especially poor women, have had to bear the brunt of the economic crisis. In response to the austerity measures introduced to solve the crisis, women have been developing a number of survival strategies. These have included acceptance of employment in export processing zones, despite the absence of union representation and the poor working conditions. They have also included increased participation in the informal sector and in contracted homework. They have expanded the size of their households in order to gain access to assistance with domestic and child care responsibilities as well as potential additional household income. They have altered their own and their children's consumption and dietary patterns, despite the resulting increase in malnutrition among both children and pregnant mothers. They have migrated in increasing numbers, particularly to the US and Canada, in order to seek employment and obtain income which can be returned as remittances to their dependents left behind.

The project argues for increased activism by women's groups, and increased collaboration between NGOs, the local communities and the political system in order to achieve the aim of an alternative development based on self-determination, participation, self-reliance, regionalism, equity and sustainability.

The US aspect of the project was concerned with the design and impact of the CBI programme on the Caribbean. It argues that the CBI programme as part of an economic policy concerned with capital rather than labour and with bilateral rather than multilateral arrangements, has acted to worsen the region's economic crisis and heighten social tensions. The project argues that US policies to date have served to integrate the Caribbean more closely to US markets, improve the US trade balance and enhance the profitability of US multinationals and finance capital. These have been achieved at the expense of the poor of the region resulting in increased poverty and social instability.

The project argues that an alternative policy needs to recognize the inextricable linkage between the standard of living of US citizens and those of the Caribbean. It also needs to recognize that sustainable and participatory development in the Caribbean serves the mutual interest of both areas. Such a policy should be concerned with

(i)   promoting measures for debt relief, expanding sugar quotas;
(ii)   developing a non-sugar trade policy aimed at promoting Caribbean development;
(iii) a migration policy concerned with improving living and working conditions in the region;
(iv)   development assistance more consistent with regional aspirations; and
(v)   reduction of US military presence in the region and creation of the Caribbean as a zone of peace.

This project is especially useful to the present exercise in illustrating the importance of factors operative in the international geo-political arena to micro-level issues of poverty among women in this region.

Lessons learnt

The three projects described contain many useful contributions to the general body of knowledge about women in development. From the perspective of the present exercise, there are several lessons worth noting.

1. The wealth of data and research experience on women in the Caribbean now available provides a rich base on which to build policies, plans and programmes designed to improve the lives of women. Planners can no longer claim the absence or the insufficiency of data as a constraint to the formulation of appropriate policies and plans for women in development.

2. The available data clearly demonstrate the pivotal role occupied by women in Caribbean societies; the extent to which they participate in, benefit from and are excluded from development plans and projects; and the manner of and extent to which they are affected by events in the international arena. Planners can no longer claim that men and women benefit to the same extent from development activity.

3. Caribbean women are perfectly capable of assessing their life situation, of describing the contextual factors which shape that situation, of articulating their needs and of prescribing possible solutions. Planners need to listen to their voices.

4. Despite social conventions which marginalize women's issues there are male technical personnel in government ministries and agencies who are willing to listen to women's views, to participate in women's development projects and to rethink traditional approaches to development. Planners need to develop and expand that capacity within their agencies.

5. The research experience has highlighted the need to develop an integrated, participatory approach to women's issues regardless of whether the focus of the development activity is policy-making, planning, project implementation or research. Specialists in each of these areas must be prepared to apply their theoretical insights and practical experience to a team effort devoted to development issues.

6. Planning for women at the national level needs to take into account not only macro-level issues and indicators but also micro-level factors, many of which may be non-quantitative, but which are vital to an understanding of women's lives and to the design of realistic plans to assist women.

7. The development of indicators illuminating women's situation requires the creative application of standard statistical procedures to both traditional and non-traditional data sources.

8. Networking among researchers and between researchers and practitioners is highly developed. It is a structure on which they themselves will continue to build and on which planners must build, if the plans they design are to bridge the gap between macro and micro.

Identifying women's invisibility

The brief overview of the three regional studies highlights some of the major issues to be considered in developing plans and projects, whether or not women are directly involved. Each of the projects reviewed provides evidence that neither women nor their problems/concerns are homogeneous. Women are differentiated physically by age, culturally by ethnic group, socially by class grouping, occupational status and household structure — to name a few. The problems/concerns of women in each of these groups and sub-groups, also differ in kind, and intensity, even though it may be argued that all women in the region are confronted by the double subordination of gender and the economic dependence (impoverishment) of the region. Identification of different groups of women and of their general and specific problems thus becomes the first priority in attempting to establish appropriate indicators.

Concern with indicators of the situation of women stems essentially from a concern with the invisibility of women's contribution to development. This invisibility manifests itself in the CARICOM region in several ways. Inadequate provision for women in national development plans, as evidenced by the two plans reviewed later is one manifestation. The absence or limited mention of women in major regional policy documents is another. For example, after sixteen years of existence, the CDB mentioned women for the first time in the 1986 annual report of its President (Demas, 1986). The influential CARICOM report on the development prospects of the region makes only passing reference to women in its discussion on unemployment, while there is no mention of women in the prescriptive section focusing on the development of human resources (Bourne, 1988). Another kind of invisibility is to be found in the disregard of women's knowledge in the design and implementation of development projects. The Jamaica IDRP-II project described earlier provides an example of this. Yet another example of invisibility lies in existing official statistical systems in which data, though collected by sex, may not be disaggregated, tabulated or even published; qualitative data are not collected to supplement available quantitative data; reliance continues to be placed on the traditional approach to data collection which was inadequate to reflect the reality of women's lives or to guide the design of programmes to meet women's needs (CARICOM, 1986).

These varying examples of invisibility which, incidentally are not unique to the Caribbean, have resulted in numerous responses and calls for the development of appropriate indicators to measure the situation of women (UN INSTRAW, 1983a, b and c, 1884a and b, 1987; UNESCO, 1981). However, despite a general awareness and acceptance of women's invisibility there is still a sense in which identification remains somewhat hazy.

Much of the early women's literature on women in development which touches on the question of the invisibility of women concentrated on the statistical invisibility of women's economic activity occasioned by their heavy involvement in the informal sector and in unpaid labour in family enterprises. With the identification of the poorest amongst these 'invisible' groups came the identification of their needs. Increased economic activity for women was seen as a universal need. Access to land, credit and appropriate technology was seen as the specific needs of rural women.[8] Housing, transportation, day care services and skills training were identified as the major needs of poor, low-income urban women. Differences in levels of participation and access to facilities between men and women were assumed to signal a 'gender gap' which needed to be filled by specific development initiatives in order to increase women's visibility.

With the progress of the UN Decade came recognition of the multifaceted nature of women's activities many of which are necessary but 'non-economic'. In effect, the link between production and reproduction became more evident, gradually leading to a better appreciation of the need to look not only at the factors impinging on women who were, or wanted to be, economically active, but also at groups of women who were particularly vulnerable because of specific 'non-economic' difficulties in their personal circumstances.

Up until the Forward Looking Strategies (FLS) it may be argued that the tendency had been to concentrate research and development efforts on increasing the visibility of groups operating on the margins of the economy but nevertheless making a significant economic contribution at the household and community level. But the FLS specifically recommended that 'Basic to all efforts to improve the condition of these women should be the identification of their needs and hence the gathering of gender-specific data and economic indicators sensitive to conditions of extreme poverty and oppression.' (UN, 1985b, para. 282)

This implies a need for a wider definition of 'silent' or 'invisible' women than one based exclusively on their economic activities, a closer examination of the visibility/invisibility issue and a distinction between women and their problems, both of which may include elements of visibility and invisibility. This remaining section of the paper attempts to provide a framework within which such recognition may take place.[9]

Fundamental to the analytical framework prepared here is the assumption that women and their roles have traditionally been accorded lower status in Caribbean societies than men. Related to that assumption is the proposition that women bear an unequal share of social reproduction work in relation to men; and that productive work in exchange for cash, in which men are involved to a greater degree than women, is accorded higher status than the social reproductive work of women. A second set of assumptions revolve around the fact that women's work includes economic and non-economic activities both of which tend to be downplayed or ignored in the development literature of the region. Thus women, their activities, their problems and concerns remain largely invisible to policy-makers, planners and, often, to women themselves. Thirdly, the framework assumes that the invisibility of women stems directly from a gender ideology which adheres to a hierarchical and asymmetrical division of labour in favour of males which is manifested in various ways and in different spheres of activity.

Together these assumptions contributed to the identification of five interrelated types of visibility operative at three different levels, each being a precondition of achieving a higher level. Movement from lower to higher levels need not be unilinear, but the direction of the movement represents a move from recognition of the existence of gender disadvantage to action designed to reduce or eliminate that disadvantage. A schematic representation is shown in Figure 1.

The first and basic level consists of two types of visibility. Conceptual

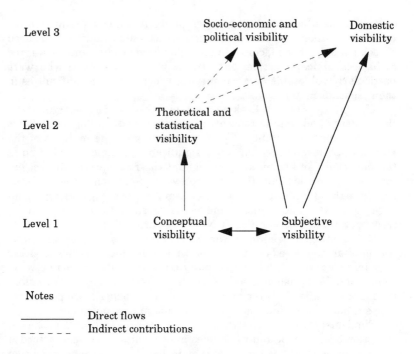

Fig. 1. Relationships between levels of visibility

visibility represents the perception of external observers that a particular sex is subject to a gender disadvantage. This is evident in the prevailing gender ideology of a society, the extent to which that ideology is articulated and the way in which it operates. Subjective visibility reflects the recognition by individuals themselves of the contributing effects of gender domination on their own attitude, behaviour, material and emotional circumstances. The difference between the two types of visibility is essentially one of perceptions. Sometimes the perceptions of the researcher and researched may coincide, but often they differ on several dimensions including problem diagnosis and prescription of solutions.

The second level of the scheme consists of theoretical and statistical visibility made possible by the generation and analysis of quantitative and qualitative data. This level of visibility stems directly from the conceptual visibility at Level 1. It makes possible the identification of trends, patterns of gender domination and explains the mechanisms which perpetuate that domination. At this level, begins the process of understanding how the gender system operates and what kinds of action may be needed in order to minimize elements of disadvantage.

The third and final level of the scheme consists of two types of visibility — the socio-economic/political and the domestic. The former derives from increasing the power resources of the disadvantaged, from the removal of legal and political barriers to advancement and from the introduction of social policies designed to create an environment free of gender domination. This type of visibility flows directly from action external to the household. Domestic visibility, based on action at the individual and household level, is reflected in a changing system of gender relations in which male and female roles are structured in a more egalitarian manner than previously. This level of visibility flows directly from the conceptual and subjective and indirectly from the theoretical and statistical.

Beyond the general question of identifying different types and levels of visibility is that of distinguishing between the visibility of women (or groups of women) and that of their problems. Available evidence suggests that some groups of women, e.g. women in petty trading, may be readily identified by conventional statistics. But in the absence of micro-level research, their problems, concerns and needs remain invisible. In effect, the group may have achieved a limited amount of statistical visibility (Level 2) but without the identification and articulation of their problems, without the introduction of mechanisms to solve their problems, the chances of moving up to Level 3 visibility are slim. Another kind of example may be found in the case of destitute women. Their problems may be highly visible through their visual presence on the streets and perhaps through human interest stories in the press, i.e. theirs is a Level 1 conceptual visibility. But without their numerical identification and categorization in a census or special purpose survey they remain 'invisible' and their chances of progressing to Level 2 visibility and beyond are also slim.

The separation of these aspects of visibility thus becomes an important precondition for operationalizing the analytical framework. The first step in the process was to group women in terms of social (including household structure, age, socio-economic status, ethnic group, marital status, organizational groups); and economic (occupational group, outside of labour force) categories. From these a selection was made of those groups which available research and local knowledge suggested were experiencing specific problems. That short list of groups was then arranged in a four-cell matrix according to the visibility or invisibility of either the women or their problems. The criteria adopted for each cell were as follows:

Women visible: • group clearly identified in available statistical systems;
                 • group can be visually identified.
Women invisible: • group either not identifiable in statistical systems or identified as small proportion of population;
                 • group not usually seen.

Problems visible: • problems articulated and discussed in public;
research data available;
• effects of problems can be clearly seen.
Problems invisible: • little known or heard about problems;
• effects of problems not easily seen.

Applying this conceptual framework to information yielded by the different levels of research available yields the categorization appearing in Table 1. From this it is clear, that although available research provides valuable information about Caribbean women as a group, little is really known about a wide range of sub-groups whether the discussion is concerned with economic participation, social status groups or marginalized groups.

The groupings are not of course mutually exclusive. There may be some double-counting, e.g. élite women may also be in the minority ethnic groups — thus compounding their invisibility. There may be some contradictions, e.g. prostitutes may be easily identified in the areas they frequent and may thus be considered 'visible' but that does not mask the 'invisibility' of their needs which are seldom articulated. Differences in terms of such criteria as motherhood, class alliances, involvement in the formal or informal sector, are not introduced into the model. This is not to deny the existence or importance of such differences, but simply to reflect a recognition that such differences, while affecting the degree of visibility or invisibility within specific groups, do not really alter the categorization of the overall groups. Thus, for example, the group 'disabled women' may be statistically disaggregated in terms of socio-economic status. But unless specific information is available to elucidate the problems of each of the sub-groups, the total group may still be considered 'invisible'. The important point is that the constituent sub-groups are bound together by common identifiable needs by virtue of being in the same overall category. But their involvement in different social or economic sub-groups also yields another set of needs, specific to the particular sub-groups to which they belong. This combined, yet differentiated needs structure creates specific difficulties for planning authorities conditioned to think of women as a homogeneous group.

Category I: Women visible, problems visible

For the groups of women listed under Category I, studies exist on general issues about unemployment and manufacturing from which information can be gleaned about women. Major work on the other groups has been becoming available in recent years. From the perspective of the categorization adopted, these groups of women and their problems may be considered generally visible. They have progressed beyond Levels 1 and 2

TABLE 1
IDENTIFYING VISIBILITY AND INVISIBILITY

	Problems	
Women	*Visible*	*Invisible*
	Category I	*Category II*
		Housewives
	- - - - - - - - - -	- - - - - - - - - -
Visible	Young unemployed	Domestics
	Women in manufacturing	Women in the public sector
	Women in EPZs	Self-employed women
	Women in agriculture	Women in sales (other than trade)
	Women traders	Women in service
		(other than domestic)
		Professional women
	- - - - - - - - - -	- - - - - - - - - -
	Adolescent mothers	Divorced women
	Women who head households	Widows
	- - - - - - - - - -	- - - - - - - - - -
	Village women	Women in minority ethnic groups
Invisible	*Category III*	*Category IV*
	Elderly women	Destitute women
	- - - - - - - - - -	
	Disabled women	
	Retired women	
	- - - - - - - - - -	- - - - - - - - - -
	Victims of physical violence	Women in home production
		Women 'out' workers
		Prostitutes
		- - - - - - - - - -
		Immigrant
		(especially illegal) women
		- - - - - - - - - -
		Women in Trade Unions
		Women working involuntary
		organizations
		- - - - - - - - - -
		Elite women

Note: Dotted lines indicate change of socio-economic category.

visibility and have achieved a limited measure of Level 3 socio-economic/ political visibility but we are without data to determine the extent to which they have achieved domestic visibility. It would not however be necessarily correct to say that no further planning efforts on their behalf are required.

Category II: Women visible, problems invisible

Groups in Category II can be readily identified from census and survey data, but little is known about the specific problems they face and, in general, it may be argued that little planning is effected on their behalf at the national level. Consider, for example, the case of domestic service. This is an area of employment activity in which significant numbers of Caribbean women have been involved from the earliest days of Caribbean history. In Barbados, for example, census data suggest that the number of domestics hovered between 9,000 and 12,000 in the latter half of the nineteenth century, rose to 14,000 by 1921 and by 1980 had resumed the mid-nineteenth century level of about 9,000. These numbers represent about 17 per cent to 25 per cent of the total female work force. Yet it is an area which has been poorly served by historians, sociologists and economists alike (Higman, 1983, p. 117).

From the different perspectives of three recent studies on the subject, it is clear that despite the inherent problems involved in an activity which is not necessarily a preferred economic option, domestic service performs a critical role in Caribbean societies.

The earliest of these studies was undertaken in Trinidad in 1975 and was concerned with the working conditions of a sample of domestic workers (Mohammed, 1986). The study found that wages and other conditions of work were determined by private agreement between employer and employee. No protection was available to domestics in respect of minimum wage, sickness, maternity, old age, or disabilities. Relationships on both sides were characterized by 'a strong element of distrust'. The study identified four major needs for domestic workers. These centred around:
(i) a change in attitude towards housework and the labour performed by domestic workers;
(ii) establishment of a minimum wage commensurate with the job requirements and sufficient to meet the prevailing cost of living;
(iii) provision of inexpensive day care facilities; and
(iv) the need for domestics to organize themselves into trade unions.
These were predicated on the growing dependency of working and professional women on the services provided by domestic workers, and the need for many working-class women to find employment (Mohammed, 1986).

The Higman study traces the pattern of growth and decline in domestic service in Jamaica over two centuries, 1750–1970 (Higman, op. cit.).

He links trends in the domestic service workforce to changes in the Jamaican economy and in the social status of the servant-employing classes. He concludes that although domestic service continues to be important, the socio-economic position of domestic servants has been on the decline since the middle of the ninteenth century.

The Anderson study focuses on the domestic employment relationship in Jamaica as it relates to the domestic bonding which is necessary for its maintenance and to the prevailing intra-family sex roles which that bonding is intended to maintain. For Anderson, it is this heavy emotional investment in the domestic service relationship which separates domestic service from other types of income earning and which makes it difficult to identify essential research issues. Anderson argues that it is to the interest of both parties to maintain a relationship which tends towards mutual accommodation and in which little evidence of conflict is apparent. On the one hand, traditional high levels of labour force participation force middle-class Jamaican women to delegate more of their domestic responsibilities. On the other, domestic service is one of the most readily available employment opportunities for women with limited education and occupational skills. It is therefore to their mutual advantage for the two parties to seek and maintain a workable, long-term relationship. Those relationships which degenerate into the exploitative are usually short-lived; those which survive serve the separate interests of server and served. She concludes that taken together the beliefs and practices discussed by respondents in her study 'form a coherent ideology of domestic service which serves to maintain a structured system of class and gender relationships' (Anderson, 1987, pp. 16–17).

In effect, domestic service is contributing much more than employment for significant numbers of women. It is performing an important maintenance function in the society which goes well beyond what the employment numbers indicate. Yet, domestic servants, as a group, are not encountered in the development plans in the region, even though some territories have introduced legislation to ease their way. For example in Barbados, there is a Domestic Employers (Hours of Duty) Act which stipulates the working hours for domestics but makes no provision for a minimum wage. Domestic servants are also covered under the National Insurance Security Act; the Holidays with Pay Act and the Severance Pay Act. These legal measures serve to protect the domestic servant to a certain extent, as indeed do similar measures in other territories. But in the absence of trade union representation and the provision of programmes aimed at enhancing their employment skills domestic servants have to continue to rely on their own ability to influence their working relationship.

Women in Category II of this framework may thus be said to be progressing towards Level 2 — theoretical and statistical visibility. Their numbers are generally known; but little specific information exists about their problems, concerns and needs. Few, if any, policy measures exist on their behalf.

Category III: Women invisible, problems visible

Women in Category III represent a particularly poignant aspect of invisibility. They are either relatively few in number or cannot be identified although they are known to exist. Yet the problems which they confront have been continuously expounded, though only in the case of victims of physical violence has the case been made specifically from the perspective of women. In two other cases, disabled and elderly women, available information has been used as a basis for inclusion of programmes/projects in national development plans. Thus, for example, the most recent Development Plan for Barbados proposes in the health sector to focus on eleven major areas including:

- the development of programmes and provision of increased facilities for the disabled; and
- the implementation of a vibrant community-based programme for the elderly.

No details are given with respect to the former, but for the elderly, it was proposed to:

- upgrade the existing geriatric hospital;
- establish a geriatric service in the major Government Hospital;
- establish homes for the ambulant elderly; and
- develop Community Health Teams to maintain the aged in their homes.

In similar global terms, the Minister of Employment, Labour Relations, Community Development and the Environment proposes to:

- expand the provision of home help and housing for the elderly;
- make greater use of existing facilities to establish day care centres for the elderly.

It may be argued that in this territory the provision of appropriate facilities and custodial care at least ensures that the physical needs of elderly women and men are being addressed. But a recent survey of the elderly in that territory suggests that although significant achievements have been realized in meeting 'tangible' needs, much remains to be done. There are still sizeable pockets of inadequate provision, of unmet needs and of lack of knowledge about available services. And the question of non-tangible needs still has to be addressed (Brathwaite, 1985 and 1986). To that list may be added the absence of separate analysis of the problems of elderly men and women.[10] Over 60 per cent of the sample in that survey were women yet their physical circumstances, the nature and extent of the problems they experience or their knowledge and use of available services, remain unanalysed (Nurse, 1986). Thus, from the perspective of this framework, elderly women remain invisible in terms of their specific problems.

When we turn to the group of women victims of physical violence, the position is much more hazy in terms of numbers involved, but information about the women affected is slowly coming to hand. A recent study commissioned by the Bureau of Women's Affairs in Barbados revealed that between 1977–1985 an average of 50 cases of rape and 26 cases of indecent assault were reported per year (Jordan, 1986). These were cases of major indictable crimes which were dealt with summarily. Not included were minor crimes which either never reached the court or were dealt with in a magistrate's court. In 1985, 192 reports of such non-sexual physical violence were received. Of these 156 or 81 per cent were committed by males against females. Included amongst these are 82 cases of beating which resulted in minor or no physical injury — classified as 'minor crimes'. No record is available of the number of beatings which are not reported to the police.

The conclusion would seem to be that the relatively low number of indictable crimes which reach the court mask a much higher number of minor crimes which either never reach the court or are unreported. They also mask the terrible psychological scars which women develop after these incidents and the inadequacy of existing police and legal systems to provide adequate support services. According to one study of domestic violence among East Indians in Guyana:

'It is only when husband-wife violence is pushed to the point where the female partner is seriously or fatally injured that she is not discriminated against by the police.' (Shiw Persad, 1988)

That study concludes that since recourse to the law has proven unsatisfactory and support from friends and relatives ineffective '... many abused wives are kept in a web of cultural, religious, economic and ideological trappings of an underclass.' (Shiw Persad, op. cit.)

In effect, in the context of this paper such women remain invisible, but studies such as those cited are slowly making their problems visible.

In terms of the framework, women in Category III may be said to have progressed beyond Level 2 and to be slowly gaining Level 3 — socio-economic/political visibility — in terms of measures being introduced to alleviate their situation. Yet it would be correct to say that not very much is known really about these women beyond their numbers.

Category IV: Women invisible, problems invisible

In this group are to be found those women about whom least is known whether in terms of identifying the numbers involved or the problems experienced. These could be viewed as the most 'invisible' of all groups; for although they are known to exist, data are either sketchy, e.g. women in trade unions, or non-existent, e.g. élite women. But even amongst this group, information is slowly being extracted.

The WICP employed the category 'home production' to identify those women who engaged in agriculture or handicraft for sale on an occasional basis as a supplement to their home service (housework) activities. Between 6 per cent and 11 per cent of the samples were found to be so engaged. These women were located mainly in rural areas and resorted to such activities when they could find money to purchase raw materials and a ready market for their produce. It was a device to help fill up their spare time, with little semblance of permanency and little hope of significant returns.

A 63-year-old WICP respondent in Antigua recalls her occasional involvement in the production of handicraft from seeds — a skill she learnt from her mother. 'I had was to do a little thing to keep life easier, you know. Couldn't just sit down so with your hands in your lap all the days.'

She and her children would collect the seeds from trees in rural areas, boil and dye them and string them into jewellery, belts, tablemats and the like for sale during the tourist season. However, the government cut down the trees, ploughed up the land for an agricultural project and seeds now have to be bought. Loss of a free source of raw material, high cost of replacement and lack of sales, through competition from other types of handicraft have forced her out of the market and eliminated her single source of income earning. Increasing age and deterioration in vision have further reduced her ability to earn income from the only skill she has. She is now fully dependent on her only daughter, who used to help with the seed handicraft, but who is now involved in sewing garments for sale to tourists. She grows vegetables for household use and would sell any occasional surplus to neighbours. Also, she might still do occasional beadwork from her last remaining supply of seeds, because 'You may get them sell, if not at the same price, just to say you get rid of them'.

Women like this respondent can only be identified in a survey. They are not included in official statistics as workers, their problems of marketing and sales are not articulated by any collective, and their chances of being included in any project or programme aimed at improving their situation are minimal. Further, if they are elderly as in this case, their invisibility is further compounded.

Consider a more organized group — women in trade unions. In one sense, these should be a highly visible group by virtue of the prominent role played by trade unions in the economic life of the territories in the region since the 1930s. In another, they are highly invisible since their numbers on membership rolls are not known, even though they have been involved in the trade union movement from its inception. They are outnumbered 3 to 1 at decision-making levels, thus the impact they have had on bringing women's issues to bear on conventional union approaches to labour policy has been minimal (Bolles, 1988; Gloudon, 1986). Further, little is known about the problems which they confront as they attempt to enter and remain in an area traditionally regarded as a male domain.

Thus both the women and their problems remain invisible.

Women in Category IV remain firmly at the lowest level of visibility, Level 1 — conceptual. Their numbers are unknown, their problems are unknown, no policy measures protect them. In effect, groups in this category may be considered invisible.

The conclusion to be drawn from this analysis is that while general information about Caribbean women is available, that for specific groups of women is generally lacking. In terms of the proposed model, most groups have not progressed beyond the first level of visibility. For the few groups for which some information is available, it may be said that they have attained a measure of statistical visibility. However, in the absence of planning and policy measures on their behalf they have been unable to move much beyond the second level of visibility.

Routes to visibility

If women are to be enabled to expand and improve their life prospects, then specific efforts need to be made to transform their 'invisibility' into genuine visibility. Further that visibility must not only be limited to statistical visibility, i.e. Level 2 of the model, but should be extended to the third and higher level. This involves the design and execution of specific strategies based on the realities of how women perceive themselves, determine their personal goals, allocate priorities and negotiate action. Lesson 3 learnt from the Chapter describing recent research is relevant here. Caribbean women can and do engage in an ongoing process of assessing their situation and devising action. Table 2 identifies the range of strategies which have been and are being used to attain the highest level of visibility. Strategies are linked to different types and levels of visibility through a series of perceived or stated objectives. From this it is evident that the achievement of a specific level of visibility rests on a combination of strategies in which information and networking figure prominently.

Four case studies are used to demonstrate alternative strategies for moving from invisibility to different levels of visibility and the effect this movement has or has not had on the approach to national development planning for women. The first case study demonstrates the use of research as a vehicle for achieving conceptual visibility and moving towards statistical visibility. Illustrations are taken from a variety of studies on women in agriculture. The second case study illustrates how research followed by collective action of the researched helps to strengthen visibility at Levels 1 and 2 and to start the move towards socio-economic and political visibility. A UNECLAC study on women traders supplies the example. The third case study illustrates a participatory action programme as a mechanism for achieving Level 3 visibility. The WAND project in Rose

TABLE 2
OBJECTIVES AND STRATEGIES FOR ATTAINING VISIBILITY

Visibility level	Type of visibility	Visibility objective	Visibility strategies
Level 1	Conceptual visibility	(i) Identification that a particular sex is suject to a gender-disadvantage	(a) Representation/articulation by group members (b) Identification by service agencies (government, NGOs, and media) (c) Research
	Subjective visibility	(i) Sensitization of disadvantaged group to recognize the inhibiting effects of gender domination	(a) Group self-analysis (b) Mobilization and education
Level 2	Theoretical and statistical visibility	(i) Establishment of pattern of domination and disadvantage (ii) Identification of mechanisms which maintain invisibility (iii) Identification of statistical indicators (iv) Assessments of extents of gender disadvantage	(a) Interviews (b) Case studies (c) Group discussion (d) Statistical research
Level 3	Socio-economic and political visibility	(i) Reduction/removal of gender disadvantage (ii) Increasing power resources of disadvantaged group	(a) Mobilization (b) Education/training (c) Legal reform (d) Gender-balancing distribution policies (e) Networking
	Domestic visibility	(i) Re-working of gender-based domestic division of labour (ii) Recognition and strengthening of male domestic responsibility	(a) Education (b) Mobilization/education of male groups (c) Family policy (d) Networking

Hall, a village in St. Vincent, provides the example. A fourth case study draws on the experience of a women's theatre collective to illustrate the use of drama to intensify Level 1 visibility and move directly to Level 3. The fifth and final case study demonstrates the use of regional networking as a strategy for attaining each level of visibility. The experience of Directors of Women's Bureaux in the region is used in this illustration.

The strategy of research: women in agriculture

This strategy has been employed by groups external to the researched group (CAFRA, 1988; FAO, 1988; Knudson and Yates, 1981; Springer, 1983). Data are gathered from both primary and secondary sources. Planners may or may not be involved in the research process, but considerable effort is expended in disseminating the results as widely as possible. Individual studies focus on specific territories or crops, but taken together the studies provide planners with a wealth of information.

Available statistical data on employment in agriculture suggest a significant and steady decline in the absolute and relative numbers of the working population engaged in agriculture. Much of this decline may be attributed to the declining role of agriculture in the region. Evidence of the latter may be found in the declining share of agriculture in national GDP, declining levels of production, declining proportions of arable land under cultivation, declining returns on export agriculture and increasing food import bill. Each of these factors is evident in varying degrees in individual territories.

According to the 1980 Census, the proportion of the working population engaged in agriculture across the region ranged between 6 per cent and 37 per cent (Table 3). Of these between 2 per cent and 37 per cent were women. Within the female working population, between 1 per cent and 22 per cent were engaged in agriculture. Together these indicators suggest that few women are involved in agriculture. Yet the most casual observation in any Caribbean territory reveals that significant numbers of women are indeed involved in a wide range of agricultural tasks. Some of this occurs on large-scale plantation-type holdings where women are employed mainly as agricultural labourers (Springer, op. cit.). This is the case on the sugar cane, cocoa, coconut and rice estates and is readily identifiable and measurable. A considerable amount of female agricultural activity, however, is concentrated in small-scale peasant production, some of which is primary but much of which is secondary to the main activity of either the woman, her partner or both (Knudson and Yates, op. cit.; CAFRA, op. cit.). Production is primarily for domestic consumption, with the surplus being sold on the local market, if possible. Because this type of productive activity is considered an extension of traditional domestic activity, much of it is not identified in national statistical systems.

TABLE 3

INDICATORS OF WOMEN IN AGRICULTURAL OCCUPATIONS, 1980

Territory	Proportion of women in total working population in agriculture	Proportion of female working population in agriculture
Jamaica [1]	n.a	n.a
Trinidad and Tobago [3]	15.7	4.6
Guyana	9.5	8.9
Barbados	3.2	5.6
Belize	36.6	8.4
St. Lucia	23.5	19.0
Grenada [2]	24.7	19.1
St. Vincent	22.4	17.3
Dominica [2]	17.9	20.6
St. Kittes/Nevis	30.1	22.1
Montserrat	22.1	7.7
Turks and Caicos	25.4	9.5
High	36.6	22.1
Low	3.2	4.6

Notes: 1. Census taken in 1982.
2. Census taken in 1981.
3. Data refer to activity in past week. For all other territories reference period is this past year.

Source: 1980/81 Population censuses.

Thus, one micro-level study estimates that just under half of rural St. Lucian women engage in substantial farm work whereas the census data indicate only 19 per cent of employed women in agriculture. A third area of activity in agriculture is the marketing of agricultural (including fishing) produce in which women are known to be predominant but which is not reflected in the statistics.[11] Two other groups of women who work in the agricultural sector are field technicians, and professionals, both of whom are usually employed by the Ministry of Agriculture. These are very few in number but virtually no data exist about their lives and work.

Information coming out of recent studies is slowly providing a clearer picture of the lives of rural women in agriculture, and detailing their hopes, aspirations and needs. The following stories highlight some of the findings from these studies.

A SMALL-SCALE CULTIVATOR

Linda, a 43-year-old WICP respondent from St. Vincent, has been a self-employed cultivator since 1965. Linda first became involved in agriculture as a young girl helping her parents in their vegetable garden and selling the produce in town. She also learnt about soils and plants in her Nature Study classes in primary school. Shortly after their marriage, she entered into independent agricultural production when her husband went to the USA on a farm labour contract scheme and she had to find something to do to help maintain herself and the children. On his return, they bought a heifer and from there built up a livelihood based on his livestock tending and her gardening.

She cultivates root crops and vegetables on about one-and-a-half acres of land under a type of share-crop arrangement in which her husband tends cattle for the landowner in exchange for the use of the one-and-a-half acres. The landowner receives a portion of the produce and the remainder is sold. Produce is reaped on Fridays and transported by donkey to her house where it is sorted and packaged. On Saturday, the produce is taken by bus to town for sale to the market women there.

Preparation of the land is carried out in a 'swap labour' arrangement by which a male friend helps her husband for a day and the husband, in turn, is obligated to the friend to return his labour on another day. Linda performs all the other tasks of crop production using hoe and cutlass, walking each day to her land in the mountain which is about one hour's distance from home (WICP data).

A PLANTATION WORKER

Didi is a 67-year-old East Indian woman, a descendant of indentured labourers, who started to work in the cane fields of Trinidad and Tobago at the age of 10. Starting from the lowliest task of weeding, which was the lowest paid agricultural task assigned to women labourers, Didi has risen to become a cane cutter, an occupation usually associated with males. Her husband is also a sugar worker. They have ten children, two of them having been born in the cane field. With innovation and thrift Didi has worked to improve the living standard of the family, transforming their house made of mud into a spacious property filled with furniture and appliances.

Didi is unable to read or write but she has been a union steward fighting resolutely for the rights of her fellow sugar workers. She was the major instigator of a famous strike in 1973, and again in 1975. She has been instrumental in gaining maternity benefits for women in the sugar industry in her territory. Didi has resolutely refused repeated offers of the job of field foreman in order to retain the freedom to agitate on behalf of her fellow workers (Haniff, 1988).

A HIGGLER

Miss Tiny is a Jamaican higgler whose entire working life has been spent in selling.[12] Born in 1935, her work experience started as a child when she was left to guard the produce of her mother who was herself a rural higgler. After the birth of her first child she migrated to Kingston at the age of 16 and became a 'tray girl', i.e. selling small items of agricultural produce which she bought from country folk. This she did for five years during which time she had two children for one father and four for another. With the latter she established a common law household and tried operating a food shop, a short-lived experiment.

Miss Tiny then became a fish vendor buying and selling small quantities of fish from the large fishing boats which came into Kingston. As business improved, she began to buy larger quantities of fish until she realized that it was more economical to buy directly from fishermen in the country. This necessitated travelling to the country in the evening, waiting for the boats, sleeping on the beach, making the purchase and returning next morning early enough to catch the market business. Miss Tiny bought a freezer and a van which her son learnt to drive.

As the fish vending business improved, Miss Tiny was able to buy and furnish her own home by 'throwing partners' — a form of rotating credit association. But in 1980, the van was stolen and the fish vending business collapsed. Miss Tiny immediately entered the international higgler business through the good offices of a woman friend. She travels mainly to Panama to seek items which are scarce in that territory but available in Jamaica, using the exchange gained to purchase in Panama items for resale in Jamaica (Haniff, 1988).

These three vignettes barely touch the surface of the myriad features which characterize the lives of Caribbean women in agriculture. Details provided by several other studies provide a picture which may be summarized as follows:

Demographic characteristics. Their average age is over 40; educational attainment levels are generally low, ranging from none to completed primary; they live in a married or common law union, with several claiming household headship even though a male partner was present; their average family size ranges between four and seven; their households tend to be two or three-generational with all members being involved in one or other of the farming activities.

Farm work. Invariably entry into farming occurred through lack of knowledge and training in anything else and having been raised in an agricultural community. Work days are long and divided between household chores, child care, travel (usually walking) to and from the farm site or estate, working the land, and often selling the produce. In addition, some of them produce handicraft, raise livestock and maintain kitchen gardens from which they earn additional income. One study has demonstrated that thirteen of the sixteen waking hours of the farm woman are spent in work activities (Odie-Ali, 1986).

Information about agriculture. Knowledge about farming usually comes from parents, partner and other farmers either by word of mouth or by observation. Agricultural extension officers did not figure prominently as sources of information — they were regarded as being either unreliable, unable to provide what was required, or providing impractical advice — 'sterile help' as one woman farmer put it. But some women do credit extension officers with providing valuable assistance.

Decision-making. Women participate significantly in decision-making on the farm. Independent decisions are taken in respect of what crops and livestock to produce, farm improvement, marketing strategies and hiring of labour. Decisions about credit, extension of farmland and crop protection, are made jointly with her partner. Decisions about the use of money realised from the sale of their own produce are the woman's prerogative. Invariably such monies are used for household maintenance purposes and for emergencies. Savings garnered through informal rotating credit associations are applied to the purchase of house and furnishings.

Access to land. Although nothing in Caribbean jurisprudence excludes women from land ownership, the traditional pattern of male ownership or control of land still persists. Where women gain access to land it is usually acquired through inheritance either from her father or her husband. Ownership through direct purchase though not unknown is less frequent. Access is also possible through leasehold, renting, squatting, each of which creates considerable insecurity of a tenure. Particularly in the smaller territories the average size of plots farmed by women is less than three acres, i.e. the lower end of the minimum range of 1–5 acres used in official statistics (Knudson and Yates, op. cit.; CAFRA, op. cit.).

Problems. The major problems identified by women farmers centre on access to supplies (fertilizer, pesticides, weedicides etc.), access to credit, transportation to markets and praedial larceny. For women in agricultural wage labour the major need is for adequate representation of their interests by trade unions. For women selling agricultural produce, their need is for transportation and marketing arrangements.

The strategy of research has resulted in the identification of the nature, extent and quality of women's contribution to the agricultural sector, the quantification of the problems experienced by women working in that sector and the enumeration of suggestions for alleviating these problems. In several cases, planners and policy-makers joined researchers in the interpretation of data, development of recommendations and dissemination of results. Yet minimal returns are evident in terms of policy action directed towards women in agriculture. Indeed, one commentator has concluded 'agricultural and rural development policies and programmes in several Caribbean countries still do not include a perspective on gender, and appear not to have been influenced by the wealth of data which now exist on women in this sector' (Ellis in FAO, 1988, p. 43).

In the context of the model, the strategy of research may be said to have propelled women in Caribbean agriculture towards theoretical and statistical, i.e. Level 2 visibility.

The strategy of research and mobilisation: women traders

One of the visible effects of the recent economic crisis has been women's increased involvement in the informal sector (Rivera, 1989; Le Franc, 1989). This results partly from women's own initiative, partly from increasing government advocacy of small business and partly from NGO activity backed by donor financing, which attempts to assist small businesses by providing skills training and credit.

Caribbean women have been involved in informal sector activities from the earliest days of the history of the region. Initially concentrated in domestic service and trading in locally cultivated foods, these women had little or no education, and came from either a rural farm or urban unskilled labour background. Now, the range, character, and organization of activities have changed. Domestic service is still important, though declining. Other services are provided by women's small business enterprises, and trading has expanded to include street foods and manufactured goods, some purchased on buying trips in neighbouring territories. In some territories, traders export local products and import basic commodities. Guyanese traders, for example, sell locally manufactured gold jewellery, garments, and straw baskets in neighbouring territories and buy food, medicinal drugs and school supplies to sell at home. Traders from Grenada and St. Vincent take fruits, vegetables, and shellfish into Trinidad and return home with hardware, lumber, building materials, and household supplies for resale. The volume and content of such trade are determined by shortages in the importing country and the gains that can be captured from currency conversion on the various transactions. Some territories experience little or no reverse trading. 'Suitcase traders' from Trinidad and Barbados, for example, purchase consumer items overseas for resale at home.

Traditional traders have now been joined by men and younger women, who are likely to have secondary education and, often, white collar or lower-level professional experience. Participation of professionals increased significantly in the 1970s because of fewer jobs, government restrictions on importing consumer items, and, in the case of Jamaica, several devaluations of the local currency.

A recent study on women traders in the Caribbean has identified four critical aspects of the issue:

1. Where women predominate in informal sector trading activities the trade is generally in wearing apparel and light goods, popularly referred to as 'the suitcase trade'; and fresh agricultural produce.

2. Data, especially hard data which would allow serious analysis on the situation of women engaged in this sector, are practically non-existent or inaccessible.

3. Hard data on traders who travel within the region to sell agricultural produce — the so-called 'inter-island traders' — are more accessible than data on the 'suitcase traders'.

4. The trading activity of the 'inter-island traders' is confronting critical problems. Without remedial action it is threatened with disintegration. The implications of this might be loss of a vital service in the food supply for the region; and loss of income for a large group of women in the sub-region who are sole providers for their households (UNECLAC, 1988). The following information derives from the UNECLAC study:

TRADERS IN FRESH AGRICULTURAL PRODUCE — EASTERN CARIBBEAN

'Ramona, a thirty-nine year old St. Lucian, has been trading in Barbados for two years. She has five children and lives with her common-law partner. She reached standard four in primary school. She grows bananas on rented land in St. Lucia and says that she started trading because she could not get a job. She trades in grapefruit, mandarins, oranges, plantains and coconuts. While the boat MV Stella S is in dry dock she buys peanuts in Barbados for resale. She goes to Barbados every four to five months. She usually spends about four weeks in Barbados — never shorter than this — and sometimes stays as long as seven weeks. Ramona indicates that she won't make a profit if she goes and returns with each boat trip.

'When in Barbados, she lives with her brother who himself gets assistance from their mother in St. Lucia. Ramona brings food. She does not pay for accommodation.'

'Veda of St. Vincent is a large trader. She is thirty-six years old, divorced with seven children. She left secondary school at seventeen, having reached the third form. She has been trading for nine years. She trades in mangoes, plantains, coconuts, oranges, grapefruit, tangerines and sometimes nutmeg and eddoes. She travels to Barbados often by LIAT while her goods are shipped there. She usually spends three days in

Barbados living with her Barbadian boyfriend who is the father of her last child. She stores her goods at her boyfriend's house.'

These capsule portraits of a small (Ramona) and a large (Veda) trader merely hint at the considerable effort involved in organising and maintaining these trading activities in the Eastern Caribbean. It has been estimated that about 1,300 traders operate out of five Eastern Caribbean territories. The majority of traders are women from rural areas whose average age is over 35 and who have at least a primary education. Most of them live in a residential union with a male partner and several children — the average ranges between five and ten. Traders purchase, and often grow some of their produce in their own territory and travel to neighbouring territories for their resale. Some traders purchase commodities for resale at home; most simply purchase items for their own households.

The entire process of production or purchase, packaging, transportation, marketing and return travel is organized and supervised by each trader individually (Figure 2). It is heavily dependent on the creation and maintenance of a wide network of female and male contacts who provide information and services at each stage of the operation. An examination of the activities involved in the trading cycle suggests a heavy workload extending, on average, to 10 hours per day over a period of a few days to two months. The length of the trading cycle is determined by the distance between the territories involved and the number of territories visited in a single trading trip. Returns are reported as being minimal, with the majority facing financial losses which result in a high dropout rate. Yet, 'the image persists that traders earn substantial amounts of money and therefore do not need any organised assistance'. (UNECLAC, op. cit., p. 8)

But it seems that in reality, success stories are limited to merely a few. Of particular interest has been the efforts of traders in different territories to organize themselves into associations. The most successful and the only one currently operational, is the Dominican Hucksters' Association which was established in 1981 to promote the interests of hucksters by providing technical and financial assistance. So far, the Association has initiated a training project in basic costing and pricing and a pilot project on collective purchasing and post-harvest services. It provides insurance coverage and credit facilities by which members can obtain a sixty-day, short-term loan of US$300. It has launched a public relations programme using a multi-media approach based on radio, newspaper and a Newsletter. Despite these initiatives, the UNECLAC report warns that these efforts to improve the trading practices of traders to enable them to enter and compete in the formal trading sector may be detrimental to female traders who are generally less able to enter the formal sector.

The study identifies the needs of women traders as follows:

1. Recognition needs to be given to the vital service which traders and trading performs. Traders are the main exporters of agricultural produce in intra-Caribbean trade. Trading provides an opportunity for self-im-

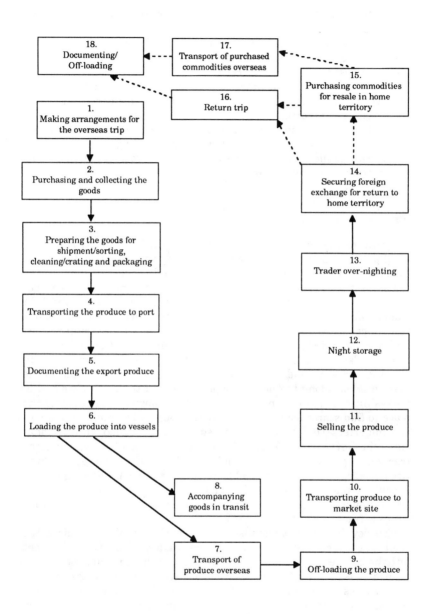

Fig. 2. The traders activity cycle

provement and the development of entrepreneurial skills to significant numbers of women.

2. The working conditions of traders are deplorable. Long hours, exposure to the elements, lack of protection for produce, liability to physical abuse are just some of the factors.

3. The situation of traders is steadily deteriorating due to shrinking markets in the food-importing countries and increasing competition in the agriculture-exporting sector.

4. Increasingly restrictive national and regional trading requirements limit the ability of traders to adjust to the hostile trading environment.

5. Without incentives and government support to upgrade the trading sector, traders will disappear.

INTERNATIONAL TRADERS

Up until the mid-1970s traders consisted essentially of sellers of agricultural products with a sprinkling concentrating on non-edible items of local manufacture. With difficulties in national economies resulting in import restrictions and tighter foreign exchange controls came shortages in basic consumer items and the opening up of a new area of activity for traders. Jamaica and Guyana were the two territories in which women traders capitalised on this opportunity. For Jamaica, the countries visited were Grand Cayman, Haiti, Curacao, Panama and the US (mainly Miami) (Taylor, 1986, 1988). The foods traded were foreign foodstuff, clothing, footwear and appliances. Goods were sold in Kingston in the main market, along the main shopping street in the city centre and in makeshift booths in shopping plazas. 'Bend down' plazas became the place to find scarce foods brought into the country by 'informal commercial importers' (ICIs) as they were subsequently called. In November 1987, the Government Revenue Board recorded 3,084 ICIs as registered traders, 60 per cent of whom were located in the Kingston Metropolitan Area. Among the latter group 90 per cent were women. These figures refer only to registered traders, but unknown numbers of women bring in smaller quantities of goods for resale from their homes — the so-called suitcase traders.

Survey data permit a statistical profile of the typical Jamaican ICI (Le Franc, op. cit.). She is about 33 years old, a mother of two who went into the business on her own initiative because she was unemployed and needed to assist with family expenses. She started the business with her own savings and has been in it for about five years. She has had some secondary education and been engaged in a non-manual job immediately before entering into trading. She earns approximately J$1,000 (US$182) per week, most of which is reinvested to keep the business going. Her approach to business is highly individualistic, with little or no support and involvement from family members. Her business practices are highly conservative — she sells mainly at retail, she restricts her search for supplies to a single country, she confines herself to a single selling location, she sells a limited and particular set of goods. The result is that, as Le Franc puts it 'stable security (takes) easy precedence over risk taking and aggressive profit making', thus dampening the extent of capital accumulation possible. This is not to deny that traders do seem able to enjoy a lifestyle which suggests access to considerable sums of money, even though these may not reflect real wealth. But in the absence of written records of income and expenditure, no firm statement about the profitability of these ventures is possible.

In the early 1980s, the Government attempted to regulate the activities of traders by introducing a programme to clear the streets of sidewalk vendors. In the process some vendors suffered physical violence and damage or confiscation of their goods by the police. In response, vendors began to create associations to protect their interests. The United Vendors Association eventually became the umbrella organization of the ICIs. The Association provides a range of services to members including counselling, security, a development fund and assistance to obtain small business loans. It has been instrumental in establishing two additional shopping arcades for vendors, an identification system for vendors, four chapters outside of the Kingston Metropolitan Area and a savings fund to develop a co-operative enterprise.

One study indicates two major features of trading with policy implications (Taylor, 1988). First, there is the ambivalent attitude of Government. On the one hand, efforts are made to curtail trading activities by introducing various regulatory measures; on the other hand, various concessions are made in recognition of the service which is being provided. Secondly, there is the need for further strengthening of the Associations, through assistance from NGOs rather than government.

This case study illustrates how the strategy of research may serve to strengthen Level 1 and, to a certain extent, Level 2 visibility. But to consolidate that position and to begin to move towards Level 3, collective action is necessary in the groups own self-interest. Individual networking allows individual traders to function. Networking to create associations enables individual traders to function a bit more effectively. However, without the provision of infrastructure and other support by the government, the ability to attain Level 3 visibility is severely curtailed.

The strategy of participatory action: village women

Rose Hall is a small rural village community in northern St. Vincent with a population of 1,500 persons. Like women in similar communities within and outside the Caribbean, the women of Rose Hall face myriad problems of poverty. Low income, few and inadequate facilities, large families, poor returns on their main economic activity — agriculture, marginalization on the fringe of St. Vincent's development thrust. The list seems endless. But the women of Rose Hall also have a strong potential for leadership, a strong vision of what they wish for their families and community and a burning desire to attain that vision.

Recognizing the potential of that scenario, WAND initiated in 1980 a pilot project for the Integration of Women in Rural Development in Rose Hall. The objectives of the project were to:

1. Develop and test a participatory methodology as a model that could integrate women more fully in the process of rural development.

2. Develop in rural women self-esteem, self-confidence and an ability to accept leadership and decision-making roles in their community; and

3. Provide information on Women and Development issues that could influence policies of national governments in the region (Ellis, 1986b).

Over the life of the project, the women and men of Rose Hall developed a package of activities based on their own assessment of their needs, their own system of prioritizing action, their own project and programme designs and their own evaluation procedures. The entire process was based on a continuing dialogue between a Community Working Group, established to administer the project, and the entire community.

At the outset of the project, WAND organized a three-week training workshop in Participatory Approaches to Community Needs Assessment, Programme Planning and Evaluation. Participants included women from the community, members of the project working group, extension officers from government departments and NGOs working in the area. Apart from exposure to certain concepts and techniques, participants also learnt about their own skills and abilities and how these could be used to greatest advantage to the benefit of themselves and the wider community. This process of self-discovery and collaboration represented the basic tool for the furtherance of project objectives.

Through the aegis of the pilot project, the people of Rose Hall identified and participated in a number of activities including the following:

RESEARCH

In recognition of the need for information to inform social action, great stress was placed on research which was identified, designed, and conducted by community members. Using this approach several types of survey were conducted. A basic household survey was undertaken to develop a profile of the community. Special purpose studies were undertaken to develop a sense of community spirit, e.g. an oral history survey of the oldest members of the community produced a history of Rose Hall. Baseline surveys were a prerequisite to any action programme proposed, e.g. a survey on adult literacy levels in the community preceded the establishment of an adult education programme; a survey of the size, characteristics and needs of the population under 5 years of age preceded the building of a pre-school. The research which is carried out by a team over the entire community is usually 'simple, direct, uncomplicated, specific and short' (Ellis, 1986c, p. 146).

Dissemination of research findings also adopts participatory approaches. The preferred approach is to present the findings to a mass meeting of the community, using techniques of the creative arts. This is followed by general discussion and decisions on appropriate action to follow. This open discussion represents another aspect of the ongoing community-wide evaluation built into the entire process.

TRAINING

Following the inaugural workshop which was spearheaded by WAND, community members took over the planning and conduct of workshops which they identified as critical to community needs. As in the case of the first workshop, the objective was to teach members how to recognize their own skills and how to harness these to the betterment of the community. A wide range of topics were covered including personal development, interpersonal relationships, problem-solving techniques, programme planning, project development, proposal writing, evaluation and small business management (Ellis, 1986b). In addition, skills-training classes were conducted in income-related areas such as sewing, food preparation and preservation, record-keeping and agricultural practices.

As in the case of the research, the community members determine the type, content, form, timing and direction of the training programmes and classes. They depend on their own skills, only rarely using resource persons from outside the community.

ACTION PROGRAMMES

With the confidence of knowledge provided by the research and skills provided by the training, the community was able to progress to the planning and implementation of a wide range of community-based projects. These have included:

- income-earning projects, e.g. sweet making, sewing of uniforms for school children, boy scouts and girl guides;
- building of a pre-school;
- establishment of a farmers' group which buys seeds and fertilizer in bulk, develops contacts with Ministry of Agriculture personnel, or-

ganizes visits to other agricultural areas on the island etc.;
* establishment of a handicraft centre for girls;
* establishment of an adult education programme which provides literary training, agricultural information and home improvement skills; and revitalization of a branch of the National Council.

These activities in which both women and men participate are coordinated by the Community Working Group, three-quarters of whom are women. Women are therefore both contributors and beneficiaries of a development process which they themselves control.

COMMUNITY MOBILIZATION

Although the Community Working Group was charged with the responsibility of implementing the project, and although it continues to be responsible for community activities even now that the pilot project has ended, the Community Working Group has never acted alone. It has always been conscious of the need to ensure that community members are actively involved in all aspects of planning, implementation and evaluation. Continuous informal discussions are maintained with individuals and groups. Formal community meetings provide the forum in which decision-making takes place. This continuous process of building self-confidence has enabled the community to lobby on its own behalf at whatever level is considered necessary. Thus national planners, policymakers and non-government organizations have been approached, as have regional agencies and international donors. As a result the level of assistance which Rose Hall has received for its many projects is remarkably high.

CONCLUSION

Because of the internal cohesiveness of Rose Hall and the readiness of that community for change, the introduction by WAND of participatory methodology was especially timely. It enabled the community to develop a technique for collective action geared to meet the development needs as defined by the community itself. It also enabled the community to draw systematically into their system the very planners and policy-makers whose national development plans were making little difference in the village life of Rose Hall.

The range of strategies employed in Rose Hall served to clarify gender issues and to sensitize community members to recognize and respond to the inhibiting effects of gender disadvantage. In the process of that response knowledge about the situation and needs of women in the community became widely available, i.e. visibility Levels 1 and 2 have been attained. Through self-help measures the community seems well poised to attain Level 3 visibility.

The strategy of popular theatre: SISTREN, a women's collective

SISTREN, a Jamaican women's theatre collective, was founded in 1977 as a part-time voluntary, recreational drama group consisting of thirteen women employees of the Special Employment Programme which was introduced by the 1972–80 government of Michael Manley in an effort to provide temporary unemployment relief. Of the 14,000 low paid, low-status temporary workers, 10,000 were women. It was 13 of these women who approached one of the women tutors from the Jamaica School of Drama for assistance to produce a play for presentation at a workers' week concert. The tutor, Honor Ford Smith, reports 'I asked them what they wanted to do a play about'. They replied 'We want to do plays about how we suffer as women. We want to do plays about how men treat us bad'. She asked 'How do you suffer as women?' (SISTREN, 1986, p. xxii). So began the process of drawing on their individual experiences to develop dramatic presentations which analyse the critical issues affecting women and the wider society.

By 1988, the collective had become a fully fledged company producing its own plays, touring abroad, publishing, undertaking research, training its members, conducting community workshops. In addition, it has developed a screen-printing project as a means of generating income. In the process, SISTREN has acquired a substantial local and regional following, and a tremendous international reputation. According to Ford Smith, SISTREN is often projected 'as a successful model of a grassroots women's organisation... as a unique way of organising, as an example of popular theatre in action, the empowerment of working class women, and of effective working class self-management' (Ford Smith, 1989, p. 15).

The original aims of SISTREN were to:

(i)   analyse and comment on the role of women in Jamaican society through theatre;

(ii) organize into a self-reliant co-operative enterprise; and

(iii) to take drama to working-class communities. (SISTREN, 1986)

These aims have remained intact, resolving themselves into the following activities:

- it offers an educational service to women and men on issues of gender in Jamaica and the Caribbean;
- it acts as a catalyst for, and participates in campaigns and actions directed at introducing specific changes in the situation of women;
- it performs popular theatre;
- it produces a magazine;
- it conducts and publishes research on issues affecting women;

- it prints and sells T-shirts and wallhangings. (Ford Smith, 1989)

Basing its work on the personal experiences and individual testimonies of women, SISTREN has developed a drama methodology which allows its members as a collective, to identify themes and improvise dialogue which explores and analyses the events and forces shaping the lives of poor women. Thus, for example, *Bellywoman Bangarang* explores the theme of sexuality, mothering and society; *Muffet Inna All a We* deals with woman's constant struggle to control her own destiny; *Bandoolu Version* examines the issues of destructive male/female relationships; *Youth and Youth Know Yuh Truth* explores the issue of unemployment and single motherhood. The presentation of these works to the public, the media attention they attract and the link a presentation may have with a particular contemporary issue have together assisted SISTREN in its aim of stimulating societal changes beneficial to women. Thus, for example, *Bandoolu Version* coincided with the struggle of Jamaican women to secure appropriate legislation for maternity leave. The legislation was passed.

Initially, SISTREN operated in a supportive context. An organized women's movement existed in Jamaica at the time. The government of the day pronounced and implemented policies which legitimized popular expression. For SISTREN this implied access to state facilities, including services of a tutor, office and rehearsal space, from the Jamaica School of Drama, assistance with training from the Women's Bureau. With a change of government in 1980, all this ceased. National priorities changed. Co-operative and community efforts were closed down. The women's movement collapsed, SISTREN was declared subversive and banned from radio and television. Without government infrastructural support, however limited, and no source of local funding SISTREN was forced to rely on external funds for its very existence. Together these events have meant that throughout the 1980s, SISTREN was functioning in a less than sympathetic, even a hostile, environment.

Paradoxically, the level and range of activities increased and the organization thrived. The silk screen textiles project was started. Design themes were linked to issues being explored in the drama productions. A research and documentation section began the process of documenting the organization's activities and airing issues on women. A series of activities, a film, a newsletter, later transformed into a magazine, a book on life stories of the original members, and booklets for public information and education resulted from this effort. Alliances were built with local, regional and international groups. A workshop programme was initiated in which members travelled throughout the country building and working with community groups using the drama methodology.

In a searching analysis of the first twelve years of SISTREN, its Artistic Director identifies a number of financial and administrative difficulties affecting the work and potential impact of the organisation. She concludes that the dictates of international funding agencies exacerbated internal contradictions in the collective structure. As a result, the organization became constrained in its ability to deliver to the community, to clarify its administrative structure and to satisfy the needs of members for personal development (Ford Smith, 1989, pp. 12–13).

Yet despite the many problems, SISTREN has done much to increase the visibility of women in Jamaica generally and the women of SISTREN in particular. It has done so by grounding its work in the personal experience of women by developing a particular form of participatory action which stresses women's creativity and by teaching women how to organize to effect change. For its members, this has translated into greater self-awareness, greater self-reliance, increased skills and a deeper sense of commitment to women in Jamaican society.

As an example of a strategy to increase visibility, SISTREN illustrates the linkage between conceptual and subjective visibility at Level 1; the move to Level 2 using research and documentation; and the move to Level 3 using education, mobilization, networking to stimulate both policy changes for all women and behavioural changes within their own households.

The strategy of regional networking: directors of Women's Bureaux

Following the establishment of the UN Decade for Women, women in the Caribbean hosted a sub-regional meeting in 1977 which produced a Regional Plan of Action (Seminar, 1977). Among the several recommendations in the Plan was one calling for the establishment of institutional machinery.

'Every territory in the region should establish a national mechanism for the integration of women in development in keeping with the structure of its government. This might range from the establishment of Women's Bureaux, National Commissions on the Status of Women within the structure of governments, to official recognition and utilization of non-governmental National Councils of Women's Organizations. Whatever the mechanism adopted, the following functions would need to be performed:

(a) Data collection and research.
(b) Participation in the formulation of national plans, policies, and programmes to achieve equality between the sexes and the full integration of women in the development process at all levels.
(c) Co-ordination of programmes affecting women.
(d) Monitoring and evaluation of on-going and future plans and programmes, with a view to ensuring that the interests and concerns of women are reflected, and the involvement of women as beneficiaries and participants is assured.

(e) Documentation and dissemination of information, public relations, and publicity.

(f) Promotion of innovative pilot projects.

(g) Guidance and advisory services.

(h) Liaison with regional and international bodies (Regional Plan of Action, 1977).

That sub-regional plan was later incorporated into ECLA's regional plan for the integration of women in the social and economic development of the Caribbean which was submitted to the UN.

This call resulted in an acceleration of activity in territories which had been active before the decade (notably Jamaica and Guyana), by positive responses in several territories and by the creation of the full-time post of Women's Affairs Officer in the CARICOM Secretariat in 1980. By the end of the Decade, the position was that seven territories had formally established units within government departments, one had established a full fledged ministry and four had allocated responsibility for women's affairs to officers within a specified ministry.[13] In addition four territories had appointed short-term Commissions whose term of office had already ended and three had on-going Standing Advisory Committees or Councils. The region could thus be described as having in place the institutional mechanism for advancing women's affairs. Table 4 presents the current situation.

However, the historical experience of these entities strongly suggests that the creation of institutional mechanisms by itself did not effectively anticipate, identify and develop assistance strategies for the various needs of women.

Critical to the operation of these entities is the location of the Director (or officer responsible for Women's Affairs) within the civil service structure. Throughout the Caribbean governments have been, and continue to be, the largest single employer of both male and female labour. However, women are concentrated in the lower clerical grades and in the teaching service. Virtually no women are found in the two most senior grades (Permanent Secretary and Senior Assistant Secretary) and those who do, achieve those posts on the basis of professional qualifications rather than length of service which is the more usual criterion. A few women are to be found at the intermediate grades (e.g. Assistant Secretary).

As officers responsible for a discrete unit within a Ministry, Directors of Women's Affairs should be treated as Departmental Heads in terms of level of appointment, salary, emoluments etc. In practice, Directors are appointed at one or two levels below the Permanent Secretary, i.e. either on par with or one level below all other Departmental Heads. Where there is no Director, but simply an officer responsible for Women's Affairs, that person is usually even further down the line. This means that programme proposals and budgets have to be approved by at least two senior personnel before unit requests are included in the annual esti-

TABLE 4

NATIONAL MACHINERY FOR WOMEN'S AFFAIRS IN THE COMMONWEALTH CARIBBEAN

| Territory | Date of establishment/Duration | | | Ministry | National Commission | Advisory Council/Commission |
	Desk	Bureau	Department			
Jamaica	1974	1975				1972 to present
Trinidad and Tobago				1975[1]	1975	
Guyana		1980		1976[2]		1976 to present
Barbados		1984	1976		1976–78	1984–1986
Belize		1981			1982	
St. Lucia				1981[5]		
Grenada	1979	1983		1979–83	1976	
St. Vincent	1985		1987	1984[6]		
Dominica	1980	1983		1978[3]		1983 to present
Antigua	1980		1989[4]			
St. Kitts/Nevis	1981			1984 to present		
Montserrat				1983[7]		
British Virgin Islands				?		
CARICOM Secretariat		1978				

Notes: Ministry refers to the Ministry in which an existing officer was assigned responsibility for Women's Affairs except in the case of Grenada and St. Kitts which had full fledged Ministries of Women's Affairs for the periods stated.
1. Permanent Secretary in Women's Affairs   2. Ministry of Cooperatives   3. Ministry of State   4. Directorate
5. Ministry of Community Services and Chief Community Development Officer
6. Ministry of Tourism, Information and Culture and Coordinator of Women's Affairs
7. Ministry of Youth and Community Development

Source: Various reports

mates of expenditure for the Ministry or in the Ministry's section of the national development plan. Unless the Director has a very forceful personality or the relevant Minister has a particular interest in the work of the Unit, Directors have been able to do little to ensure adequate representation of their units in budgets and national development plans. Thus, these women remain invisible not only in terms of their location in the administrative system of which they are part, but also in terms of the work which they do, the allocation of resources to that work and the representation of that work in the major planning documents of the system.

To counteract this triple invisibility, women's bureaux have collaborated with each other, through the combined assistance of the CARICOM Secretariat and the Commonwealth Secretariat, in a slow process of building their institutional capacity. In this regard, the experience of collaboration between Women's Desks in the region is of particular interest. The initial effort centred on a seminar in 1981 'Strengthening National Machinery for the Integration of Women in Development' which was sponsored by the CARICOM Secretariat, through its Women's Desk, and the BWA of Jamaica. Two of the five objectives of the seminar were to develop understanding about public administration, and increase the skill of participants in analysis and planning (CARICOM, 1981).

Specialists in these two areas provided women's bureau personnel with insights into how their units were located within national public administrative systems and planning processes.

Two years later the CARICOM Secretariat, in collaboration with the Commonwealth Secretariat, embarked on a programme of activities aimed at continuing the process of strengthening national machinery for women in the region. The programme started with the preparation of case studies of the management, organization and structure of six Women's Desk/Bureaux[14] (Gordon, 1984). This was followed by a workshop consisting of the directors of the six agencies, the four consultants who prepared the Studies, the CARICOM Women's Affairs Officer and two resource persons from the Commonwealth Secretariat. Over two and a half days this group discussed the reports and prepared a document outlining the needs and identifying the supports required for effective performance. The group was then joined by Permanent Secretaries responsible for the six Women's Desk/Bureaux who spent the next two days preparing proposals for mechanisms which could assist both Permanent Secretaries and Bureaux Heads in better managing the bureaux.

The 1983 assessment provided compelling evidence of other types of constraints. These included overambitious objectives, inadequate staff and other resources, ineffective or non-existent links with other branches of the public service, and financial constraints. Together these factors acted to influence negatively the methods of operation of the Directors and to limit the initiatives they wished to undertake (Gordon, op. cit.).

Despite these constraints, the six bureaux in the study had, individually or collectively, achieved singular achievements in developing supplementary structures for the implementation of their programmes; implementing legislative reform to improve the rights of women; developing production projects; and improving self-awareness. But these achievements have not blinkered bureaux from recognizing that an important gap in their activities relates to their apparent inability to mobilize women at the community level in order to ensure women's involvement in the diagnosis of their needs and the prescription of solutions.

The 1983 workshop was therefore followed by one in November 1985 which looked at strategies to strengthen the impact of bureaux and to implement the UN Forward Looking Strategies. The meeting of 11 Bureau heads and four Permanent Secretaries concentrated on recommendations in the areas of institution building, training and policy formulation (Commonwealth Secretariat, 1985). Also recommended was the establishment of sectoral/parish/regional committees to ensure a two-way flow of information between community and policy-maker with the bureaux as the conduit (Commonwealth Secretariat, 1985). It is not clear to what extent this recommendation has been implemented. The one Director who had effectively set up such a system even before the original workshop is no longer in the post.

Earlier in that same year, the Third Meeting of CARICOM Ministers responsible for Women's Affairs had identified as a priority the formulation of a national policy on women as part of an overall programme for strengthening the national machinery (CARICOM, 1985). To support this and to follow up on the recommendations of the November meeting, the Commonwealth Secretariat provided a Consultant in 1987 to assist requesting bureaux with the preparation of policy statements. To date six of the bureaux have benefited from that assistance, one is working on a statement independently and one has had a White Paper on the subject for many years. What is not yet clear is the extent to which those statements are merely administrative productions or are based on dialogue and discussion with NGOs and women at the community level. Further, it is far from clear whether these statements have provided the basis for the plans included in current national development plans. In the two territories whose plans are discussed later, it is known that no WID policy statement exists for one — Barbados — even though considerable information exists. For the other — St. Vincent — a WID policy statement is known to be available though not announced. It is not known whether its contents are reflected in the proposals outlined in the current development plan.

Parallel to the efforts to develop policy statements in individual territories, there has been a rapid endorsement of international instruments related to women. Thus, for example, all thirteen CARICOM member states have signed the UN Convention on the Elimination of Discrimination Against Women. To date, ten of these have ratified that convention.

Yet the major policy document of at least the two territories in these examples reveals a systematic exclusion of reference to women in the various sector analyses and plans. Even in the brief section devoted to women there is no mention of male/female or even female/female differentials on any dimension. And this despite the fact that the major areas identified as critical by planners — unemployment, poverty and inequality of income — are the very areas in which research has shown women to be at the greatest disadvantage.

While the fundamental institutional and resource problems faced by Directors cannot really be solved by them as individuals or even in a collective, there are two regional resources available which have been instrumental in helping them to meet other problems. The WAND unit, has been instrumental not only in the establishment of several Women's Desks but also in the provision of training and technical assistance on Bureau and NGO projects in a wide range of areas in individual territories.

The CARICOM's Women's Desk has been a useful mechanism for ensuring the discussion of WID issues at Ministerial level through a series of biennial meetings of Ministers responsible for Women's Affairs initiated in 1981 (CARICOM, 1981, 1983, 1985, 1988). Further, it has been instrumental in organizing training workshops in a number of areas intended to assist Directors in executing their administrative functions (see Table 5). Regional seminars organized by CARICOM have usually been followed either by specific assistance at the national level, by national seminars based on the original regional one or a combination of the two. Thus, for example, the seminars concerned with assessing national machinery (November 1983 and November 1985) were followed by the provision of a consultant who provided individual Bureaux with assistance in the drafting of national policy statements. The regional seminar on Management for Development (April 1988) has been followed by a series of national-level workshops on the same topic.

The activities of these two regional agencies working in collaboration with Directors has resulted in the maintenance of a strong regional network permitting sustained collective action, cross-fertilization of views and strategies, access to knowledge, information and mutual emotional support. Yet, there remains a sense in which the Bureaux and their Directors remain a marginalized group within their respective bureaucracies. At the policy level, this is reflected in the general absence of national policy statements on women; and the general absence (or limited mention) of provision for WID programmes in budgets and national development plans.[15] At the practical level, the lack of staff and inadequate budgetary allocations and low status of Directors continues to militate against the ability of the bureaux to meet their demands and to encourage a dependence on international finance. There are, however, isolated cases of Directors who have succeeded in circumventing these difficulties.

The Women's Desk, now styled Directorate of Women's Affairs, in

Date	Type and place of activity		Collaborating Institutions
1979	Seminar: Preparing Women for Effective Leadership	Jamaica	CARIWA
January 1980	Regional Meeting of Officials Concerned with the Greater Involvement of Women in Development	Guyana	—
March 1981	First Meeting of Ministers Responsible for Women's Affairs	Domnica	National Governments
November 1981	Seminar: Strengthening National Machinery for the Integration of Women in Development	Jamaica	Jamaica BWA; UWI
March 1983	Second Meeting of Ministers Responsible for Women's Affairs	Guyana	National Governments
May 1983	Workshop: Strategies for Increasing Development Opportunities for Women in the Caribbean	Barbados	Commonwealth Secretariat
November 1983	Workshop: Assessing National Machinery	Barbados	Commonwealth Secretariat
May 1984	Seminar: Women in the Industrial Development Process	Guyana	UNIDO
April/May 1984	Seminar: training Women for Effective Participation in Conference Diplomacy	Trinidad and Tobago	National Governments
May 1985	Third Meeting of Ministers Responsible for Women's Affairs	Antigua	National Governments
November 1985	Workshop: Ladies in Limbo Revisited	Belize	Commonwealth Secretariat
July 1986	Workshop: Data Collection and Statistical Analyses on the Situation of Women in the Caribbean	Barbados	IDRC
April 1988	Fourth Meeting of Ministers Responsible for Women's Affairs	St. Kitts	National Governments
April 1988	Workshop: Management of Development – Effecting Change	Guyana	CIDA; National Governemtns

Source: Information supplied by CARICOM Secretariat, Women's Desk.

61

Antigua was established in 1980 as part of the Ministry of Education, Culture, Youth, Women's Affairs and Sports, in which location it has remained ever since. Initially staffed by a Director and a typist (with no typewriter!), the Directorate now boasts a staff of fourteen: the Executive Director, Assistant Director, Public Relations Officer, six Project Officers, two Secretaries/Typists, two trainee Office Assistants and one Cleaner/Messenger. The Directorate has also grown in terms of its physical assets from a single desk in the Ministry to two buildings, one on a quarter acre of land, and a range of office, kitchen and sewing furniture and equipment. This makes Antigua the territory with the largest establishment for Women's Affairs amongst the public sectors in the region.

No explicit national policy statement on women exists. Efforts by the Directorate to activate such a statement proved unsuccessful through lack of support in 1981 and through severe editorial changes by the Minister in 1985. A third attempt based on widespread discussion of a draft throughout the island and a refined version prepared through the CARICOM Secretariat/Commonwealth Secretariat project mentioned earlier is currently before Cabinet. Despite this absence of a formal policy statement, mention is usually made of women and the Directorate's programmes in the Annual Throne Speech in which Government's plans for the year are outlined. In addition, Government has signed and ratified the UN Convention for the Elimination of Discrimination Against Women. These actions together with recent upgrading of the Desk to a Directorate suggest the existence of an implicit policy on Women's Affairs in this territory.

The programme of activities of the Directorate has moved from one concentrating exclusively on food production, preparation and preservation to one embracing a variety of skills training, classes in health and physical education, course in stress management, workshops on issues affecting women, research, publication of informative material. Present plans envisage the construction, on three acres of land donated by the government, of a complex consisting of a convention centre, an administrative block, residential accommodation unit and training centre. Also planned is the establishment of a bus service for rural women traders, a centre for children who have dropped out of school, a literacy training programme and several research projects. In effect, starting from a focus on traditional activities, the Directorate is gradually developing a broader based programme which is anchored in the stated needs of Antiguan women.

Funding is obtained from several sources. The government provides an annual operational budget and the provision of salaries and infrastructural facilities. Individual ministries, local sponsors and external donor agencies provide funds on an ad hoc project basis. Funds from the income-generating projects are funnelled back into the Directorate towards recurrent expenditure. Except for government funds received through the estimates, all other funds are sought and obtained on the initiative of the Directorate.

As in the case of other Directors in the region, the Antigua Director is located in the public service structure which links to the main decision-making body, Cabinet, through the relevant Ministry. In theory, proposals for budgetary allocations and development plans are channelled through the Ministry to the Planning Unit, thence to Cabinet for ratification. However, in Antigua there is no national five-year development plan but Departmental plans and estimates are co-ordinated by the Department of Planning within the Ministry of Finance and Economic Development during the annual budgetary exercise. The basis of determining the actual allocation of resources however seems rather unclear. According to the Executive Director, requests from the Directorate, usually within the range EC$25,000 — 30,000, are always cut back to EC$10,000 without consultation and without giving her a chance to defend her submission. This she counteracts by lobbying for major items of need. Thus, for example, the extension of its first building, the allocation of the second building, the forthcoming new building, the bus for the proposed bus service have all been obtained by lobbying on the basis of need and insufficient allocation of resources.

Such levels of government support in the absence of a formally announced policy statement raises the question of how was the Director able to achieve such support. Her basic strategy rests on a combination of personal contact, letters of intent, close relations with community-based groups, networking at the regional and international levels and widespread use of the print and electronic media. Prior to her appointment, the Director was a Specialist Supervisor in Home Economics in which capacity she had established a number of women's clubs dealing with family living, family nutrition and health. Working with and through those and other groups, enabled her to build the programme, on the basis of a broad target audience and within an environment receptive to the work of the Directorate. Maintaining close links with regional and international agencies particularly through the programmes of the CARICOM Secretariat enabled her to upgrade her knowledge, skills and self-confidence and to access external funding sources. By deliberately pursuing and maintaining a higher media profile for the Directorate, public awareness of its work is not only high but also serves to encourage support and commitment of government, NGOs and individuals. As a result the Directorate enjoys a very positive image in the Antiguan community which the Government cannot afford to ignore. All of this has been achieved on the initiative of a single woman using her wide-ranging social and political contacts, her refusal to be stymied by bureaucratic obstacles, her enthusiasm and passionate commitment to the task of assisting women to improve the quality of their lives.

The example of regional networking as a strategy to counteract the invisibility of Women's Bureaux illustrates that much depends on the throughput from the national level. The particular form the networking process has assumed under the guidance of the CARICOM Secretariat has yielded many personal gains to individual Directors in terms of knowledge, skills, and self-confidence. As a group, Directors of Women's Affairs may be said to have achieved a measure of conceptual and subjective visibility through their networking. But except in isolated cases the translation of these into higher levels of visibility for all women through greater government commitment in policy-making, development plans and budgetary allocations has been very lethargic. Much of this relates to limited resources at the national level and attitudinal blockages on the part of male decision-makers. But much is also due to uncertainty about the location of the bureaux in the planning process and mechanisms for ensuring that bureaux plans are reliably reflected in national plans. The next phase in the institution-building process would thus seem to be a workshop on the processes and techniques of planning for women's development in these territories. The workshop should examine the role of the bureaux in the planning process and the steps which could be taken to reflect more clearly the needs of women and government proposals to meet those needs through bureaux activities. Further, bureaux must be able to identify how those needs are being met by non-bureau programmes and projects both within and outside the public service. Accordingly, participants in the workshop should not be restricted to women's bureaux personnel.

The common thread

The five examples used in this section illustrate not only different strategies for attaining visibility but that two vital ingredients in the process are information and social networks. The former will be discussed in the next section of the paper. The latter takes the form of dynamic, informal structures which provide women with the information, material assistance, protection, self-confidence and emotional support to enable them to initiate and/or maintain their activities. Members of these networks may be kin or non-kin, colleagues or friends, ties may be close or distant, strong or weak, active or dormant. The important point is that these structures possess a flexibility which allows the woman to use them as circumstances in her life history change.

Thus Miss Tiny, the Jamaican higgler was able to draw from her network of higgler friends one contact who introduced her to the business of international trading when her fish-vending business failed. Agricultural traders from the Eastern Caribbean continually develop and draw on contacts from a wide network in order to obtain assistance in dealing with the various activities in the trading cycle. The women of Rose Hall depend on their network of family, friends and neighbours in the community to make the community programmes work. The women of SISTREN depend closely on each other for support in virtually all aspects of their lives. The Directors of women's bureaux constantly appeal to their regional network of colleagues for information, training and mutual support. They also rely on informal networks within their respective public sectors in order to carry out their functions. And all of the women, in these various groups, like other women throughout the region, rely on kinship networks for assistance with child care, household emergencies and so on. None of the studies reviewed analysed these networks. Rather their existence was just cursorily mentioned. No information is therefore available on which to base a detailed discussion of this phenomena in this paper.[16] However, while available data do not permit a close understanding of the dynamics of the network systems, they do allow a general awareness of the role they perform in supporting the work activities of women.[17]

A development strategy which fails to recognize the existence and importance of these networks therefore fails to recognize a critical reality of women's lives. They also miss the opportunity to build on an existing form of social relationship which is already designed to provide mutual support and with which women are already familiar.

Indicators for planning for women in development

The importance of information in moving women from invisibility to visibility has been evident from the illustrations used in the previous section. This reflects one aspect of the numerous calls made in individual territories and regional meetings for reliable information about the real situation of women. WID specialists familiar with women's issues need to find acceptable measures for filtering that information into national development plans. Planners knowledgeable about planning techniques, need to become familiar with women's issues and to develop measures to include that information into national development plans. The previous sections of this study have drawn attention to a number of issues related to women which need to be considered if development plans are to address the needs of women. Included amongst these issues are the range of factors influencing the ability of women to participate in and benefit from development; the range of activities in which women can and do engage; the range of strategies they use to enable them to carry out their responsibilities; the range of strategies used to bring the situation of different groups of women to the attention of development planners. Overshadowing these has been the limited attention paid to women's issues in current development plans and the limited resources allocated to those issues.

Both at national and regional level, a number of initiatives have taken place over the years to sensitize planners to these issues. Fundamental to these initiatives has been an understanding that development planning based on a sectoral approach often fails to provide the integrative solution to women's concerns which is required. Thus, to provide employment without day care facilities, family planning services without skills-training programmes, or housing without employment is to indicate that the linkages between these various programmes are not recognized. For women, these links are vital. Planners in the Caribbean have been exposed to these issues through seminars, workshops, conferences, research reports, media presentations, public discussions. Yet somehow this information is not being filtered into plans and programmes with periodic, specific, and realistic objectives designed to meet the interests and needs of women. Part of this may be related to the lack of clear objectives of the government agency responsible for women's affairs and the consequent difficulty of translating these objectives into the language and techniques of planning. Part may be linked to bureaucratic resistance to matching official rhetoric about women with firm commitment to provision of resources. Part is undoubtedly due to the difficulty of transforming micro-level issues which are not easily quantifiable to macro-level statistical indices.

One possible approach to the problem is the production of a series of social and economic indicators which are simple to produce and easy to understand. Such indicators should depict disparities between different sub-groups of women and between women and men over time. The importance of indicators in development planning for women has been recognized in many countries. In Thailand, for example, a recent study insists that:

'Indicators for women's development are essential for policy formulation, planning and programming as well as for evaluation of programmes and projects directed towards the development of women. These indexes describe the present situation and status of women, and if collected as time series indicators, could show the past trend and pattern of changes from which guidelines could be developed for planning for the future. In addition these indexes could serve as warning signals against negative aspects of development. More importantly, they also could be used as targets and objectives for development.' (UNESCO, 1987, pp. 139–40)

The question of devising appropriate indicators of women's participation in socio-economic development has occupied the attention of several UN agencies for many years, INSTRAW and UNESCO being particularly prominent (UN, 1983a, b, and c, 1984a and b, 1985a, 1987; UNESCO, 1981). At a UNESCO meeting in 1980, it was agreed that such indicators should:

measure change over time, refrain from seeking simple composite indices or profiles of women, differentiate or disaggregate among groups of women, stress comparison within a society rather than attempt cross-cultural generalizations, compare the relative condition of women with that of men, and be complemented by or able to pick up the contextual macro and micro variables that affect women's socio-economic participation. (Buvinic, 1981, p. 13)

It is important to recognize that all indicators are not necessarily quantifiable and that some quantitative indicators do not necessarily measure the total situation being described. For example, the studies on domestic service cited earlier clearly indicate the numerical importance of this form of employment for large numbers of women. However, such statistics reveal nothing about the links between the domestic service workforce and the social relationships between domestic and employer or the effect of those links on the lives of those involved. Thus, it is not surprising to find no specific plans for these women in available development plans. A different kind of example comes from women in rural areas who are primarily engaged in agriculture. Available quantitative measures suggest that only limited numbers of women are so engaged. Yet the micro-level studies reveal not only much larger numbers, but also a considerable amount of variation in the type of agricultural activity in which women engage. Concomitantly, the range of problems they encounter and the range of programmes that could assist them is also varied. Yet the development plans don't even acknowledge women's involvement in agriculture.

Perhaps one of the major stumbling blocks is the small-scale nature of the studies which unearth the micro-level issues and their probable inability to meet stringent requirements of representativeness. Another possible stumbling block may be the way in which the statistical material from these studies is presented. Is enough attention paid to methodology? Is the analysis tightly linked to macro-level issues? Can the recommendations/prescriptions be linked to available plans or do they require totally different institutional arrangements?

One possible approach to confronting this issue is to present indicators in the form of a system or model which attempts to answer the following questions:
• What are the parameters of the society with which we are dealing?
• How do women fit into the society?
• What are the institutional arrangements in place to
   assist women?
A model attempting to provide such answers for the Caribbean was first presented at the UNESCO meeting in 1980. That paper argued that a system of indicators should reflect

... the operation of sexual differentiation in areas other than education and employment, the conventional indicators, should reflect notions of differential power and authority between the sexes and should reflect the heterogeneity of the sub-group women. Ideally, such an approach requires both quantitative and qualitative measures. The quantitative measures should indicate the differential representation of men and women in different areas of activity, the differential exercise of rights and responsibilities, the differential control over material rewards. Qualitative measures should indicate the perception of the individuals concerned of their own and their group's position in several spheres of activity and in the society as a whole. (Massiah 1980, p. 14)

The original Caribbean model envisaged a system consisting of three panels. The first was concerned with the structural features which impinge on the society's efforts to develop. The second panel was intended to reflect the situation of women, while the third was intended to reflect the institutional arrangements in place to enable women to participate in and benefit from development efforts. Within the second panel, it was proposed that indicators should be arranged in the context of three themes — sources of livelihood, emotional support, power and authority — rather than in sectors. These themes were devised to reflect more clearly the integrated reality of women's lives which, it was felt, the sectoral approach obscured.

The suggested framework may be summarized as follows:

PANEL I   RESOURCES
Human: population, education, health, social conditions
Physical: land, mineral resources
Economic: patterns of property ownership, performance of economic resources
Social mobility: socio-economic groups, incidence of social mobility, equality of opportunity

PANEL II   STATUS OF WOMEN
Sources of Livelihood: involvement in production process, levels of income, alternative/supplementary sources of income, access to productive resources.
Emotional support: involvement in reproductive unions, extent of motherhood, job satisfaction, leisure activities including involvement in informal cliques/ associations.
Power and authority: autonomy in family union; participation in political organizations; participation in socio-economic organizations; office-holding in organizations; management/supervisory positions in formal economic sector

PANEL III   LEGAL PROVISIONS

| National institutions: | constitutional guarantee of equality of sexes; universal adult suffrage; political independence; women's Bureau/Commission; paid maternity leave |

A review of the available data sources from conventional statistical systems, i.e. population censuses, sample surveys and administrative records suggests that even with the present and known deficiencies, there is enough to produce broad profiles of the situation of women (Appendix II). The surveys reviewed in this study suggest that while they have produced valuable information, they have been small-scale, localized investigations the results of which cannot be generalized to the country as a whole. However, the data they produce can be used to complement data from official national sources. Together these two sources provide, in this region, a sufficiently acceptable base on which to build such a system of indicators on the situation of women.

The remainder of this section of the study presents indicators for one territory, Barbados, using a combination of census and other official data and survey data from other sources within the framework proposed in 1980.[18] The model is applied for the years 1970, 1980, and, where possible, 1985 or the nearest year for which relevant data are available. Results are shown in Tables 6 to 13 and definitions of indicators in Appendix III.

While the data presented are for the entire island, the entire model or subsections thereof may be adapted for particular groups of women. However, efforts to disaggregate indicators in a population of a quarter of a million need to proceed with caution. Two problems adhere to this question — the definition of the groups (e.g. urban and rural, socio-economic categories) and the availability of detailed data disaggregated in that way. While it may be possible to produce tabulations from census data in the required format, this often may not be possible for survey data where the numbers are so much smaller. A more realistic approach would be to undertake 'ad hoc' case studies of particular groups of women as the need arises. In Barbados, for example, regardless of the definition adopted for urban and rural, census data suggest that the male and female populations are relatively evenly spread throughout the country. So, too, are gender differences in terms of worker rates, occupational groups, educational attainment, mortality levels and so on. However, for specific details on any specific group, e.g. housewives, the census is particularly unhelpful.[19]

As in the original model, rates, ratios or percentages are used for the indicators concerned with the structural features of the society. Where the position of one sub-group of women is being compared to another, the proportion that sub-group comprises of all women is used. This corresponds to Boulding's 'Distribution Index' (Boulding, 1976). Where the position of women is being compared to men, the proportion which women constitute of the total group is used. This corresponds to Boulding's 'Index of Femaleness' (Boulding, op. cit.). A gender gap is said to exist when this proportion diverges from one-half. For those indicators reflecting the characteristics of national institutions, the age of the relevant institution is used. For the specific concerns of this assignment, certain indicators which were not discussed in the original model are now included while others have been omitted. Also, in keeping with the recommendations from the UNESCO 1980 meeting, composite indices have been avoided.

Barbados: a case study

According to a recent indicator study on the status of women in ninety-nine countries, Barbados with a score of 74 points placed among a group of twenty-three countries which earned a rank of 'Good'. Barbados and Jamaica, with a score of 73.5, were the only developing countries in that group. Only seven countries in the sample, none of which were developing countries, attained scores of 80-89.5 which placed them in the category 'Very Good'. None of the countries achieved a score of 90 and over which would have ranked them in the 'Excellent' category.[20] (Population Crisis Committee, 1988)

Evidence such as this would seem to suggest that women in Barbados are sufficiently well advanced as not to require any specific developmental assistance from their government. This, in fact, is a view often expressed by key officials.[21] But closer examination of more detailed indicators provides evidence of groups whose numbers or problems are not reflected at the national level and which may be considered invisible. The indicators presented in the remainder of this paper attempt to identify some of those groups. The discussion proceeds in the context of the panels identified earlier.

PANEL I: RESOURCES

Human resources

Population

The indicators in this panel, shown in Table 6, suggest that Barbados is a small population of about one-quarter of a million with slow rates of growth, low birth and death rates. The sex ratio in both the total population and the population of working age suggests a relatively even balance between the sexes. The dependency ratios point to a gradually aging population in which the relative share of aged dependents is increasing.

TABLE 6
INDICATORS OF THE SITUATION OF WOMEN IN POPULATION, BARBADOS, 1970–80

Population	1970	1980
Total population		
Male	100,000	116,000
Female	125,000	128,000
Annual rate of growth	0.2	
Crude birth rate	19.8	
Crude death rate	8.9	
Sex ratio: total population	886	899
Sex ratio: population 15–44	903	943
Youth dependency ratio	678	495
Old age dependency ratio	152	176
Population aged 65+	19,500	25,500
Male distribution index	6.2	8.9
Female distribution index	10.1	12.0
Proportion female	64.7	60.1
Urban population	98,000	97,000
Male distribution index	40.5	39.1
Female distribution index	42.3	40.2
Proportion female	54.2	53.3
Rural population	137,700	147,300
Male distribution index	59.5	60.9
Female distribution index	57.7	59.8
Proportion female	52.2	52.1

Sources: CARICOM, n.d.; UWI, 1976.

The increasing proportion of the elderly, almost two-thirds of whom are women, suggest that elderly women are an invisible group which should be targeted for greater attention.

Geographically the population remained relatively evenly spread between St. Michael, the main urban parish containing Bridgetown, the capital, and its suburbs, and the rest of the territory.[22] Women comprise just over half the population in both urban and rural areas.

Education

Turning to the quality of the population in terms of education, it is evident that both girls and boys are taking advantage of the available facilities (Table 7). At primary level, virtually full enrollment has been maintained for both boys and girls, with girls forming half of the enrolled

TABLE 7
INDICATORS OF THE SITUATION OF WOMEN IN EDUCATION, BARBADOS, 1970–1980

Education and Training	1970			1980		
	Proportion of male population	Proportion of female population	Female proportion of total population	Proportion of male population	Proportion of female population	Female proportion of total population
Enrollment at						
Age 5–14	97.5	97.8	50.1	97.6	98.2	50.0
Age 15–19+	39.5	44.1	52.8	39.7	47.5	54.5
Certification of population 15+						
Secondary Certificate	7.1	6.4	52.5	12.8	14.9	57.9
University Degree/Diploma	2.2	1.1	37.4	4.6	3.2	44.5
Vocational training for current occupation	12.8	7.6	42.1	29.2	15.4	37.9
Educational attainment of population aged 15+						
None	0.1	0.1	62.4	0.6	0.6	54.0
Primary	22.1	27.2	60.1	51.1	53.8	55.2
Secondary	75.2	70.9	53.5	41.9	40.7	53.2
Tertiary	1.6	0.6	32.1	3.9	2.1	38.5
Years of schooling						
Less than 5	7.9	9.8	60.2	2.2	2.6	58.8

Note: Data processing errors are believed to have produced a reversal of the primary and secondary categories [CARICOM, Vol. 1, n.d.]

Sources: CARICOM, n.d.; UWI, 1967.

population. At secondary level, the enrollment rates for boys increased only marginally, whereas that for girls increased by some three percentage points. When levels of certification are considered, significant differences begin to appear. Less than 20 per cent of the adult population have achieved secondary level certification, with females comprising three-fifths of that group. At University level, only 3 per cent of the female population has acquired degrees or diplomas, representing about two-fifths of all persons with such qualifications. These indices represent increases since 1970, so that a case for improvement may be argued. Similarly low but improving indices obtain for vocational training. With less than 40 per cent of the trained working population being females, there continues to be room for improvement.

Overall levels of educational attainment, again show no appreciable difference between rates for males and females at the different levels. Further, there is evidence that such differences as exist are closing at the primary level, where the gender gap is slightly in favour of the females, and at the secondary level. At University level, however, there are no signs of any significant change in the 'gender gap' over the period with females constituting less than 40 per cent of the University trained population.

Health

A history of considerable expenditure on health has paid off in terms of very favourable indicators for both males and females (Table 8).

Life expectancies now exceed 70 years for both sexes with a difference of five years in favour of the females. That level of difference has remained steady since the decade of the 1960s. Infant mortality rates have declined from 46 in 1970 to just 13 in 1984, reflecting not only better pre-natal and child care at the institutional level, but also within the home. Maternal mortality has been traditionally a minor cause of death. This rate has declined from 14.3 per 10,000 live births to 2.4 in 1980 and has risen slightly to 6.9 in 1986. It should be noted that the years 1981-83 witnessed no maternal deaths. Low mortality among women in the reproductive years has been a feature of adult female mortality in this territory. In 1960 the probability that a woman aged 15 would die by age 45 was 6 per cent. By 1970 this had been reduced to 2 per cent after which it rose slightly to 3 per cent.

Two other indicators of female mortality relate to deaths due to cancer of the breast or cervix. Prevailing rates in 1984 were 30 and 25 per 100,000 women respectively, the highest rates obtaining for any individual cause of death afflicting women only. Indeed cancers represent the leading cause of death among women in 1984, contributing to a potential loss of 12.8 years of life from that disease (PAHO, 1986). Women suffering from this disease should therefore be considered another group of 'invisible' women who merit special attention.

TABLE 8

INDICATORS OF THE SITUATION OF WOMEN IN HEALTH, BARBADOS, 1970–84

Health	1970	1980	1984
Life expectancy at birth			
Male	65.8	70.2	n.a.
Female	70.8	75.2	n.a.
Infant mortality rate	46	25	13
Mortality rates of children			
Aged 1–4 years	2.2	0.8	0.7
Maternal mortality rates	1.4	0.2	0.7
Mortality rates due to			
Cancer of breast	n.a.	n.a.	25.1
Cancer of cervix	n.a.	n.a.	29.6
Probability of women dying between the ages of 15–45	1.9	3.0	n.a.

Source: PAHO, 1986.

Households

An important feature of women's ability to manage their lives relates to their household responsibilities. In Barbados, approximately one-fifth of the population of both sexes lives alone, while females contribute just under one-half of all persons living alone (Table 9). Among the population living alone, 43 per cent are aged 65 and over and of these 59 per cent were women in 1980, an increase from 56 per cent in 1970. Here again, is another area of vulnerability for elderly women and one pointing to the need for assistance.

The proportion of households headed by women has remained relatively steady increasing from 43 per cent to 44 per cent between 1970 and 1980. Approximately one-third of all adult females and one-half of adult males are household heads. The size of households for which heads are responsible has declined for males from 4.2 to 3.6 but remained stable at 3.7 for females. Available data for 1980 do not permit an estimate of the proportion of women who head households and are not in a residential union. In 1970 that percentage stood at 42 per cent. However the 1980 census does provide data on household headship and family type. According to this, 37 per cent of nuclear families, 57 per cent of extended families and 49 per cent of composite families are to be found in households headed by women.[23] This may be viewed in terms of the proportion of female household heads in each family type. According to this, 57 per cent head nuclear families, an unidentified number of which are single person

TABLE 9
INDICATORS OF THE SITUATION OF WOMEN IN HOUSEHOLDS, BARBADOS, 1970–80

Households	1970			1980		
	Proportion of male population	Proportion of female population	Female proportion of total population	Proportion of male population	Proportion of female population	Female proportion of total population
Single person households	17.4	22.5	49.2	21.8	22.2	44.3
Population 65+ living alone	24.9	37.3	55.8	29.3	41.0	59.4
Household heads	53.5	30.9	42.9	50.3	33.9	43.9
Mean household size						
Male heads		4.2	—	—	3.6	—
Female heads		3.7	—	—	3.7	—
Household heads						
Never married	27.8	54.3	59.6	30.4	53.5	58.0
Not in a reproductive union	n.a.	41.9	—	n.a.	n.a.	n.a.
In workforce	83.6	45.5	289.1	77.1	48.9	33.3
Unemployed	10.3	6.6	41.6	9.0	12.2	33.3
With primary level education only	30.6	47.5	49.5	n.a.	n.a.	n.a.

Sources: CARICOM, n.d.; UWI, 1976.

families, 37 per cent head extended families and 7 per cent head composite families.

Almost 50 per cent of female household heads were in the 1980 workforce, increasing somewhat over the 1970 figure but considerably lower than the percentage for male household heads at both dates. The proportion of unemployed women who head households has risen from 6.6 in 1970 to 12.2 in 1980 while the female proportion of unemployment amongst all household heads has risen dramatically from 42 per cent in 1970 to 70 per cent in 1980. This points to another vulnerable group — unemployed women who are household heads.

Physical resources

Land

Barbados is a tiny island of 430 km but it ranks among the world's most densely populated countries. This is reflected in the population density which has been over 500 persons per square kilometre for many years reaching a high 567 in 1980 (Table 10).

The arable land area which stood at 200 km in 1964 is reported to be declining rapidly. Although we are without the quantitative data to support this, there is growing visual evidence of this phenomena. It must therefore be assumed that the densities relating population to the arable land are even greater. These measures, while of limited methodological validity, indicate the extent of the pressure of the population on the available land resources. Thus, whether in terms of total land area or arable land area, it is evident that Barbados is a heavily populated island.

Two other indicators of the utilization of land resources have been selected. The first relates to the only known mineral resource available in the island — oil — which was discovered during the 1970s. From a starting position of zero in 1970, Barbados was producing 300,000 barrels of crude oil by 1980 and almost 700,000 by 1985 amounting to more than half its domestic requirements. In addition by 1985 it was exporting refined oil to the tune of two million barrels, representing 8 per cent of the exports from the Commonwealth Caribbean.[24] Even though Barbados remains a net importer of petroleum and derivatives, the existence of a mineral resource base does provide a potential development asset from which women could benefit. Female involvement in the mining sector is virtually non-existent.

The second indicator related to land resources is agriculture which has traditionally been the mainstay of the Barbados economy but which is undergoing severe stress right now. This is evidenced in the declining output and contribution of agriculture to GDP and the declining employment in agriculture. With regard to the latter, female employment in the

TABLE 10

INDICATORS OF THE SITUATION OF WOMEN IN RELATION TO PHYSICAL RESOURCES,
BARBADOS, 1970–85

Physical resources	1970	1980	1985
Land			
Density	547	567	n.a.
Arable land density	807[1]	n.a.	n.a.
Employment in agriculture			
Proportion of male workforce	16.4	10.9	7.3
Proportion of female workforce	14.7	8.4	6.4
Female proportion of agricultural workforce	36.5	36.6	40.6
Exports of refined oil	—	931[2]	2,322[2]
Employment in mining, etc.			
Proportion of male workforce	0.59	0.46	n.a.
Proportion of female workforce	0.06	0.05	n.a.
Female proportion of workforce in mining	5.94	7.17	n.a.
Economy			
GDP per capita	1,135[7]	6,186[7]	8,663[7]
Contribution to GDP of			
Agriculture	13.9	9.8	6.9[3]
Manufacturing	10.8	10.9	13.0[3]
Public sector	14.7	14.9	13.8[3]
Percentage of government expenditure on			
Health	16.7	16.3	13.0[6]
Education	20.4	21.1	18.4[6]
All social services	n.a.	52.8	49.4[5]
External debt	31.4m[7]	319.8m[7]	794.8m[7]
Index of retail prices	7.0[4]	14.4	3.9
Unemployment rate			
Male	7.5	7.4	13.2
Female	12.3	15.1	24.1
Female proportion	52.6	62.8	59.4

Notes:
1. 1964.
2. Thousands of barrels.
3. Provisional figures for 1983.
4. 1972.
5. 1984.
6. 1987.
7. $Bds based on $US equivalent given in IADB, 1986 [US$1 = Bds $2].
Sources: CARICOM, n.d.; UWI, 1976; IADB, various years; Barbados, 1988.

agricultural sector declined from 14.7 in 1970 to 8.4 in 1980 and 6.4 in 1985. Male employment in agriculture was minimally higher than female at each date. The proportion of agricultural employees who were women remained steady at 37 per cent.

Economy

Here the concern is with the performance of the main physical resources and the extent to which the returns from those resources are reinvested in the human resources in the form of social services.

This sector provides compelling evidence of an increasing per capita income for the Barbados population. From just under US$600 in 1970, per capita income has risen to over US$4,000 by 1985, suggesting considerable economic growth, most of which occurred during the 1970s.[25] The new trend was characterized by declining agriculture, manufacturing which expanded during the 1970s and contracted during the 1980s, tourism which grew fairly steadily and a public sector which also remained steady during the 1970s but declined thereafter.

A major feature of recent trends in the economy is the rapidly escalating external debt outstanding which grew from US$15.7 m in 1970 to US$397.4 by 1985. This affected not only the foreign exchange reserves and balance of payments position but also the ability of the government to deliver social services to the population. Thus, central government expenditure in social services decreased in both real and per capita terms, particularly after 1980. Indeed, a recent study places Barbados among countries with the most severe cuts in per capita GDP and Health and Education expenditures (Commonwealth Secretariat, 1989). That study has shown that government expenditure on health declined by 21 per cent between 1980 and 1984. The proportion of government expenditure allocated to health moved down from 16.7 per cent in 1970 to 16.3 per cent in 1980 and by 1987 had reached 13.0 per cent. In education, the corresponding proportions were 20.4 per cent, 21.1 per cent and 18.4 per cent. For all social services, the decline since 1980 has been from 52.8 per cent to 46.2 per cent in 1982 after which there was a slight rise to 49.4 per cent in 1984.

To summarize, the findings of the first panel, then, Barbados, a small-densely populated territory shows signs of low population growth and an aging population. That population has been relatively favourably equipped in terms of education and health, with only few signs of gender differences at the national level in terms of outcome indicators. In terms of housing, there are significant numbers of households headed by women, but no real difference in the size of households headed by men and women. There are, however, sizeable differences in the characteristics of female and male household heads particularly in terms of unemployment.

The capacity of the land to support its population is limited by its physical size, the use of the land for agricultural production, and the limited availability of mineral resources. However, the human capacity to manipulate the available physical and economic resources is evidenced by an economy which, on the surface, experienced significant growth during the 1970s. But increasing external debt, growing unemployment and increasing inability to provide social services during the 1980s signal an economy which may be in danger of experiencing considerable difficulties in the 1990s.

The two sectors in this panel have highlighted four groups of women which may be considered invisible in the context of this study:

* elderly women
* elderly women who live alone
* unemployed women who head households
* women suffering from cancer of the breast or of the cervix.

Earlier in this report, reference was made to the provisions for the elderly in the current development plan, although elderly women have not been singled out for special attention.

In similar vein, the development plan speaks in general terms about unemployment but fails to identify any specific sub-group among whom unemployment is particularly severe. Thus, neither women nor sub-groups of women are targeted for specific employment creating strategies. Accordingly, no proposals exist for unemployed women who head households.

Similarly, it would be expected that the high rates of cervical and breast cancer would be reflected in related health programmes for women. Instead in the Ministry of Health's contribution there are general statements such as: 'Special attention will be given to those suffering from diabetes emeritus, hypertension and cancer' (Barbados, 1989a, p. 77). 'Expansion of the cancer screening services so as to follow up 100 per cent postnatal clients and provide routine pap smears and relevant education to women' (Barbados, op. cit., p. 79).

But the point has to be made that the fact that no direct reference is made to certain groups or situations does not necessarily mean that nothing is being done. What the plan does reflect is a planning philosophy which assumes that national level plans automatically cover the needs of all groups in the society. Such a philosophy fails to acknowledge, hence to provide for, the differential needs of the various groups in that society.

PANEL II: STATUS OF WOMEN

This section of the model seeks to describe the situation of women at a particular point in time or over a specific period and to relate it to that of men. In the process, attention is drawn to areas in which women are at an advantage and those in which they are at a disadvantage. This is the section of the model which lends itself most readily to disaggregation. Thus indicators may be produced at the national level, as is done here, or for any sub-group of women.

Sources of livelihood

Involvement in the productive process

The total labour force grew from 91,000 in 1970, to 108,000 in 1980 and 113,000 in 1985. Women constituted 40 per cent, 45 per cent and 47 per cent of the labour force on each of these dates. Within the labour force, workers account for about 93 per cent of the males and about 87 per cent of the females at both census dates and 86 per cent males and 76 per cent of the females in 1985. Among workers, employment for wages accounts for over 90 per cent of both male and female workers, while self-employment has risen from 8 to 13 per cent among males and fallen from 8 per cent to 7 per cent among females suggesting some decline in the importance of self-employment among women during the period (Table 11).

Despite this similarity of the male and female distributions on these two indicators, the relative position of women appears mixed in terms of the proportion which women constitute of these two categories of workers. The female share of the paid workforce amounted to only 39 per cent in 1970 increasing to 44 per cent in 1980 and 1985 at which level it seems to have stabilized. Among the self-employed, females accounted for 39 per cent in 1970, but 33 per cent and 31 per cent respectively in 1980 and 1985.

The occupational distribution of the paid workforce also provides initial evidence of a gradually narrowing gender gap. In the agricultural sector, in 1980, 8 per cent of the female working population and 11 per cent of the male working population were engaged in agriculture. But of the total population so engaged just 36 per cent were women. Further, the detailed listing of occupations for the 1980 Population Census reveals that over 98 per cent of women in Barbadian agriculture are involved as 'agriculture and animal husbandry workers', i.e. as agricultural labourers. The corresponding proportion for men is 80 per cent. Only 1 per cent of women in agriculture are designated farmers and one-half of 1 per cent as farm managers. By contrast, 4 per cent and 5 per cent of men in agriculture are found in these two categories. The familiar picture of women being at the lowest level of a sector is here compounded by the declining importance of this sector in the economy to which reference has already been made. Hence another vulnerable group of women is immediately identified.

In non-agricultural occupations the position of women has not undergone much change. During the 1980s over 90 per cent of the female work-

TABLE 11
INDICATORS OF LIVELIHOOD AMONG WOMEN, BARBADOS, 1970–1985

Involvement in the productive process	1970			1980			1985		
	Proportion of male population	Proportion of female population	Female proportion of total population	Proportion of male population	Proportion of female population	Female proportion of total population	Proportion of male population	Proportion of female population	Female proportion of total population
Sources of livelihood									
Employment for wages	91.7	91.4	38.8	89.8	93.2	43.9	86.2	91.8	43.5
Self-employment	7.9	8.0	39.3	10.0	6.6	33.1	12.7	7.5	31.2
Employment in non-agriculture	83.7	85.4	39.3	89.1	91.6	43.4	93.7	93.5	43.8
Employment in professional and technical	9.5	9.3	39.4	9.8	11.6	46.9	9.9	11.2	50.0
Index of dissimilarity of occupational groups		36.3			34.0			38.2	
Unemployment population aged 15-24	83.9	87.1	54.3	85.9	77.7	59.5	57.0	50.0	56.2
Other sources of income									
Remittances	n.a.	n.a.	n.a.	0.8	1.8	71.5	n.a.	n.a.	n.a.
Local (other than self)	n.a.	n.a.	n.a.	10.2	33.1	79.1	n.a.	n.a.	n.a.
Pensions and other public assistance	n.a.	n.a.	n.a.	11.5	15.6	61.1	n.a.	n.a.	n.a.

Sources: CARICOM, n.d.; UWI, 1976; Barbados, 1988.

ing population has been engaged in these occupations, increasing from 85 per cent in 1970 proportions similar to those obtaining for males. The proportion which women comprise of the total workforce in non-agriculture has increased from 39 per cent in 1970 to 44 per cent in 1985, most of the increase occurring during the 1970s. Among these women, three groups merit separate attention on the strength of changes in their size. Women in the informal sector, perhaps the most difficult group to identify, have traditionally been regarded as operating on the fringes of the economy. Domestic service, petty trading and dressmaking were the three areas usually associated with women's activities in these areas on the basis of general observation. A more sophisticated approach has been proposed by a recent study in Jamaica which attempts to allocate industries to different labour market segments on the basis of the number of workers involved and a specified skill index (Anderson, 1987).[26] According to this approach, the informal sector consists of all small-scale industries i.e. those with less than 10 workers, and a skill index lower than 14. On this basis, the informal sector is shown to comprise small-scale agriculture; a protected informal segment consisting of private household workers; an unprotected informal segment consisting primarily of small-scale food manufacture, petty trading, and small-scale services; and a segment consisting of informal crafts.

No study of the informal sector of Barbados is currently available. However, if the Anderson model is accepted, it is evident that sizeable sections of the Barbados female work force can be located in these segments, e.g. 68 per cent of female service workers in the 1980 Census are classified as maids; 19 per cent of all female sales workers are street vendors; 52 per cent of all female production workers are classified as tailors, dressmakers and related workers. Even if the discussion is restricted to only these three categories, the predominance of women is evident. Together, the females in these three groups account for 30 per cent of the total female workforce and 90 per cent of all workers in those groups. Because of the labour intensive nature of these activities, the low returns and the relative absence of protection, the women in these groups may well be in need of special assistance. Yet the lack of both quantitative and qualitative data suggests that this group represents another example of invisibility.

The second sub-group among women in the non-agriculture occupations, to which attention might be drawn are women in the manufacturing industries. Much of the employment available in this sector is provided by export-oriented industries, especially in electronics and garments. Although many of these factories were locally owned, many were also foreign-owned companies with an expressed preference for women. In the absence of other alternatives these manufacturing concerns represented a significant employment opportunity for poor women either within factories or at home on a 'home-work' basis. But the rates of pay were low, health and safety standards were poor and trade union membership was restricted.[27]

The 1980s have witnessed cutbacks in employment and the closure of over 100 factories. The resulting unemployment highlights the vulnerability of women in this sector to economic and technological changes, worker exploitation and the inability or unwillingness of governments to act on their behalf when negotiating terms. They also provide examples of what can happen to women when development plans are gender blind.

The third sub-group among women in non-agriculture occupations are women in professional occupations. Their number has risen marginally from 9 per cent in 1970 to 11 per cent in 1985 of the total female working population while the equivalent per cent for males remained steady at 10 per cent. Simultaneously, women have been comprising an ever growing proportion of the total professional population. From 39 per cent in 1970, the proportion of women professionals increased to one-half by 1985. Most of this may be attributable to shifts in the structure of the female professional population. Traditionally, nurses and teachers, comprised the bulk of women professionals — over 90 per cent. But by 1980, this proportion had fallen to just under 80 per cent, with a corresponding increase of 'other' professionals from 12 per cent to 21 per cent. Included in the 'other' groups are such groups as architects and engineers, accountants, life scientists, statisticians, creative artists. In effect, the widening range of professional occupations in which Barbadian women are participating reflects not only rises in educational attainment but also widening economic opportunities. But numbers remain small and research information about their circumstances and needs is almost non-existent. Thus invisibility becomes an issue for another group of women.

When the occupational distributions of males and females are compared, the resulting index of dissimilarity declined minimally between 1970 and 1980, then rose thereafter. However the level of the index suggests that despite changes in the occupational patterns and the relative similarity of male and female distributions, there persists a relatively high degree of gender differentiation in the occupational structure of this territory.

Access to productive resources

Fundamental to the ability of a people to develop their own capacities must be the provision of basic infrastructure. But availability must be accompanied by accessibility. Indicators to illustrate accessibility of services provide clues as to areas of need to which infrastructural development projects may be directed.

For Barbados, access to basic services such as pipe-borne water, electricity, suitable toilet facilities, cooking fuel other than wood appears to be of an acceptable level. Indicators illustrating this are readily available from census data. However indicators of access to services for specific groups need to be devised from special purpose surveys in which questions of women's access and control of resources and the derived benefits are specifically addressed. Thus, for example, although women traders in Barbados probably benefit from the basic services provided by the government, their particular occupation requires access to a number of other services. Credit, technical assistance (e.g. accounting), security for themselves and their produce, primary market, insurance coverage, counselling are some of the services they may require. But the magnitude of the need and the range of areas remain unknown. The same may be said of the several other 'invisible' groups identified.

It is therefore recommended that a series of small-scale surveys be undertaken of specific groups of women with a view to developing measures illustrative of their several needs.

Conclusion

Census and labour force survey data suggest that Barbadian women rely primarily on paid employment as their main source of livelihood. Other survey sources indicate that at least three other sources are important — the husband/partner, children and other relatives. Few Barbadian women appear to be self-employed. Patterns of occupational distribution suggest some amount of change but not enough to offset the relatively high level of gender dissimilarity. This makes it possible to identify groups of women whose location in the distribution renders them vulnerable or invisible.

Emotional support

Reproductive unions

Sizeable proportions of Barbadian women within the reproductive ages have never been married but by the time they reach age 45, the converse is true. This suggests that the age at which women marry is relatively high, a conclusion supported by the indicator of the singulate mean age at marriage which is well over 30 years — and increasing with only minimal differences between women and men (Table 12). But that does not mean that no other type of reproductive union has been experienced or that childbearing had not already begun before marriage. On the contrary, the proportion of women in some form of reproductive union is high, though apparently declining from 50 per cent in 1970 to 44 per cent in 1980.

A high incidence of motherhood prevails both among women in unions and those who are not, 90 per cent of whom are mothers. Contraceptive use is also high. One survey taken in 1980/81 placed the proportion of ever use among women aged 15-49 at 63 per cent and current use at 37

TABLE 12

INDICATORS OF EMOTIONAL SUPPORT FOR WOMEN, BARBADOS, 1970–80

Emotional support	1970	1980
Reproductive unions		
Proportion of population 15–64 ever married		
Male	39.9	33.3
Female	43.3	37.9
Mean age at marriage		
Male	36.5	37.6
Female	34.1	36.1
Proportion of women 15–44 in unions	50.1	43.8
Mothers per 1000 women in unions (14–66)	888	885
Mothers per 1000 women not in unions (14–64)	905	903
Contraceptive use (15–49)		
ever use	n.a.	62.9
current use	n.a.	36.9
Motherhood		
Mean age at first birth	22.6	22.1
mean age at last birth	33.5	33.7
Mothers per 1000 women (15–44)	644	643
per 1000 working women	611	650
per 1000 housewives	822	850
per 1000 married women	899	883
per 1000 common law women	910	890
per 1000 visiting women	366	387
Children per mother (15–49)	3.7	2.7
per working mother	3.6	2.7
per housewife mother	3.9	3.2
per married mother	4.3	3.1
per common law mother	3.9	3.2
per visiting mother	2.6	2.7
Births per 1000 teenage women (15–19)	94.1	70.8
Job satisfaction		
Job as source of satisfaction	n.a.	38.2
Rank position of job as source of satisfaction	n.a.	1
Community involvement		
Group membership		34.4
Participation in activities		70.0
Membership of committees		23.0
Community involvement as source of satisfaction		39

Sources: CARICOM, n.d.; UWI, 1976; Nair, 1982; WICP unpublished data.

per cent (Nair, 1982). A companion study of males conducted in 1982 reports almost identical levels of usage among males in the same age range. Ever use stood at 61 per cent and current use at 37 per cent (Lewis and Heisler, 1985). A more recent study conducted in 1988 provides evidence that current contraceptive use among all women in unions is 55 per cent and 62 per cent among non-pregnant, fecund women in unions (Jagdeo, 1989). These relatively high rates of usage suggest a society in which although a high premium is placed on motherhood, firm steps are being taken to protect the woman from the burden of large numbers of children.

Motherhood

Although Barbadian women may be said to be heavily involved in childbearing as suggested by indicators of proportions of motherhood, their actual fertility levels are low and declining. Child/woman rates, among women in the reproductive age range have declined from 2.4 in 1970 to 1.8 in 1980, and child/mother rates from 3.7 to 2.7. These declines coincide with a lengthening of the interval spent in childbearing. Declines obtain among working and non-working women and among women in different types of reproductive unions.

Childbearing among adolescents has been on the decline since 1970 in terms of absolute numbers, the proportion of total annual births occurring to teenagers and the adolescent fertility rates.

Job satisfaction

The rationale for this indicator stems from an increasing awareness that women gain emotional satisfaction from activities outside of their involvement in reproductive and mothering activities. Evidence from at least one Caribbean study suggests that a job or income-earning activity provides a sense of self-esteem and control over one's life to which women attach much significance. WICP data indicate that the three most highly rated qualities about their job that women mention are the job itself, the income earned and the people they work with. Together these three accounted for almost 80 per cent of the responses to the question 'What do you like most about your job?' Examples of responses related to the job itself include: 'Meeting people and the responsibility that it entrusts on me'; 'Influencing the direction in which the institution goes; giving advice of one kind or another'; 'I feel responsible knowing that I am doing things for older people'; 'I like at the end of a lesson and a day the feeling that the children have gained something that would help them'.

In other words, the fact of a challenging job, the opportunity to establish social relationships away from home and to contribute to household income provides a measure of satisfaction to women which should not be overlooked. Of course, these are not necessarily different from men. But the point is that women are now articulating these as needs which must be taken into consideration in the design of plans, programmes and projects on their behalf. It is not entirely valid to claim that women work (i.e. work for income) to get out of the house or to upgrade the lifestyle of their households, as is often said about middle-income women, or out of sheer necessity, as is often said about low-income women. Women may work for all of these reasons but they also work because they want to work for their own self-development.

In the Preface to the current Development Plan, the Prime Minister of Barbados states '... development is really about people's hopes and aspirations for improvements in the quality of their lives.' (Barbados, 1989, p. (i)) If this is accepted and women see a job as providing those aspirations, then indicators should reflect those perceptions. Data from the WICP suggest two indicators of job satisfaction. The first is percentage of responses in which 'the job itself' is included in reply to a question what do you like most about your job. In the Barbados sample 38 per cent of the responses from employed women included 'the job itself'. The second possible indicator is the rank position of 'the job itself' amongst all responses to the same question. For Barbados, the rank position was 1. Together these two indicators suggest that a job is indeed an important source of emotional support for women.

Community involvement

Here again recourse needs to be made to micro-level studies. The WICP data indicate that about 34 per cent of the Barbadian sample belonged to organizations of one kind or another with 70 per cent of that number being highly active. The overwhelming majority — over 90 per cent — of the sample considered membership in organizations as being of importance to women. Reasons varied from those clustered around self-development (39 per cent), meeting new people (23 per cent) and getting away from home (18 per cent). In the words of one respondent, 'It helps me become a person outside the home'.

In other words, Barbadian women are looking beyond the home environment for sources of emotional support or psychological satisfaction. Involvement in community organizations represents an important source of such support.

Conclusion

National level data on mating and fertility suggest that Barbadian women are involved in different types of reproductive unions, eventually marrying at a relatively high age. Childbearing occurs both within and outside of the several union types but has been declining steadily, irrespective of age, union type or economic activity. Besides mating and childbearing, women also gain satisfaction from their job and from their involvement in community organizations. These various levels of activity together contribute to the woman's self-perception of her value as a human being.

Power and authority

The final area considered of importance in an assessment of women's situation relates to the power and authority wielded by women in Barbados (Table 13). In Barbados, the principle of equality of women and men and non-discrimination on the ground of sex is enshrined in Section II of Chapter 3 of the Constitution. This suggests that Barbadian women and men have the same rights and responsibilities in every area of civic life. However, the legal provision of rights often is not reflected in the practical enjoyment of power and authority. A variety of sources need to be tapped in order to develop indicators of power and authority in key areas.

In the area of the family, women's power and authority may be gaged first from the pattern of household headship. It may be argued that women who head households exercise a considerable degree of autonomy in the management of these households, even though many of them may be very poor. At the other end of the scale, it may be argued that where households are headed by men, the degree of women's autonomy within the households is restricted. And at some point within the scale, there may be found incidences of jointly headed households which imply an egalitarian system of management.

Census data provide ample evidence of high levels of female headed households, as was shown in Table 9. Without digressing to address the concepts of 'household' and 'headship' adopted by those censuses, it is clear that levels of that order represent a significant reality in the lives of Caribbean women. Large numbers of them do bear sole responsibility for their households. Survey data provide an interesting caveat. Not only is the proportion of female headed households slightly lower than census data suggest, but there is a small proportion (5 per cent) of jointly headed households. This may indicate a new trend among women who are now recognizing their own contribution to their households (Powell, 1986). Alternatively, it may be simply the uncovering of a category of household which the census was not designed to catch. Whichever it is, the implication is that household headship is not necessarily a simple demarcation between male and female autonomy. An important consideration is the process by which decisions are made within the household.

This introduces the second set of indicators of power and authority in the familial setting — women's perceptions of the pattern of decision-making in their households. WICP data suggests that for women in residential unions, women tend to be the main decision-makers in matters

TABLE 13
INDICATORS OF POWER AND AUTHORITY OF WOMEN, BARBADOS, 1970–85

Power and authority	1970	1980	1985
Family			
Household headship	42.9	43.9	n.a.
Decision-making			
Women only	n.a.	4	n.a.
Partner only	n.a.	—	n.a.
Joint	n.a.	6	n.a.
Economic			
Employment in administration and management			
Proportion of male workforce	2.1	2.6	4.7
Proportion of female workforce	0.4	0.8	2.7
Female proportion	10.7	19.0	28.9
Ownership of financial assets	n.a.	50.0	n.a.
Political	(1971)	(1981)	(1986)
Membership in			
House of Representatives			
Male	23	26	26
Female	1	1	1
Senate			
Male	10	9	8
Female	1	3	4
Cabinet			
Male	10	9	12
Female	—	1	—
Membership on statutory boards	(1970–71)	(1980)	(1985)
Total membership	388	565	565
Female proportion	12.4	14.0	22.8

Sources: CARICOM, n.d.; UWI, 1976; WICP, unpublished data;
Duncan and O'Brien, 1983; Barbados, Civil Lists.

related to childbearing, childrearing and routine household management. Decisions on matters such as expenditure on major household items, location of residence and the borrowing of money tend to be jointly made. But the type of union and the level of development of the territory appear to be major influences on the decision-making patterns (Powell, 1986). Further, if the views of Barbadian males are taken into account, it seems that the resources which the woman brings into the home may also exert an important influence on the extent to which women may exercise autonomy in household decision-making (Barrow, 1986*a* and *b*).

One corollary needs to be added. Virtually all the income-earning women in the Barbadian WICP sample claimed that they made their own decisions about spending the money which they earned and saved. This is somewhat mitigated by the fact that most of these funds are spent on food, clothing and other household needs and that women rank the partner's contribution to household income as the most important. Thus, the extent of the woman's power within the household appears to be fragile and dependent on her ability to maintain a balance between her autonomy and an interdependent relationship with her partner.

In the economic sphere, the indicators selected to demonstrate elements of power are focused on women in administrative and managerial occupations. There is clear evidence from census and labour force survey sources of low but increasing levels of female involvement. The proportion of the female working population engaged in these occupations has increased from less than one-half of 1 per cent in 1970 to almost 3 per cent by 1985. The corresponding proportions for males are 2 per cent and 5 per cent. Simultaneously, the proportion which females constitute of all administrative and managerial workers increased from 11 per cent to 29 per cent over the same period.

Another useful indication of the economic power of women relates to ownership of financial assets. Without access to the necessary records proxies need to be developed from survey data. The WICP data provides such a proxy based on the proportion of items owned by women in the samples which may be described as financial assets. According to that source about half of the items claimed by women as they owned included such financial assets as land, house, business equipment, livestock and the life insurance.

In the area of social participation, no source was found providing information on office holding in non-governmental organizations, trade unions and similar groups. It is recommended that studies be developed on this topic. This would require access to the records of a large number and diversity of voluntary organizations.

In the political arena, indicators were chosen to illustrate women's participation in elections, in the national legislature and on statutory boards. No sources were located with data which could allow the derivation of indicators of membership and office holding in political parties and senior executive positions in the public service. These are two important areas which require investigation.

Available electoral data suggest that Barbadian women account for over half of registered voters. Over 70 per cent of their registered number voted in the last elections for which data are available (1981 and 1986) and over half of the votes cast have been cast by women in all elections since 1951 (Duncan and O'Brien, 1983). But this apparently solid involvement of women in the political life of the territory is not reflected in their parliamentary representation. Indeed the picture is far from encouraging. Between 1971 and 1986 there have been four general elections in which candidates sought election for the 24 (27 in 1981 and 1986) seats in the House of Representatives. Within that period, only six women have contested for seats in the general elections, but only two have been successful, one of them winning the same seat in both 1976 and 1981. In the 12 member Senate, a total of 11 women have been appointed during the period, but at no time did the number sitting exceed three. Further, there has been only one woman Minister of Government in the 10 member Cabinet which prevailed up to 1981. She was first Minister of Health and then Minister of Education which post she retained after 1981 when the size of the Cabinet was increased to 12. The current Cabinet has no woman Minister. Prior to 1986, there was one woman appointed at the ambassadorial level (1974–75) and since 1986 a woman has been appointed as ambassador to the United Nations. In effect, women in Barbados are not included in the top echelons of national government and thus opportunities for direct influence on decision-making in the territory are severely limited.

One final area of political participation is membership on statutory boards where appointment is made by the political directorate. Although the selected indicators suggest a somewhat more satisfactory position than obtains for participation in electoral politics life, much room remains for improvement. At the beginning of the 1970s, there were 58 statutory boards with a total membership of 388. Female membership stood at 48 or 12 per cent. By the end of the decade, there were signs of marginal improvement with accelerating improvement into the 1980s. Female membership increased to 14 per cent in 1980 and 23 per cent in 1985. However, in keeping with the position of previous years sizeable proportions of this membership continue to be concentrated on boards of educational institutions, child care and welfare agencies. Thus, the increased female membership on boards does not necessarily reflect access to the powerful boards.

Membership of statutory boards merely reflects one aspect of political power. Occupancy of the major decision-making positions on those boards — Chairman and Deputy Chairman — represents another. In 1980, there were four boards chaired by women two of them being boards of secondary schools. By 1985 the number had increased to 10, seven of which were boards of secondary schools. Also in 1985, there were 11 boards in which the deputy chair was female, seven of them being boards of secondary schools.

Once again the position is shown to be one of limited involvement of women in the power structure of the society. Where they are allowed entry, it is into areas traditionally associated with women — education, health, child care and welfare.

PANEL III: LEGAL AND INSTITUTIONAL PROVISIONS

In this panel, the concern is with the institutional framework provided by the society to enable its women to participate fully (Table 14).

Taken together the indicators suggest that Barbados has had ample time to establish machinery to protect its women and to ensure that machinery is effective. Thirty-eight years have elapsed since the territory gained full adult suffrage and twenty-three years since the attainment of political independence and a constitution in which the principles of equality and non-discrimination is enshrined. The Women's Bureau has been in existence for the past thirteen years.

Within that general framework, many measures have been introduced to assist women, e.g. paid maternity leave has been a feature of women's economic life for the past 13 years. Women are eligible to the same employment benefits as men, e.g. paid leave during illness, national insurance provisions, old age pensions, protection at the workplace, rights to fair employment practices and so on.

These measures, however, operate to the benefit only of those who are employed by others, i.e. in the formal sector of the economy. For those in the informal sector, not only do these provisions not obtain, but there is no legal protection. Thus, immediately another vulnerable or 'invisible' group of women is thrown into relief.

Many other legal provisions in areas such as the conclusion of contracts, the ownership, acquisition, administration and disposition of property, the right to jury duty, the right to hold political office are available to women in Barbados. Yet somehow, there remain pockets of need which clearly indicate that women may not be benefiting to the fullest from such provisions.

Conclusion

The indicators for this territory tell a story of an economy with limited resources which has been able to provide a number of opportunities for its women. However, in recent times, that economy has experienced severe strains. Efforts to deal with problematic balance of payments and other macro-economic problems produced the so-called structural adjustment measures which have taken little account of social cost. The measures adopted produced a situation in which Barbados became in danger of reversing the progress made in the past, particularly in health, nutrition, education and employment. As a result women have suffered particularly in respect of rising unemployment, declining real wages, reduced social services, increasing prices of food and other basic necessities and increasing hours of work.

TABLE 14

BARBADOS — YEAR OF ESTABLISHMENT OF INSTITUTIONAL MACHINERY
FOR ASSISTING WOMEN

Year	Legislative/ Administrative mechanism	Age of institution (in years)
1942	Right to vote and sit in Parliament subject to specified property qualification requirement	47
1951	Universal adult suffrage	38
1966	Political independence	23
1966	Constitutional provision for equal rights and non-discrimination on grounds of sex	23
1976	Paid maternity leave	13
1976	Establishment of National Commission on Status of Women	13
1976	Establishment of Department of Women's Affairs	13
1984	Ratification of UN Convention 1967[1]	5

Note: In addition, between 1978 and 1982 extensive reform of family and related laws were introduced either through amendment of existing laws or creation of new ones. See Ford, 1989; Gillings, 1987.
1. UN Convention on the Elimination of Discrimination Against All Women.

All women have experienced these problems, some more than others. The indicators selected here have demonstrated how some of those groups may be identified. They also identify data gaps which need to be urgently filled if the full extent of the issue is to be understood and if appropriate programmes are to be formulated, implemented and evaluated.

Caribbean women in recent development plans

In a survey of National Planning systems in 10 Caribbean territories in 1980, the Consultant who prepared the report identified three main features characterizing development planning in the region:

(i) it has been and is closely linked with the receipt of development funds from external sources; (ii) it is geared to the restructuring of the economies;

(iii) it is loosely organized and not yet an institutionalized part of the life of the societies (Boissière, 1980, p. 1).

The link with international financial assistance was established in the 1940s with the establishment by the UK of what were known as Colonial Development and Welfare Funds. Colonial governments wishing to benefit from these funds were required to submit a ten-year programme of development expenditure. Since then governments in the region have been engaged in some variety of economic planning as part of the general development effort. The assumption appears to be that planning permits the selection of appropriate economic choices for achieving desirable social goals. That planning can also provide guidelines for determining social and political choices appears to be a minor consideration. The major concern seems to be that of providing greater government direction to the path and progress of the economy. Planners therefore concerned themselves with the application of macro-economic solutions to problems defined at the macro-economic level.

Dissatisfaction with the results of this approach led to several critiques in which stress was laid on the critical importance of the relevance of policy and hence of political processes. With that view came a recognition that the economic development plan may function both as a tool of transformation and of mobilization towards national goals. But that recognition has not necessarily affected the traditional view of planning which, as has been documented for at least one territory, continues to serve largely formal purposes. In the words of one commentator speaking about Jamaica,

They assure external financiers that the economy has the capacity to receive inflows of funds. At the same time, they help to foster the belief within the country that comprehensive policies are being formulated for the general welfare (Brown, 1975, p. 12).

The implication here is that decisions about development priorities reflect the preferences of the dominant decision-making group. When therefore interest groups lacking direct access to loci of decision-making begin to voice demands, to be 'integrated into development planning', they are striking at the very heart of a system which is not designed to accommodate the demands of powerless groups. In the case of women's groups, such a cry creates two fundamental dilemmas for the system. First, there is the assumption that government is an appropriate mechanism for ensuring that women's needs are met. The particular dilemma relates to the multi-dimensional needs of women and the question of balancing those needs against those of other interest groups which may, perhaps, be of more strategic importance to the government dominant political party. A related point has to do with the perceived cost to the government which opts in favour of satisfying women's needs. Such cost could be high in social and political terms and may well act as a disincentive to positive action.

The second dilemma relates to the assumption that development planning is a purely technical exercise which can accommodate new demands once an adequate information base is available. For planners concerned with meeting short-term goals of incumbent governments, with the effects of past policy and planning decisions and with the current state of national and international economies, the mere availability of additional material is simply not enough. And the experience of women's groups has been that even with the available data their interests are not necessarily reflected in development plans. The point at issue here is that development planning in the region is a process embedded in a particular type of public administrative system. It is concerned with meeting the wishes of a political directorate whose ultimate objective is to satisfy the immediate wishes of its electorate and those of dominant groups both at home and abroad. The process is not easily amenable to the accommodation of changing definitions of need or a long-term view of the planning exercise. Women's groups wishing to influence the process therefore face a formidable challenge. Women have traditionally not occupied positions in the upper rungs of the public service and women's groups have traditionally lacked the power to influence the political process.

The planning process

The process as it currently exists, involves a hierarchical submission of plans from individual departments, through Ministries and the Planning Unit to Cabinet and Parliament for ultimate approval (Figure 3). The process usually involves informal, interdepartmental consultation at lower levels and more formal inter-ministry consultation through a Coordinating Committee of all Permanent Secretaries. Consultation may also involve Advisory Councils (national or sectoral), and a number of parastatal agencies. Less formal and consultative arrangements may exist with various interest groups, e.g. the private sector, NGOs. But in no territory is there provision for public participation in the formulation of sector plans and projects.[28] One territory, Jamaica, has attempted to develop a plan based on recommendations from a number of Task Forces created by the government. Members are drawn from a variety of sources including government, the private sector, the UWI and non-government organizations. Each Task Force reports on a specific issue and the reports provide the basis of discussions from which the plan is formulated. The mechanism, which is still very much experimental, functions on an ongoing basis. The main concern is the heavily bureaucratic and time consuming nature of the operation.

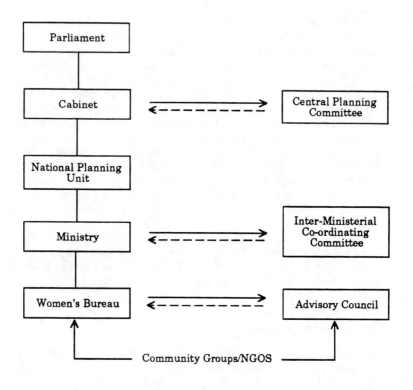

Fig. 3. The planning process

The entire process is geared towards developing a medium-term plan — usually over five years — with short-term sector plans and projects prepared from the perspective of the overall plan and reviewed annually as part of the budget exercise. One writer indicates that 'it is hardly relevant to speak of short, medium and long term planning in the region as a whole'. In a survey of 10 territories conducted in 1980, only three had five-year development plans, while none had any clearly specified long- term policy objectives (Boissière, 1980). This position has changed little since then. Without such overall guidelines and priorities, there is little consciousness of planning except in the purely budgetary sense.

Several constraints in the operation of the system have been identified. Foremost amongst these is the fundamental difficulty created by a planning philosophy which focuses on the mobilization and allocation of resources on the assumption that the overall objectives of the plan necessarily lead to benefits for all. Where issues affecting specific groups in the determination of priorities are considered, it is almost by default rather than through the activities of a specially constituted mechanism. Budgetary considerations connected with the difficulty of forecasting the level of local revenue, foreign aid inflows and the cost of necessary imported inputs represent a critical constraint limiting the effectiveness of planning. A particularly disturbing recent trend has been the emphasis being placed on Public Sector Investment Programmes. Manpower deficiencies, in terms of quality, quantity and the utilization of available skills also rank high amongst the constraints. Institutional difficulties created by uncertainties of the role of the Central Planning Unit, and inadequate consultation between the various entities involved in the process represent another hurdle. So too do data deficiencies — either general unavailability, unavailability in the desired format or availability after too long a time lag — and the absence of machinery for monitoring or evaluation on an ongoing basis.

Perhaps the most serious constraint is the precedence accorded to short-term political priorities over long-term developmental objectives. This not only prohibits the evolution of planning as a systematic process in the daily management of a society, but also creates rigidities which weaken the chances of the needs of powerless groups from being recognized and addressed. Some commentators go so far as to say that there have been no successful Caribbean development plans on the grounds that the premises of existing plans are questionable and that no dynamic process of planning really exists. Further, that the implementation of plans has been equally unsuccessful.

Planning for women in development

The administrative procedure adopted for planning purposes implies the need for a focal point within the system with formal and informal links both to other parts of the system and to the community. The placement of institutional mechanisms responsible for women's affairs within the public service suggests that governments have given women such a focal point from which to participate in the planning process. For women's bureaux/desks can legitimately channel their requirements directly through the host ministry and indirectly through other ministries sponsoring programmes/projects relevant to women. That, at least, seems to be the theory. However, in practice, results have not been particularly encouraging, as the current development plans of two territories, Barbados and St. Vincent illustrate.

BARBADOS

This territory has a long history of development planning, starting from a Sketch Plan of Development, 1946–56 which was prepared by a special committee appointed by the Governor of the day for that purpose (Barbados, 194(6)?). To date there have been 10 development plans, half of them prepared after the territory gained political independence in 1966.

In its first development plan, that of 1946–56, this territory allocated the sum of $5,000 to a 'Women's Work Bureau'. Nothing in the text of the plan or in subsequent plans indicates what this sum was intended to provide and whether anything did materialize or, indeed, what a women's work bureau really was. However, it is worthy of note that at least one territory in the region had recognized the need for including provision for women in its development plans from as far back as forty odd years ago.

A review of those early plans suggests that women's issues, insofar as the term was used, consisted of issues related to infant, child and maternal mortality. As planning philosophy became more articulated, and even though acknowledgement was given to the need for a wider interpretation of women's issues, no effort was made to identify these issues either separately or within sectoral plans. Thus, women as a group were never targeted. Since that 1946–56 Development Plan then, nothing on women's affairs appeared in development plans until the 1983–88 plan, even though a Department of Women's Affairs had been established in 1976, a National Commission on the Status of Women had been convened in 1976 and reported in 1978, and a development plan for 1979–83 had been produced. It appears that the Department construed government policy to be contained in the various international conventions and agreements which government had signed and ratified, in the recommendations of the NCSW, the National Advisory Council and the biennial meeting of CARICOM Ministers responsible for Women's Affairs.[29] Within this context, the Department developed internal annual programmes of activity which, though not reflected in the National Development Plan or in separate Departmental budgets, were partially financed by the Ministry in which the Department was located.

From the 1983–88 plan, it is clear that only minimal efforts were envisaged for enabling the Bureau to conduct its work. Further, the location at that time within the Ministry of Information and Culture appears to have limited perspectives of the function of the Bureau to a purely informational one. This is reflected in the downgrading of the Department to a Bureau and in the proposals contained in the Plan (Appendix I). One proposal focused on the use of Community Development Officers as channels of information between the Bureau and women in the community. Two proposals related to the establishment of links with government agencies and the creation of an advisory body. A fourth proposal related to the continuation of grant assistance to women's organizations.[30]

The final proposal related to the identification of projects with income-generating potential and the willingness to 'act as a channel for funding if a project is feasible and if a funding agency is willing to provide funds for its implementation' (Barbados, 1983, p. 154). As would be expected, activities flowing out of these vague proposals were sporadic, lacking in continuity and generally ineffective in meeting the overall objective of the development plan 'Change Plus Growth'.

Among its several objectives the Development Plan for 1988–93, focusing on the theme 'A Share for All', aims to improve the quality of life; reduce the pockets of poverty that exist; increase the output of goods and services; provide jobs through productive activity; and improve income distribution. Within those overall objectives, the Plan seeks to reduce unemployment to an acceptable level and provide incomes adequate to provide food, clothing and shelter for families at the lowest income levels (Barbados, 1989*a*, p. 5). In effect, employment creation is a cardinal feature of the Plan. Yet the Plan, like its predecessor, provides only general objectives for the unit within the public sector charged with responsibility for a section of the population in which 'unemployment is considered to be unacceptably high' (Barbados, op. cit., p. 17). According to the Plan,

Government, through a restructured Bureau of Women's Affairs will implement programmes geared towards: researching and disseminating information on women and promoting educational programmes on women's issues; encouraging and facilitating the further development of women's organizations; reviving the National Advisory Council on Women's Affairs to advise Government on the formulation of policies relating to women; and promoting, in collaboration with the respective governmental and non-governmental agencies and organizations, projects geared towards the fuller integration of women in national development, with special focus on employment generation for women. An inter-ministerial committee on Women's Affairs will be appointed to assess, monitor and facilitate the integration process. (Barbados, op. cit., p. 93)

No specifics are provided either in terms of targets, activities or estimated expenditures. And up to the time of writing no additional staff had been provided, and neither the National Advisory Council nor the interministerial Committee had been appointed. There is therefore little to gauge the extent to which the objectives are being met.

The priority area of employment generation is the main concern of the Ministry in which the Bureau of Women's Affairs is now located. The objectives of that Section of the Ministry are many and varied:

- to increase the total number of productive jobs available to persons in the labour force seeking employment;
- to minimize job losses and the social effects of such job losses;
- to pursue balanced economic, financial and industrial policies through which business enterprises can grow and develop, thereby contributing to job creation;
- to maintain appropriate education, training, and technology systems that will guarantee a ready supply of intelligent, diligent and trainable workers; and
- to maintain a sound health and safety regime for the purpose of minimizing job losses through illness and contributing to increased productivity level (Barbados, op. cit., p. 88).

At first glance the proposed strategies appear geared towards infrastructural improvement rather than project implementation, e.g.

- implementation of the recommendations of the Task Force on Employment;
- computerization of the records of the Labour Department and provision of more accurate and current labour market information for better utilization of human resources;
- strengthening of linkages between the National Training Board, the Statistical Service and the Labour Department (Barbados, op. cit., p. 91).

Within these general strategies, however are contained several unspecified project activities, e.g. the National Training Board conducts several vocational training programmes aimed at both men and women; the National Employment Bureau is responsible for seeking job opportunities at home and abroad for unemployed Barbadians. But here again, without targets, activities and proposed budgets, little can be said of the outcome of these efforts particularly in respect of the extent to which women benefit.

Nothing in the Plan provides information on proposed expenditure for the programmes of the Bureau of Women's Affairs (BWA). Estimates for proposed capital expenditure for each agency are provided but nothing has been allocated to the BWA. Examination of the annual estimates of revenue and expenditure indicate no identifiable budget for the Bureau. Instead its resources are included in the sub-head 'General Administration' of the Ministry. This suggests that the Bureau may not really be regarded as a viable entity within the Ministry, since the estimates for all other Departments are clearly spelt out. It is therefore not possible to make quantitative estimates of the extent to which the Bureau is financially equipped to implement the objectives listed in the Development Plan.

No specific long, medium, or even short-term Women's Development Plan exists. What does exist is a generalized 'Plan of Action' developed during a recent Workshop on 'Management and Development' — which links eight main issues to a series of suggested recommendations and strategies (Barbados, 1989b). Within that, the Bureau has carved out activities in public awareness, support systems for WID programmes, research and training for the current financial year. The evolution of the current programme of activities demonstrates the operation of the institutional framework which allows the Bureau to function even though its existence is barely acknowledged in successive Development Plans. The BWA is supposed to be guided by the recommendations from the various sources mentioned earlier as well as by ongoing consultation with women's organizations. This process allows the Bureau to identify those activities which it can manage on its own, those which require collaboration with other agencies and those which require funding assistance. It thus becomes possible to develop a programme which may not reflect extensive governmental support but which may be meeting stated and perceived needs of beneficiary groups, even if only in a limited way. In addition, the Bureau is expected to collaborate with other Departments and Ministries in the public service which are involved in activities of direct relevance to women.

An examination of the activities of the Bureau provides clear evidence of collaboration with governments and NGOs and of independent project activity (Table 15). Further, of the 212 recommendations offered by the NCSW, 190 have been implemented by government agencies including 40 of the 46 recommendations for legal reform. In addition, sectoral plans in successive development plans have undertaken action which is not specified as being a consequence of the NCSW recommendations. Thus, the fact that recent Development Plans make only minimal reference to the Bureau does not necessarily mean that the Bureau is inactive or that women's needs as represented by the Bureau are not being recognized. The absence of specified programme and project activity in the Plans does however reflect the weak resource base and chequered history of the Bureau.[31]

Since its inception there have been two evaluations of the Bureau, one by the Commonwealth Secretariat and the CARICOM Secretariat, the other by ILO (Massiah, 1983; Gillings, 1987). Both of these reports stress the inability of the Bureau to function effectively without adequate staff and other resources. This was interpreted as evidence of minimal government commitment to the Bureau as also was the absence of a policy statement or action plan, the frequent relocations and the omission or minimal mention of the Bureau in the National Development Plans. It

TABLE 15

ACTIVITIES OF BUREAU OF WOMEN'S AFFAIRS, BARBADOS, 1979–1989

Type of activity	Name	Participants	Collaborating agency
Policy formulation	On-going monitoring of NCSW Recommendations	—	—
Public education			
(i) Audio-visual	Video on 'Women in Barbados' prepared for showing at the UN End of Decade Conference	—	Government Information Service; ISER (EC), UWI
(ii) Seminars/Workshops	Towards the total integration of women, 1979	Representatives of Government and NGOs	CIM
	Civic education for effective leadership, 1981	Women's voluntary organizations	Department of Extra Mural Studies, UWI
	Sex role stereotyping, children's expectations	Teachers and Guidance counsellors	CIM
	Interpersonal relationship in the workplace, 1982	Youth leaders and representatives from women's voluntary organizations	CIM
	Issues affecting women, 1982	Community development officers	CIM
	Laws as they relate to the family, 1984	Youth leaders	CIM
	Family breakdown, 1985	Representatives of women's organizations and individuals	CIM

Table 15 (cont'd)

ACTIVITIES OF BUREAU OF WOMEN'S AFFAIRS, BARBADOS, 1979–1989

Type of activity	Name	Participants	Collaborating agency
(ii) Seminars/Workshops (cont'd)	Development of women in post-independent Barbados, 1985 (panel discussion)	General public	—
	Violence against women, 1987	Representatives of women's organizations, health workers, individuals	Government of Netherlands
	Management and development – effecting change, 1989	Representatives of government, women's organizations, women managers	CARICOM, CIDA
Training			
(i) Direct	Leadership training for women from NGOs	Representatives of women's organizations	—
(ii) Indirect	Management for Caribbean women and organization development, Jamaica, 1980	1 representative NOW	CIM
	Women and education, Uruguay, 1981	1 representative Ministry of Economic Affairs	CIM
	Mass communications media and women's image, Argentina, 1982	1 representative GIS	CIM
	Training and employment for women, Jamaica, 1982		CIM

Type of activity	Name	Participants	Collaborating agency
(ii) Indirect (cont'd)	Inter-American Year of the Family, Chile, 1983		CIM
	Income-generating projects for women in rural areas, Israel, 1983	1 representative, WID	Government of Israel
	Integration of women in industry, Guyana, 1984	1 representative, Ministry of Employment and Industry 1 representative, private sector	UNIDO
Research	Women in agriculture, 1981		
	Assessment of status of women in Barbados, 1985		
	Violence against women, 1986		
Projects	Careers showcase — annual (to provide school leavers with information on job opportunity, training requirements, etc.)	School leavers, general public	Business and professional women
	Dried fruit project, 1980–1985 (to provide training in the preservation and sale of grown fruits)	Individual women	OAS Appropriate Technology International
	Legal education/Legal aid project	General public	CIM
	— to examine and analyse laws related to women		GIS

Type of activity	Name	Participants	Collaborating agency
Projects (cont'd)	— to provide background material for a public education programme on the laws examined		
	— to organize and conduct seminars on women's rights for counsellors, social workers and City Development Officers		
Miscellaneous	Channel funds from Government to specified NGOs (annual)	Specified women's organizations	Host Ministry
	Channel funds for international agencies to small NGO projects (occasional)	Women's organizations	Host Ministry
	Classes in self-defence for women (occasional)	Individual women	Barbados Judo Association
	Promotion of Women's 10 km Road Race (annual)	Individual women	National Sports Council

Sources: Gillings, 1987; Massiah, 1983; Information supplied by Barbados BWA.

was recognized that the Bureau was performing as well as it could within the available constraints. However, both evaluators felt that few of its activities could be construed as being part of a comprehensive plan with stated objectives, priorities, schedules and programmes. Rather activities appear to develop on an 'ad hoc' basis as needs arise or special requests are made. Clearly this is too fragmented an approach to yield constructive results. And within the context of a Development Plan which claims to set out 'in a concise manner the Government's development objectives, strategies, projects and programmes for Barbados' over the next five years, this is clearly not acceptable.

ST. VINCENT AND THE GRENADINES

As elsewhere in the region, development planning in this territory grew out of the local administration's response to British government policy which linked approval of loans and grants to the preparation and approval of development plans. Three development plans followed:
Interim Development Programme, 1963–1966
Five Year Development Plan, 1966–1970
Revised Five Year Development Plan, 1969–1973
According to the current (1986–88) Plan, these early Plans 'failed spectacularly to meet their targets' as a result of a number of deficiencies. Disillusionment with planning as a tool for development followed and planning reverted to an annual budgetary exercise supplemented by economic reviews.

At the First Meeting of Planning Officials in the Caribbean held in 1979, the report on St. Vincent noted that:

apart from what were essentially economic reviews and projects carried out periodically by international and regional agencies and traditional aid donors..., economic planning in this decade has been confined almost exclusively to annual budgetary proposals; and as the territory, in the grip of the post-1973 economic crisis became forced to place increasing reliance on British grants to offset widening deficits in the recurrent budget, the British Government (through BDD) came increasingly to exercise a considerable measure of control over the capital budget. (St. Vincent, 1980)

In 1978, a Central Planning Unit was established and immediately became involved, with the help of a World Bank mission, in preparing a Public Sector Investment Programme and financing plan for 1979–1983. This Economic Memorandum as it was called, provided the framework for planning decisions which were aimed at promoting export-oriented and employment generating agriculture, industry and tourism and at satisfying basic human needs.

Up to this stage the government of the day had neither articulated a policy on women's development nor established a national body with overall responsibility for the advancement of women. At first, the Ministry of Foreign Affairs had been allocated responsibility for Women's Affairs, but no specific officer was assigned to the task. Thus, there was no real mechanism for ensuring that women's needs and concerns were channelled into the planning process. A major recommendation for St. Vincent from the WICP was therefore

that a women's desk should be established to accelerate and implement programmes aimed at improving living conditions, at ensuring female involvement in development planning and at coordinating the activities of government, NGOs and individuals. (Clarke and Cummins, 1982, p. 79)

It was further recommended that such a body

...should have a clear mandate and be provided with adequate support from Government. Such support should take the form of adequate staffing, funding and appropriate attitudes which would facilitate effective functioning. (Clarke and Cummins, op. cit., p. 79)

Following that project, an officer in the Ministry of Community Development was assigned responsibility for Women's Affairs, but this was in addition to that officer's substantive duties as Community Development Officer. To counteract this, efforts were made to work through the NGOs, but they themselves were weakly structured and starved of resources. Without a firm institutional focal point, without policy guidelines and with limited support from NGOs, it became virtually impossible to produce any significant WID activity.

With a change of administration in 1984 came a fundamental change in perspective on both development planning and on Women's Affairs. In the case of the latter, a Women's Desk was established within the Ministry of Tourism, Information and Culture and, in collaboration with the National Council of Women, it was required to be the catalyst for implementing strategies and programmes in the area of Women's Affairs. Development planning came to be seen as an ongoing process aimed at creating a favourable environment in which economic and social development could be maintained and enhanced. The 1986–88 plan, the current plan, adopts as its theme 'Growth, Diversification and Redistribution'. In this plan as in the Barbados plan, job creation and the alleviation of unemployment are the prime objectives.

The current Development Plan includes a modest programme of activities for the Women's Desk which is geared 'to foster attitudinal changes in Vincentian men and women to enhance the integration of women into National Development and lead to the attainment of equality, development and peace' (St. Vincent Estimates, 1990, p. 193). These include lobbying for legislative reform in several areas, training in different areas of agriculture, health and employment, skills acquisition, public awareness campaigns, technical assistance, providing access to credit. Close collaboration with women's organizations, government and parastatal agencies is envisaged as a critical component of the programme (Table 16). The main objective of this range of activities is described as improving the standard of living at the community level and improving the ability of women to enjoy more fully the benefits of economic growth.

No capital expenditure is envisaged for the Women's Desk. However, recent estimates indicate that the Women's Desk represented 4 per cent of the Ministry's approved budget in 1986/87 and 5 per cent in 1987/88. At that time over half of the Desk's budget was allocated to training and related expenses, with small sums allocated for the NCW (5 per cent) and research and data collection (4 per cent). The remainder goes to personal emoluments of the staff of three — only one of whom had been appointed at the time of the 1987/88 Estimates. By 1988/89, slight changes occurred in the allocations such that personal emoluments for three staff members represented 51 per cent of the budget, but the Desk continues to consist of a single person. The St. Vincent Plan clearly identifies what is expected of its Women's Desk, in terms of programme activity. However those expectations are not expressed in quantitative assessment of the impact of its achievement.

As in the other territories in the region, women in this territory benefit not only from activities of the Women's Desk but from Government programmes in other sectors of the public service. Thus, for example, women can and do benefit from efforts at alleviating unemployment through the encouragement of private sector investment, the development of skills training programmes and the intensification of family planning efforts. But again, without quantitative targets, it is not possible to assess the WID impact of these programmes.[32]

In summary, it may be said that St. Vincent is an example of a territory which entered both the Development Planning and the WID arena fairly late, compared with other territories in the region. No specific Women's Development Plan exists, however the national development plan includes proposals for a modest level of activities by the Women's Desk which suggest a good grasp of the range of issues affecting women. But in the absence of supporting data, it is difficult to comment on the appropriateness of areas and groups selected for targeting or on the strategies proposed. The absence of quantitative targets also makes it difficult to determine the extent to which objectives are being met.

TABLE 16
ACTIVITIES PROPOSED FOR WOMEN'S DESK,
ST. VINCENT AND THE GRENADINES, 1986–88

Area	Activity
Law	• Seek legal recognition of common law partnerships
	• Seek upgrading of Maintenance Act
	• Seek stricter penalties for rape, incest, assault and sexual abuse on the job
	• Seek legislation for in camera trial of such cases
	• Seek legislation for equal pay for work of equal value
	• Seek legislation re-ensuring job security for pregnant women
Employment	• Seek representation of women on parastatal agencies connected with employment, especially agriculture, industry and the public service
	• Technical assistance for women in small business and cottage industries
	• Credit for women in small business and cottage industries
	• Support efforts to establish day care centres and pre-schools
Agriculture	• Training of more female extension officers
	• Provision of gender-based statistics
Health	• Assistance to victims of violence through provision of shelter, legal aid, counselling and guidance
	• Support agencies working with drug abuse, mental health, family planning
	• Encourage increased participation of women in formulating health policies at the community level
Education	• Public awareness programmes on violence against women, the law
	• Upgrading of curricula re family life education
Strengthening of national machinery	• Increased training of Women's Desk personnel
	• Increased staff for Women's Desk
	• Seek membership of CIM/OAS

Source: St. Vincent Development Plan 1986–88, pp. 96–7.

109

CONCLUSION

If the current development plans of these two territories contain what the Governments intend to do for women through their Women's Desks/Bureau, then the conclusion cannot be escaped that much ought not to be expected. Even if what is contained in the development plans is construed as indicative plans, i.e. plans detailing Government expenditure on proposed projects, one is hard put to find indications of what government plans for women. The common missing ingredient is a policy framework within which WID plans are formulated. Such a framework provides not only general guidelines but also determines the size of the programmes which can be attempted and the contextual factors to be considered in determining programme priorities. It also provides linkages between the individual WID action plan and the larger national development plan.

In a seminal article published thirty years ago, the renowned Caribbean economist, W.A. Lewis argued that no scientific principles exist for assessing national development plans (Lewis, 1959). Rather, one proceeds on the basis of 'commonsense and experience' to make lists of what to look for, changing the lists as circumstances dictate. The three most critical items on his list were policy, the size of the plan and its priorities. If this argument still retains its validity, it is presumably possible to apply those three criteria not only to an overall development plan but also to sections thereof.

Using the information provided in the previous sections it is possible to assess the WID content of the development plans reviewed by identifying positive and negative factors on each of the Lewis criteria.

Policy

At the most fundamental level, it should be axiomatic that an explicit policy statement is required which places WID issues and the activity of WID units firmly within a national development planning process to which all branches of the public sector are committed. Such a statement would elaborate the principles guiding its formulation, establish goals and priorities and determine implementation strategies. Yet the situation in respect of policy and policy-making for women in the two territories whose development plans were examined seems somewhat ambivalent.

Positive
• Adoption/ratification of international WID conventions;
• National planning mechanisms in place;
• WID unit in place;
• CARICOM support for institution building available;

- Technical assistance to prepare policy framework available;
- NGO and community participation exists;
- Research data identifying issues available.

Negative
- Evidence of implementation of international recommendations not readily available;
- Delays in production of policy statement;
- No formal mechanism to link with other sectors of public service for policy implementation;
- No statements of objectives and strategies for WID unit in development plan;
- Limited resources for WID programme implementation limits ability of unit to integrate its programme throughout public sector.

The picture which emerges is one in which there exists a positive environment for the creation of WID policy guidelines but a negative reaction in terms of the actual production of those guidelines. This is particularly reflected in the vague proposals in the Barbados plan.

Size

Here the question turns on the resources available for implementing the stated policy objectives. It may be argued that without explicit policy statements, the question of the size of a WID plan becomes superfluous. On the other hand, the creation of units responsible for women's affairs suggests that an implicit policy exists. The question of size then becomes one of the extent to which financial, administrative and other resources are available to execute the programmes envisaged in the plans for meeting specified needs. Again the case material suggests considerable ambivalence.

Positive
- Overall needs already identified by government; and
- Basic statistical data available and disaggregated by gender;
- Research data from NGO sources emerging;
- Project support possible from international sources;
- WID unit personnel familiar with administrative system and processes;
- Formal and informal networks assist WID unit personnel to strengthen administrative ability.

Negative
- Insufficient detailed information on needs of specific sub-groups of women;

- Minimal financial provision for accomodation, staff and programme support;
- No independent operational budget available;
- Heavy reliance on external project funding;
- Institutional building relegated to agency external to public sector;
- No monitoring/evaluation of either internal plans of WID unit or overall development plan;
- Social analysis or social impact analysis not included in plan.

The dilemma here turns essentially on the allocation of scarce resources between several competing claimants, particularly in a period of serious economic difficulties. But there is also to be considered bureaucratic perceptions of the size and importance of the problem being confronted, and the ability of women to influence those perceptions. Both of the plans reviewed reflect the limited economic base of the territories concerned. In terms of size of staff, number of programmes, the strategies proposed and budgetary allocations, the St. Vincent plan seems better placed to meet the objectives identified in the 'Women's Affairs' section of its plan. The same cannot really be said for Barbados. And in both cases, the need for an ongoing monitoring system which permits a continuing process of dialogue and consultation, designed to improve the plans is clearly evident.

Priorities

If a plan is to respond to changing circumstances, there should be evidence of some prioritization of responses to changing needs. This should be reflected in strategies which include a continuing search for information, training, infrastructural development, involvement of community in programme planning and implementation and targeted action programmes. Because of the multifaceted nature of women's practical gender needs, the plans and programmes to meet those needs should reflect a multisectoral dimension. At the same time, however, those plans also need to be integrative if they are really to meet the specific needs of women. Of the two national plans reviewed, that of St. Vincent comes closest to demonstrating this kind of strategy. But even there, it is still possible to identify that ambivalence which pervades the official approach to WID planning.

Positive
- WID units committed to research, training, community involvement;
- WID unit plans emphasize need for infrastructural reform;
- proposed programmes concentrated in areas in which women have great need;
- proposed programmes reflect inter-sector links.

Negative
- Programmes of WID unit not reflected in individual sector plans;
- No mention of women in sector plans;
- No WID unit programmes included in public sector investment programmes.

Much of this ambivalence to the inclusion of women's concerns and women's programmes in development plans has been attributed to the lack of data. This, in turn, has been directly linked to the statistical 'invisibility' of women. Tinker draws attention to

the invisibility of women's work in a world which overvalues work and the unpaid economic activity of women in a world which overvalues profit (Tinker, 1987, p. 72).

She argues that these are the primary factors explaining why women have been ignored by development theorists and practitioners alike. She advocates micro-level research which links the reality of people's lives to macro-level issues. For her 'invisibility disappears when theory is not allowed to triumph over reality'. For Overholt

visibility is the starting point for integrating women into development projects and visibility also comes through data (Overholt, 1985, p. 4).

She proposes an analytic framework for integrating women into project analysis, the cornerstone of which is an adequate data basis which considers what women do and why. The framework involves four interrelated components — an activity profile; access and control profile; analysis of factors influencing activities, access and control; and project analysis.

Both of these authors are concerned with developing strategies for ensuring the inclusion of women's concerns into development programmes by methods other than merely adding a women's component. For them, the fundamental criteria is analysis and presentation of material about women in such a way as to increase their visibility and thus the ability of planners to include their concerns into planning and programme formulation. But the experience internationally, and also here in the Caribbean, has been far from encouraging even when relevant data are available. In the case of the two territories cited, the quantity and quality of data available for one, Barbados, should imply a considerably stronger input from its Women's Bureau into the planning process. But the reality is exactly the opposite. By contrast, St. Vincent with its paucity of data appears to give strong support to its Women's Desk. But again, the reality is exactly the opposite. The original question thus still stands. Why is it that so little about women's issues is reflected in national development plans in the region? The staff structure of the two cases studied provides another clue. Units staffed by a single officer or even two or three may be reflective of bureaucratic resistance to taking on board another issue to contend with in the struggle to identify priorities. But they may also be symptomatic of an inherent administrative inability of the structure of which they are part to deal not only with the specific affairs of the unit, but also with the entire business of managing Caribbean societies, planning and implementation.

The variety and magnitude of the problems facing Caribbean governments as they move into the 1990s and beyond are integrally related to the size and openness of their economies and events on the international arena. All Caribbean economies have experienced a sustained lack of dynamism in key sectors during the 1980s. Capital formation has declined, the region has moved from being a net exporter of labour to being a net exporter of capital, living standards have declined especially amongst the more vulnerable groups and new forms of deviant behaviour are becoming prevalent. All of this means that states are being overloaded by demands which they have neither the administrative nor financial capacity to meet. In this scenario, crisis management, not long-term planning, has become the preferred method of administration and women's issues stand in real danger of being further marginalized.

Planning to increase women's visibility

This review provides evidence that despite a considerable body of knowledge, ongoing strategizing of women's groups, and perfunctory attempts by governments to incorporate women's issues into development plans, the level of women's visibility has remained fundamentally unchanged. It has been argued that women in this region have achieved a measure of statistical visibility. However, socio-economic and political visibility which should be evident in fundamental improvements in the conditions of women's lives in a thorough understanding of the prevailing gender system and in systematic policy efforts to minimize gender disadvantage, continues to be elusive.

This study attempts to distinguish women and their problems and to identify elements of visibility and invisibility on each of those dimensions. This approach permits the identification of different types of needs among different categories of women. In the process it has illustrated that while economic needs are critical, perhaps even universally so, there are other needs which are just as critical even if only for the reason of making economic activity possible.

This approach also illustrated that different strategies enabled the achievement of different levels of visibility. The model developed earlier suggests that research and data production can serve to strengthen conceptual and subjective visibility (Level 1) of the group concerned and introduce theoretical and statistical visibility (Level 2). It requires collective action of some kind, e.g. mobilization to lobby government, networks to spread training opportunities, participatory action projects to move upwards to social and political visibility (Level 3). None of the cases cited suggests that the strategies used have effectively changed the gender-based division of labour in their communities. The move to Level 3 — domestic visibility is yet to be accomplished.

The strategies identified in these case studies seemed geared to meeting what has been termed the immediate 'practical gender interests' of women (Molyneux, op. cit.), i.e. those interests deriving from the roles and responsibilities expected of women in a gender-based system of division of labour. Practical gender needs arising from those interests relate primarily to women's attempts to ensure and maintain an adequate livelihood for themselves and those in their care. The strategies in the case studies focus on the satisfaction of those needs. However, confronting the underlying factors contributing to women's disadvantageous position in society, what Molyneux terms 'women's strategic gender interests' seems not to be the primary objective of the strategies identified. Rather, there seems to be the hope that in the process of securing the former, the latter will be met.

As they strive to align available resources with short-term political priorities of policy-makers, planners do not seem aware of these various distinctions. Rather, without the benefit of explicit policy guidelines, and steeped in traditional planning techniques and methodologies, planners appear incapable of introducing genuinely gender sensitive approaches to public policy planning. In a recent path-breaking article Moser makes a distinction between 'gender aware planning', i.e. the attempt to graft a women's component on to a particular sector plan; and 'gender planning', i.e. a specific planning approach which recognizes the differing roles and needs of men and women and takes these into account in the formulation of plans (Moser, op. cit.). What exists in the Caribbean are planners who may be more or less 'gender aware' but who seem unable (perhaps unwilling) to engage in 'gender planning' geared towards dismantling the veil of invisibility from women's issues.

Fundamental to that dismantling process is of course, appropriate data. The indicators suggested in this study represent an attempt to signal the range of choice available to women, planners and policy-makers using both traditional and non-traditional sources of data. This is just on illustration of the kind of indicators which may be of use to planners. There are many others. But statisticians, WID specialists and planners must begin the process of collaborating for the purpose of identifying, developing and utilizing indicators as a basis for gender planning. No longer can planners and policy-makers adopt the stance that development plans based on traditional data automatically benefit women. History has proven that to be a patently false assumption and the current economic crisis should have forced a recognition of the immensity of that falsehood, as has been demonstrated in recent research (PACCA, 1989; Antrobus, 1989).

However, the provision of suitable and reliable data, the design of appropriate indicators and even the inclusion of well-designed programmes in national development plans will not by themselves ensure effective action. The political commitment of government must be demonstrated, in theory and in fact, by an increasing willingness to recognize the centrality of women's interests to societal survival, to restructure the model of development practised in order to accommodate those interests and to revise the bureaucratic processes in which development planning is embedded.

This review provides evidence that constitutional provisions, ratification of international conventions, creation of WID units, and introduction of legal reform have been largely cosmetic, bringing little significant long-term change in the lives of women of this region. Administrative incapacity, bureaucratic resistance and financial stringency have been some of the reasons advocated for this failure. Underlying these however, is the particular top-down form of development practised in the region which permits individuals and communities little control over the decisions affecting their lives. Genuine political commitment to improving the lives of women would see efforts to ensure that women and women's organizations play a central and active role in a process of defining and guiding an appropriate Caribbean development identifying women's practical and strategic gender needs, devising and implementing strategies to meet those needs. It would see efforts to strengthen the institutional and operational capacity of women's bureaux, to assist women's groups to develop their advocacy skills, to increase the level of gender awareness among staff in Ministries concerned with economic issues. It would see efforts to involve women's bureaux more fully in the formal planning process, to incorporate women's concerns in all aspects of government activity by creating women's units in all government ministries. It would, in effect, abandon strategies which deny or trivialize gender interests, adopting instead strategies in which gender interests are closely articulated with the overall goals of social and economic development.

For planners, the task is to complement their technical capabilities with a greater sensitivity to the needs of the people for whom they are planning and a willingness to adjust the planning process to reflect that sensitivity (Williams, 1989). Much of the current criticism of development planning relates not so much to planning as an exercise, but to the particular form of that exercise and the bureaucratic conventions in which it is embedded. Greater conceptual and methodological flexibility are therefore the first priorities. In the present context, the two fundamental concepts which need to be incorporated in the planning strategy are that women play an important role in all aspects of a society, and what women and men perform different roles in society and consequently have different needs. This necessarily entails developing within planning agencies the capacity to identify the differing roles and needs of men and women in order to relate planning policy to women's specific requirements. Re-education of planners should therefore be a critical aspect in a revised planning strategy.

Methodologically a major criticism has been the formal, economistic bias of conventional planning practice with little or no regard for the social and cultural realities of people's lives. In the present context, such realities as the pervasive influence of the sexual division of labour, gender differences in attitudes to land, work, education, housing, participation in community activities, access to credit, use of social services are some of the issues which planners need to confront when ordering development priorities. But the data which inform the planning process are stunningly silent on such issues. To counteract this, the process should incorporate procedures for the collection, analysis and dissemination of such information. Special stress should be placed on dissemination as the means for encouraging dialogue with relevant social groups, and involving them in a process of identification of needs and prescribing and implementing solutions. In effect, the planning process needs to make itself accessible to groups outside the formal, technical system and to devise means of addressing and utilizing non-traditional types of information.

For women, the task is to devise strategies which would ensure commitment of the political directorate and penetration of the formal planning process. The examples of Rose Hall and SISTREN clearly demonstrate the importance of mobilization and collective action around a concrete gender issue as strategies for moving directly from Level 1 to Level 3 visibility. Their strategies not only raised public awareness but also produced direct results in terms of remedial action in specific cases. However, that collective energy has yet to be channelled towards the planning process itself. For that, stronger alliance between women's organizations and women's bureaux, closer working relationships with the media, constant dialogue with political parties and other interest groups, continuous lobbying of government is needed.

Women's groups (NGOs) need to develop an informal planning process which permits the collection, analysis and sharing of information with each other, the media, the general public and those participating in the formal, planning process. Development planning in the Caribbean may be a formal, technical exercise, but it is undoubtedly a political activity. Groups wishing access to that activity must necessarily function as political pressure groups. Women's Bureaux, by virtue of their institutional

117

genesis and location, are not placed to do so. Women's groups and organizations, by virtue of their independence and the voluntary nature of their activity, are.

The major conclusion to be drawn from the Caribbean experience is that no single strategy by a single entity guarantees success. Government, planners, statisticians and women need to be engaged in an ongoing process of dialogue, experimentation and evaluation in which all are committed to the goal of greater self-reliance for women. Only when this process is in place will women be able to perceive the end of the route to visibility.

Notes

1. Molyneux offered the initial classification in which 'interests' and 'needs' seemed to be used interchangeably. Moser distinguishes between 'interests and needs', equating the former with concerns and the latter with the means by which concerns may be satisfied. Young prefers to focus on practical needs, an empirical concept, and strategic interests, a theoretical concept.

2. National governments in the region participate in a regional organization entitled the Commonwealth Caribbean Community and Common Market (CARICOM) which maintains its Secretariat in Georgetown, Guyana. The Community consists of thirteen member states — Antigua and Barbuda, the Bahamas, Barbados, Belize, Dominica, Grenada, Guyana, Jamaica, Montserrat, St. Christopher-Nevis, St. Lucia, St. Vincent and the Grenadines, Trinidad and Tobago. Haiti, Dominican Republic and Suriname have observer status. The institutional regime within which CARICOM operates consists of: Conference of Heads of Government, Common Market Council of Ministers, 10 Standing Committees of Ministers with specified responsibility, 3 ministerial groups (which include Ministers responsible for Women's Affairs), 7 associate institutions. In addition, CARICOM works in close collaboration with a number of regional bodies. For a discussion of the operation of the system see Rainford, 1984.

3. This was the plan of action established at a meeting of women representatives of 12 governments of the English-speaking Caribbean in 1977 (see Seminar, 1977).

4. The focus on the regional agencies is not intended to obscure national efforts. It is simply intended to reduce the amount of material presented to manageable proportions.

5. The selected projects were:
   (i) The second Integrated Rural Development Project (IRDP-II) of Jamaica which was intended to increase farmers' productivity and strengthen their standard of living by providing and/or improving soil conservation and erosion control, afforestation, roads, housing, rural electrification, small farmer organisations, credit components;
   (ii) the Black Bay Vegetable Farm Project of St. Lucia was intended to move farmers from subsistence to commercial farming for both the domestic and export markets. The project provided support services in credit, management and technical assistance, the project building, machinery and equipment, irrigation facilities, fertilizers, pesticides, weedicides and marketing arrangements;
   (iii) the Tans-G-TOC Cooperative of Dominica was a community-based effort aimed at raising the standards of living of members of participating village communities. The Corporation raised funds to build a feeder road and to establish a health clinic, a consumer shop and a savings union. Other projects included a smocking programme, various adult education programmes and proposals for a fishing project and a fertilizer revolving scheme.

6. Information on findings from this project has been obtained from the preliminary draft manuscript.

7. PACCA is a US-based association of scholars and policy-makers specializing in American and Caribbean affairs. Founded in 1982, the Association is dedicated to promoting policy alternatives to the current US political, economic and social policy in the region. Up until 1987, the bulk of the Association's work had focused on Central America, however, in that year the presence of the Coordinator of WAND on sabbatical at the University of Massachusetts where one of the PACCA co-chairs was located, precipitated the collaborative research project described in this study.

8. Underlying the phrase 'rural women' is usually the assumption that all rural women are engaged in agriculture as their main source of economic activity. Thus the needs of 'rural women' are seen exclusively in terms of women engaged in agriculture.

9. It should be noted that the proposed groupings relate specifically to Caribbean conditions, but the framework is sufficiently flexible to allow the inclusion or exclusion of groups specific to other areas.

10. The survey was presented in a two-volume series consisting of a summary of the findings and detailed tabulations (Nurse, 1986). A more comprehensive analysis of the findings is to be found in Brathwaite, 1985.

11. From census data it is possible to identify a sub-group of hawkers/hucksters within the major occupational category 'sales'. But it is not possible to identify the proportion of those selling agricultural produce.

12. Originally 'higgler' was the Jamaican term for small vendors of agricultural produce, but current usage of the term extends to all kinds of vendors. Elsewhere in the region vendors are known as 'hucksters', 'hawkers' or 'traders'.

13. The Revolutionary Government of Grenada was the only government to establish a full fledged Ministry for Women's Affairs at that time. That disappeared with the demise of the Revolution and was replaced by a Women's Affairs Division in the Ministry of Health, Housing, Women's Affairs and City Development.

14. The six were Barbados, Belize, Dominica, Grenada, Guyana and Jamaica. Summaries of the case studies are presented in Commonwealth Secretariat, 1985.

15. At least three territories are known to have formally adopted a policy statement; one has had a White Paper on Equality for many years; and the remaining ones have statements in different stages of preparations.

16. No travel expenses were included in the budget for this review study so that it was not possible to pursue this analysis amongst the groups for which research reports are available.

17. The term 'work' is here used in the sense in which the WICP respondents used it, i.e. any activity which is functionally necessary for the maintenance of a woman and her household.

18. For discussion of data availability, see Appendix II. For definitions of indicators used in model, see Appendix III.

19. Perhaps if the census tapes were available, cross-classification at this level of detail might be possible but published data rule out analysis in terms of individual occupation.

20. This study devised 20 indicators measuring women's well-being in five sectors: health, marriage and children, education, employment and social equality. Data were converted to 5-point scales, with a maximum score of 20 per sector and 100 for the complete set of indicators.

21. One Prime Minister wrote in the foreword to a women's magazine issued at the beginning of the UN Decade: 'The designation by the U.N. of 1975 as International Women's Year is significant in some areas of the world. It has little meaning in Barbados... The goal of equality with men was won for them by the males a long time ago on this island.' (The Barbadienne, 1975)

22. This is a rough approximation since parts of St. Michael may be considered rural, while parts of Christ Church and St. James may be considered urban. These areas are not, however, readily identifiable in the census tabulations.

23. The approach taken in the 1980 census was to consider 'family' as synonymous with 'household'. On this basis nuclear families comprise head of household, spouse or common law partner and their children; extended families included those same categories plus other relatives of head or spouse; composite families include boarders, domestic employees or others. Single person households are included as nuclear families. This was the first census which adopted this approach.

24. About 90 per cent was exported by Trinidad and Tobago and the remaining 2 per cent by Jamaica.

25. For a detailed analysis of the economy of Barbados from the 1960s, see Worrell, 1987.

26. The skill index is a summary measure of the education and training requirements of each industry.

27. At least one factory is known to have closed when the women workers demanded trade union representation.

28. The Revolutionary Government of Grenada did introduce such procedures, but they were abandoned after the fall of that government.

29. Specific conventions/agreements with the UN and the Commonwealth Secretariat; the NCSW report contained 212 recommendations in a wide range of areas including law, employment, health, education, family, media; for explanation of CARICOM, see note 2; a National Advisory Council existed for the period 1984–86.

30. This refers to small annual subventions to a number of NGOs including the National Organization of Women, the Women's Corona Society, the Soroptomists Club, the Women's Self Help, the YWCA and the Girls' Industrial Union. Additionally, Government funds are available through the Bureau on an 'ad hoc' basis for special projects.

31. In its short history, the Department has experienced numerous relocations moving between four Ministries, five Ministers and six Permanent Secretaries:
    Ministry of the Attorney General, 1976–79
    Ministry of Labour and Community Services, 1979–81
    Ministry of Transport, Works and Community Services, 1981–82
    Ministry of Information and Culture, 1982–85
    Ministry of Labour and Community Services, 1985–present.

32. It is, of course, possible to conduct individual impact assessment studies of each programme. But that was beyond the scope of the present exercise.

Appendix I

Proposals for Bureau of Women's Affairs contained in Barbados Development Plan 1983–1988

The Government considers that Women's Affairs should be seen within the broad context of community development. It is Government's intention to assist women in organizing themselves at the community level so that they can participate more fully in community matters many of which directly affect their welfare and to ensure that as many women as possible participate in the productive sectors of the economy.

Women's Affairs and Community Development fall within the same section of the same Ministry and it is proposed that the Community Development Officers who already have direct contact with the community will investigate and feedback the felt needs aspirations and plans of women whilst also disseminating information from the Department to the community.

It is also proposed to establish close links with the agencies of Government especially concerned with women so that on-going concerns of women, as they relate to those agencies, can be discussed, and an input from women's affairs can be made when decisions have to be made on matters which will affect women.

It is also proposed to establish a body made up of persons drawn from a cross section of the community to advise the Minister on the interests of women generally.

The Government will continue to grant assistance to women's organisations which are engaged in socially desirable programmes.

The Government is aware of the high unemployment among women and it is committed to ensuring that as many women as possible participate in the productive sectors of the economy. It will be endeavouring to identify projects which have income-generating potential and will act as a channel for funding if a project is feasible and if a funding agency is willing to provide funds for its implementation. (Barbados, 1983, pp. 153–154)

Appendix II

The data

A great deal of statistical material is generated by a number of agencies, regional, governmental and non-governmental. As a general rule, official data collection in each territory is executed mainly by the Statistics Department which is usually responsible for the collection of statistics on employment, income, migration, tourism, trade. This is supplemented by the social statistics collected by the various ministries on such areas as health, education, crime, social security and so on. Such an arrangement leaves considerable room for variation in scope and quality of statistics both within and between territories. In many instances, the material is irregular, unrelated, scattered and, in many instances, deficient. Much of this is reflective of the stage of statistical development in the individual territories, which in effect, is related to the stage of economic development.

At the regional level, the most comprehensive and consistent effort at production, publication and analysis of data has been the population censuses which were taken on a regional basis in 1946, 1960 and 1970, with plans to repeat the regional approach for the 1980 census. No other set of statistics is treated in this way at the regional level. General compilations of regional statistics have been produced by CARICOM and the OECS. Topic-specific compilations for the region are occasionally published by one or other of the regional institutions. For example, CARICOM has published a Digest of Regional Trade Statistics, a task formerly performed by ISER on behalf of the smaller territories. The School of Education, UWI has published a compendium of educational statistics for the region drawing on material from the various Ministries of Education.

Other compilations are produced by international organizations. For many years, UNECLAC has produced an Annual Report on the Economic Activity in Caribbean countries which is based on data provided by the various national statistical offices and agencies as well as by the various Caribbean regional integration organizations. The World Bank has recently published a volume which reports on the integration experience in the region, half of which is devoted to a compilation of relevant regional statistics. Each year the British Development Division in the Caribbean publishes an Economic Report for individual territories which contains compilations of relevant statistics for those territories. In each of the examples given, the focus has been on economic statistics, partly due to the concern of the specific organization but also to the dearth or inadequacy of social statistics. But whether the material is published at the regional or national level, no systematic application of indicator analysis appears to have been attempted.

In the context of women in the development of the region, the data at hand do permit a quantitative assessment of the differences between males and females in respect of education, household structure and employment and provide a statistical summary of mating patterns and levels of fertility. But even this limited material has only been used by one territory — the Bahamas — for the production of a compendium of statistics on women.

Appendix III

Definitions of indicators

Table 6

Crude Birth Rate: births per 1000 population
Crude Death Rate: deaths per 1000 population
Sex Ratio: males per 1000 females
Youth Dependency Ratio: population under age 15 per 1000 population of working ages 15–64
Old Age Dependency Ratio: population 65 years and over per 1000 population of working ages 15–64

Table 7

Enrollment:
• primary level: proportion of population aged 5–14 enrolled in primary school.
• secondary level: proportion of population aged 15–19+ enrolled in secondary school.

Table 8

Life Expectancies: the average number of years of life which an individual at birth could expect to live under prevailing mortality patterns.
Infant Mortality Rate: deaths of infants under one year of age per 1000 live births.
Child Mortality Rates: deaths of children aged 1–4 per 1000 population.
Maternal Mortality Rates: deaths of women from complications arising from pregnancy or childbirth per 10,000 live births.

Table 10

Gross Domestic Product per capita: value of total output of goods and services at current market prices per person.
External Debt: value of total debt owed to foreign sources.
Index of retail prices: percentage change in consumer prices.

Table 11

Employment: work for pay or profit.

Index of Dissimilarity: proportion of population which would have to change in order to make two distributions identical.

Unemployment: those who are actively seeking work or who are available for work but have no work, i.e. work for pay or profit.

Table 12

Reproductive Union: union between man and woman within which sexual activity and childbearing take place.

Married Union: partners are legally married and sharing a common household.

Common Law Union: partners are not married but share a common household.

Visiting Union: partners are neither legally married nor sharing a common household.

Job Satisfaction: percentage of responses in which 'job itself' included as source of satisfaction. (WICP)

Community involvement: percentage of responses in which 'self-development' included as reason for importance of community involvement. (WICP)

Table 13

Decision-making: number of decisions in which women only, partner only or joint rank first — out of maximum of ten. (WICP)

Ownership of financial assets: percentage of items owned which are financial assets. Includes land, house, business equipment, livestock, life insurance. (WICP)

REFERENCES

Anderson, Patricia. 'Informal Sector or Modern Labour Market? Towards a Synthesis', *Social and Economic Studies*, 36 (3), 1987: 149–176.

Antrobus, Peggy. 'Women and Planning: The Need for an Alternative Analysis'. Paper presented at Second Disciplinary Seminar in Women and Development Studies, UWI, Cave Hill, Barbados, April 3–7, 1989.

Barbados. *A Ten Year Development Plan for Barbados — Sketch Plan of Development, 1946–56,* Barbados: Advocate Company Ltd., 194(6).

_____. Bureau of Women's Affairs. Workshop on 'Management for Development — Effecting Change'. *Draft Report.* Mimeo, 1989b.

_____. Ministry of Finance and Planning. *Barbados Development Plan 1983–1988: Change Plus Growth,* Bridgetown: Government Printing Department, (1983).

_____. Ministry of Finance and Economic Affairs. *Government of Barbados Development Plan 1988–1993: A Share for All,* Bridgetown: Government Printing Department, (1989a).

_____. National Commission on the Status of Women. *Report,* Bridgetown: Ministry of the Attorney General, 1978. 2 vols.

_____. Statistical Service. *Labour Force Report,* 1981–86, Bridgetown: Government Printing Department, 1988.

_____. Statistical Service and Ministry of Agriculture, Food and Consumer Affairs. *Barbados: Report on the Pilot Study on Socio-Economic Indicators.* November 1981. Mimeo.

Barrow, Christine. 'Male Images of Women in Barbados' in Joycelin Massiah, 1986a, Part II: 51–64.

_____. 'Autonomy, Equality and Women in Barbados'. Paper presented to XI Annual Conference of the Caribbean Studies Association, Caracas, Venezuela, 1986b.

Boissière, Noel. 'Survey of National Planning Systems in Latin America and the Caribbean — a Sub-Regional Report' in UNECLAC, 1980.

Bolles, Lynn. 'Stuck in Second Gear: Women Trade Union Leaders in the Commonwealth Caribbean'. Paper presented at Second Disciplinary Seminar on Women and Development Studies, UWI,Cave Hill, Barbados, April 3–7, 1989.

_____.'Women Leaders in the Caribbean Labour Movement'. Paper presented to XIII Annual Conference of the Caribbean Studies Association, Pointe-à-Pitre, Guadeloupe, May 1988.

Boulding, Elise et al. *Handbook of International Data on Women.* New York: Wiley, 1976.

Bourne, C. *Caribbean Development to the Year 2000: Challenges, Prospects and Policies.* London: Commonwealth Secretariat/Caribbean Community Secretariat, June 1988.

Brathwaite, F. 'The Elderly in Barbados — Problems and Policies'. Paper presented to the XIII International Congress of Gerontology, Rockefeller Center,

New York, July 12–17, 1985.

_____. (ed.) *The Elderly in Barbados.* Bridgetown, Barbados, Carib Research and Publications Inc., 1986.

Brown, Adlith. 'Planning as a Political Activity: Some aspects of the Jamaican experience', *Social and Economic Studies*, 24(1), 1975: 1–14.

Buvinic, Mayra. 'Introduction' in UNESCO, *Women and Development: Indicators of their Changing Role.* Socio-economic Studies 3, Paris, UNESCO, 1981.

Caribbean Association for Feminist Research and Action. *Women in Caribbean Agriculture Research /Action Project. Overall Report and Summary of Main Findings.* December 1988. Mimeo.

Caribbean Community Secretariat. *Women's Affairs. Seminar on Strengthening National Machinery for the Integration of Women in Development. Kingston, Jamaica, November 22–28, 1981.* Report. 1981. Mimeo.

_____. *Women's Affairs. First Meeting of Ministers with Responsibility for the Integration of Women in Development, Roseau, Dominica, 1981. Report.* Georgetown: CARICOM Secretariat, 1981. Mimeo.

_____. *Second Meeting of Ministers with Responsibility for the Integration of Women in Development, Georgetown, Guyana, March 17–18, 1983.* Report. Georgetown: CARICOM Secretariat, 1983. Mimeo.

_____. *Third Meeting of Ministers with Responsibility for the Integration of Women in Development, Dickerson Bay, Antigua, May 16–17, 1985.* Report. Georgetown: CARICOM Secretariat, 1985. Mimeo.

_____. *Women's Affairs. Fourth Meeting of Ministers with Responsibility for the Integration of Women in Development, Basseterre, St. Kitts and Nevis, April 28–29, 1988.* Report. Georgetown: CARICOM Secretariat, 1988. Mimeo.

_____. *Meeting of Statisticians, Women in Development Personnel and Researchers, St. Michael, Barbados, July 29–31, 1986.* Report. Georgetown: CARICOM Secretariat, 1986. Mimeo.

_____. 1980/81 *Population Census of the Commonwealth Caribbean, Barbados.* 3 vols. Kingston: Statistical Unit of Jamaica, n.d.

Chaney, Elsa. *Women of the World — Latin America and the Caribbean.* Washington D.C.: US Department of Commerce/Bureau of the Census and USAID/ Office of Women in Development, 1984.

Clarke, Roberta. 'Women's Organisations, Women's Interests' in Joycelin Massiah 1986a, Part II: 107–155.

_____. and Diane Cummins. Report on St. Vincent Workshops 1982. Paper prepared for Women in the Caribbean Project Conference, Barbados, September 12–16, 1982.

Commonwealth Secretariat. *Women and Development Programme. Workshop on Ladies in Limbo Revisited. Belize City, Belize, November 11–15, 1985. Record.* London: Commonwealth Secretariat, 1985. Mimeo.

_____. *Engendering Adjustment for the 1990s.* Report of a Commonwealth Expert Group on Women and Structural Adjustment. London: Commonwealth Secretariat, 1989.

Demas, W. Men, *Women and Children in Development.* Statement of the President of the Caribbean Development Bank at the Sixteenth Annual Meeting of the Board of Governors, Caracas, Venezuela, May 14–15, 1986. Mimeo.

Duncan, N. and O'Brien, K. *Women and Politics in Barbados, 1948–1981.* Cave Hill, Barbados: ISER(EC), 1983.

Ellis, Patricia (ed.) *Women of the Caribbean.* London and New Jersey: Zed Books, 1986*a*.

—————. 'From Silent Beneficiaries to Active Participants', 1986*b* in Ellis 1986*a*.

—————. 'Methodologies for Doing Research on Women and Development' in IDRC, Manuscript Report. Women in Development: Perspectives from the Nairobi Conference, Ottawa: IDRC, 1986*c*.

Food and Agriculture Organization of the United Nations. Regional Office for Latin America and the Caribbean. *Caribbean Women in Agriculture.* Santiago, Chile: FAO, 1988.

Ford Smith, Honor. Ring Ding in a Tight Corner: A Case Study of Funding and Organisational Democracy in SISTREN, 1977–1988. Toronto: Women's Programme, ICAE, 1989.

Gillings, Scarlett. Review of the Barbados Women's Bureau. Study prepared for the ILO Sub-Regional Office, Port-of-Spain, Trinidad and Tobago, October 1987.

Gloudon, Barbara. 'Caribbean Women and the Trade Union Movement' 1986 in Ellis, 1986*a*.

Gordon, Shirley (ed.) *Ladies in Limbo: The Fate of Women's Bureaux — Case Studies from the Caribbean.* London: Commonwealth Secretariat, Women and Development Programme, 1984.

Haniff, Nesha. *Blaze a Fire — Significant Contributions of Caribbean Women.* Toronto: Sister Vision, 1988.

Hart, K. (ed.) *Women and the Sexual Division of Labour in the Caribbean.* Kingston, Jamaica: Consortium Graduate School of Social Sciences, UWI, 1989.

Higman, B.W. 'Domestic Service in Jamaica since 1750' in B.W. Higman (ed.) *Trade, Government and Society in the Caribbean, 1700–1920.* Kingston, Jamaica: Heinemann, 1983.

Inter American Development Bank. *Economic and Social Progress in Latin America. Annual Report 1972, 1980–81, 1986, 1988.* Washington D.C.: IADB, (various years).

International Labour Organisation/UN Research and Training Institute for the Advancement of Women. *Women in Economic Activity: A Global Statistical Survey 1950–2000.* Santo Domingo, Dominican Republic: ILO/INSTRAW, 1985.

Jagdeo, T. *Caribbean Contraceptive Prevalence Surveys, 4 - Barbados.* IPPF/WHR. Mimeo 1989.

Joekes, Susan. *Women in the World Economy.* New York and Oxford: Oxford University Press, 1987.

Jordan, Merna. *Physical Violence Against Women in Barbados, 1977–1985.* Report prepared for the Bureau of Women's Affairs, Barbados, 1986.

Knudson, Barbara and Barbara Yates. *The Economic Role of Women in Small Scale Agriculture in the Eastern Caribbean — St. Lucia.* Barbados: UWI, WAND, 1981.

Le Franc, Elsie. 'Petty Trading and Labour Mobility: Higglers in the Kingston Metropolitan Area' in K. Hart (ed.) *Women and the Sexual Division of Labour in the Caribbean,* 1989: 99–132.

Lewis, G.L. and D. Heisler. *The Barbados Male Family Planning Survey: Country Report 1982,* Bridgetown: Barbados and Columbia, Maryland: Barbados Family Planning Association and Westinghouse Public Applied Systems, 1985.

Lewis, W.A. 'On Assessing a Development Plan', *Economic Bulletin for Ghana,* 3 (6 and 7), 1959.

McKenzie, Hermione. 'The Educational Experiences of Caribbean Women' in Joycelin Massiah 1986a, Part II: 65–105.

Massiah, Joycelin. 'Indicators of Women's Participation in Development: A Preliminary Methodological Framework for the Caribbean'. Paper prepared for UNESCO meeting of experts on the indicators of women's participation in socio-economic development, Paris, April 21–24, 1980. Edited version in UNESCO, 1981.

_____. 'An Assessment of National Machinery for Women in the Caribbean. Two Case Studies: Barbados and Dominica'. Paper prepared for Commonwealth Secretariat/CARICOM Secretariat Workshop, Barbados, November 8–11, 1983. Extracts in Gordon, 1984.

_____. *Report of the Conference on the Role of Women in the Caribbean, Barbados, September 12–16, 1982.* Barbados: UWI, ISER(EC), 1983.

_____. (ed.) Women in the Caribbean. Special Issue. *Social and Economic Studies,* 35(2 and 3), June and September 1986. (1986a)

_____. 'WICP: an Overview' in Joycelin Massiah 1986a, Part I: 1–29. (1986b)

_____. 'Work in the Lives of Caribbean Women' in Joycelin Massiah 1986a, Part I: 177–239. (1986c)

_____. 'Postscript: The Utility of WICP Research in Social Policy Formulation' in Joycelin Massiah 1986a, Part II: 157–181. (1986d)

Mohammed, Patricia. 'Domestic Workers', 1986 in Ellis, 1986a.

Molyneux, Maxine. 'Mobilization Without Emancipation? Women's Interests, State and Revolution in Nicaragua', *Critical Social Policy,* Vol. 4, 1984/85.

Moser, Caroline. 'Gender Planning in the Third World: Meeting Practical and Strategic Gender Needs', *World Development,* Vol. 17 (11), 1989: 1799–1825.

Nair, N.K. *Fertility and Family Planning in Barbados - Findings from the Contraceptive Prevalence Survey 1980–81.* Bridgetown, Barbados and Columbia, Maryland: Barbados Family Planning Association and Westinghouse Health Systems, 1982.

Nurse, J. 'Epidemiological Survey of the Aged: Barbados', July 1986. 2 Vols. Mimeo.

Odi-Ali, Stella. 'Women in Agriculture: The Case of Guyana' in Joycelin Massiah 1986a, Part I: 241–289.

Overholt, Catherine et al. (eds.) *Gender Roles in Development Projects.* Connecticut: Kumarian Press, 1985.

PACCA. 'Alternative Visions of Development in the Caribbean'. Draft manuscript, 1989. Mimeo.

Pan American Health Organisation. *Health Condition of the Americas, 1981–84.* Washington D.C.: PAHO, 1986.

Population Crisis Committee. Country Rankings of the Status of Women: Poor, Powerless and Pregnant. Population Briefing. Paper No. 20, June 1988.

Powell, Dorian. 'Caribbean Women and their Response to Familial Experiences', in Joycelin Massiah, 1986*a*, Part I: 83–130.

Rainford, R. 'The Decision Making Process and the Institutional Fabric of CARICOM', in IADB/CARICOM, *Ten Years of CARICOM,* Washington D.C.: IADB, 1984.

Rivera, Marcia. 'Women in the Caribbean. Underground Economics' in N. Girvan and G. Beckford (eds.), *Development in Suspense.* Selected Papers and Proceedings of the First Conference of Caribbean Economists, Kingston, Jamaica: Friedrich Ebert Stiftung and Association of Caribbean Economists, 1989.

Seminar on the Integration of Women in Development in the Caribbean. Report. (Social Welfare Training Centre, Department of Extra Mural Studies, UWI, Mona, Jamaica, June 6–10, 1977).

Sen, Gita and Caren Grown. *Development Issues and Alternative Visions.* New Delhi: Institute of Social Studies Trust, 1985.

Shiw Persad, Basmad. 'Domestic Violence: A Study of Wife-Abuse among East Indians of Guyana'. Paper presented at XIII Annual Conference of the Caribbean Studies Association, Guadeloupe, May 25–27, 1988.

SISTREN (with Honor Ford Smith). *Lion Heart Gal: Life Stories of Jamaican Women.* London: The Women's Press, 1986.

Sivard, Ruth. *Women... a World Survey.* Washington D.C.: World Priorities, 1985.

Springer, B.G.F. 'The Role of Women in Agriculture in Three Eastern Caribbean States — Grenada, St. Lucia and St. Vincent'. Paper prepared for UNECLAC, 1983. Mimeo.

Stamp, Patricia. *Technology, Gender and Power in Africa.* IDRC Technical Study 63e. Ottawa: IDRC, 1989.

St. Vincent. 'Development Planning in St. Vincent' in UNECLAC, 1980.

St. Vincent and the Grenadines. *Development Plan 1986–1988: Growth, Diversification, Redistribution.* St. Vincent: Ministry of Finance and Planning, 1986.

————. *Estimates 1989/90.* St. Vincent Ministry of Finance and Planning, 1990.

Taylor, Alicia. 'Women Traders in Jamaica: The Informal Commercial Importers'. Paper presented for UNECLAC, March 1988.

————. Donna McFarlane and Elsie Le Franc. 'The Higglers of Kingston' in Marianne Schmink et al. (eds.) *Learning about Women and Urban Services in Latin America and the Caribbean.* New York: Population Council, 1986.

The Barbadienne. Souvenir Magazine for International Women's Year. Barbados: Business and Professional Women's Club, 1975.

Tinker, Irene. 'Street Foods: Testing Assumptions about Informal Sector Activity by Women and Men', *Current Sociology,* 35(3), 1987.

United Nations. Department of International Economic and Social Affairs, Statistical Office and International Research and Training Institute for the Advancement of Women. *Compiling Social Indicators on the Situation of Women.* New York: UN, 1984*a*. Series F, No. 32.

_____. _____. *Improving Concepts and Methods for Statistics and Indicators on the Situation of Women.* New York: UN, 1984*b*. Series F, No. 33.

United Nations. Economic Commission for Latin America and the Caribbean. *Meeting on Women in Development Planning, Christ Church, Barbados, May 12–14, 1980.* Report. UNECLAC, 1980. Mimeo. E/CEPAL/CDCC/63.

_____. _____. *Second Meeting of Planning Officials in the Caribbean, Kingston, Jamaica, May 29 – June 2, 1980.* Report. UNECLAC, 1980. Mimeo. CEPAL/CARIB 0/7.

_____. _____. 'Women in the Inter Island Trade in Agricultural Produce in the Eastern Caribbean'. Paper presented to Fourth Regional Conference on the Integration of Women into the Economic and Social Development of Latin America and the Caribbean, Guatemala City, Guatemala, September 27–30, 1988. Mimeo. LC/L.485/CRM.4/9.

_____. _____. 'Comparative Status of Women in Selected Caribbean Countries as indicated by selected social, economic, demographic and legal parameters'. July 1989. Mimeo.

United Nations. International Research and Training Institute for the Advancement of Women. *Workshop on Statistics and Indicators on the Social and Economic Situation of Women particularly in the Informal Sector, Colombo, Sri Lanka, October 12–16, 1987.* Report. Mimeo.

UNESCO. Statistical Office and International Research and Training Institute for the Advancement of Women. *Meeting of Expert Group on Improving Statistics,* June 1983*a*. Mimeo. ESA/STAT/AC.17/9; INSTRAW /AC.1/9.

_____. _____. 'A User's Perspective of Social Indicators on Women', prepared by the Branch for the Advancement of Women, UN Centre for Social Development and Humanitarian Affairs, March 1983*b*. Mimeo; ESA/ STAT/ AC.17/6; INSTRAW /AC.1/6.

_____. _____. 'The State of Statistics on Women in Agriculture in the Third World'. Prepared by Constantina Safilivo-Rothschild, April 1983*c*. Mimeo. ESA/STAT/AC.17/7; INSTRAW /AC.1/7.

_____. World Conference to Review and Appraise the Achievements of the United Nations Decade for Women: Equality, Development and Peace. 'Selected Statistics and Indicators on the Status of Women — Report of the Secretary-General'. Nairobi, Kenya, July 15–26, 1985*a* A/CONF.116/10.

_____. _____. 'Forward Looking Strategies for the Advancement of Women'. Nairobi, Kenya, July 15–26, 1985*b*.

United Nations Educational Scientific and Cultural Organisation. Division for

Socio Economic Analysis. *Women and Development: Indicators of their Changing Role,* Paris: UNESCO, 1981.

_____. _____. *Women's Concerns and Planning: A methodological approach for their integration into local, regional and national planning.* Paris: UNESCO, 1986.

United Nations Educational, Scientific and Cultural Organisation. Division of Study and Planning of Development. *The Results of a demonstration project in Thailand.* Paris: UNESCO, 1987. Mimeo.

_____. _____. *International Symposium on Methods for the Integration of Women's Issues in Development Planning, Paris, October 5–9, 1987,* Final Report, 1987. Mimeo. DEV 87/CONF. 801/15.

University of the West Indies. *Census Research Programme. 1970 Population Census of the Commonwealth Caribbean.* Kingston, Jamaica: UWI, 1976, 10 vols.

University of the West Indies. *Census Research Programme. Women and Development Unit. Planning for Women in Rural Development — A Source Book for the Caribbean.* Barbados: WAND, 1983.

Williams, Gwendoline. 'Women and Public Policy: Beyond the Rhetoric of Integration to a Focus on "Mainstreaming" Gender Analysis in the Development Planning Process'. Paper presented to Second Disciplinary Seminar in Women and Development Studies, UWI, Cave Hill, Barbados, April 3–7, 1989.

World Bank. Recognising the 'Invisible' Women in Development: The World Bank's Experience. Washington D.C.: World Bank, 1979.

Worrell, D. (ed.) *The Economy of Barbados, 1946–1980.* Bridgetown, Barbados: Central Bank of Barbados, 1982.

_____. (ed.) *Small Island Economies — Structural Performance in the English-Speaking Caribbean since 1970.* New York: Praeger, 1987.

Yudelman, Sally. *Hopeful Openings: A Study of Five Women's Development Organizations in Latin America and the Caribbean.* Connecticut: Kumarian Press, 1987.

Young, Kate. 'Reflections on Meeting Women's Needs' in Kate Young (ed.) *Women and Economic Development: Local Regional and National Planning Strategies.* Oxford: Berg/UNESCO, 1988: 1–30.

Abbreviations

ACEP	Asociación Colombiana pasa el Estudio de la Poblation
AID	Association Internationale de Développement
BDD	British Development Division
BWA	Bureau of Women Affairs
CAFRA	Caribbean Association of Feminist Researchers and Activists
CARICOM	Caribbean Community
CBI	Caribbean Basin Initiative
CDB	Caribbean Development Bank
DWCRA	Development of Women and Children in Rural Areas
ECLAC	Economic Commission for Latin America and the Caribbean
ENDA	Environmental Development Action in the Third World
FLS	Forward Looking Strategies
FAO	Food and Agriculture Organization of the United Nations
ICIs	International Commercial Importers
IFAD	International Fund for Agricultural Development
ILO	International Labour Office
INSTRAW	International Research and Training Institute for the Advancement of Women
IRDP	Integrated Rural Development Program
ISER(EC)	Institute of Social and Economic Research (Eastern Caribbean)
LIAT	Leeward Islands Air Transport
NCSW	National Commission on the Status of Women
NCW	National Commission onWomen
NGO	Non-Governmental Organization
NOC	National Occupational Classification
PACCA	Policy Alternatives for the Caribbean and Central America
PAM	Programmes Alimentaire Mondial
SEWA	Self Employed Women's Association
SIDA	Swedish International Development Authority
TYRSEM	Training of Rural Youth for Self Employment
UK	United Kingdom
UN	United Nations
UNICEF	United Nation Children's Fund
US	United States of America
UWI	University of the West Indies
WAND	Women and Development Unit
WICP	Women in the Caribbean Project
WID	Women in Development
YWCA	Young Women's Christian Association

Chapter II

Women's role in the informal sector in Tunisia

El Amouri Institute

The informal sector in Tunisia

A safe haven in hard times or a new panacea?

The State sector expanded in Tunisia throughout the 1960s and 1970s and the free-market economy developed alongside, forming the two facets of a strategy whose watchwords were modernization, organization and industrialization. This State-advocated strategy was inspired by a desire to construct a new society; all it did, in fact, was to speed up the decay of social bonds and to provoke multiple forms of resistance. The workers deliberately undermined the logic of productivism while the farmers, attached to age-old forms of social bonds and organization, refused to introduce new cropping methods. State and society formed two worlds where ways of thinking and feeling diverged and where value systems were different, if not actually contradictory. Eventually, the failure of national accumulation, the end of complementarity between agriculture and industry, the burden of debt and the public-sector deficit cleared the way for new and original forms of economic activity. Areas of autonomy now appear more frequently outside the organized forms in the small private sector and in the increasingly important informal sector.

Workers in this sector account for 40 per cent of all non-rural employment. Home-based production, small-scale business and the the multiple activities frequently related to it, have made it possible to understand certain economic forces, particularly the strategies for life and survival deployed by urban populations.The sector highlights a new and original interconnection between the economic and the social and shows that, despite the important role still played by capital and large industry in certain sectors, the formal economy in no way organizes the whole of society.

The informal sector concerns especially newly-arrived city-dwellers who set great store by mutual solidarity and seek to re-establish ties as strong as the ties of blood. The solidity and dynamism of these forms of social cohesion allow the individual to form bonds and provide the individual with the permanent support of allies. Imported techniques are adjusted from time to time to adapt them to specific operations. A segment of the production process may be modified or, even more often, a machine may be diverted from its initial function. Workshops become centres for education and for young people who have done badly in school and equip them with advanced qualifications. Some see it as a form of 'galloping industrialization',[1] of 'intense entrepreneurial dynamism'. Others look upon it as an exemplar of the primary accumulation of capital, as a safety-valve, in as much as it allows society to adapt to the economic mutations that become necessary during periods of transition. It would, however, be a mistake to confine the informal sector to urban areas and to forget the part played by women in challenging a certain form of development that uproots more than it integrates, that divides more than it joins together. But is the role played by women limited to the traditional divisions of sexual roles or does it transgress them to usher in a new relationship between the sexes?

Origins

As was the case in all of the formerly colonized countries, the Tunisian economy was in disarray at the end of the 1950s. Successive governments had to run a country full of urgent social expectations; there was a general aspiration to education and health facilities, agriculture was performing very poorly, and although the urban artisan class was substantial, accounting for 76.8 per cent of the manufacturing sector, its productivity was feeble.

By opting for a modernist ideology and a policy of all-out industrialization, the politicians, dazzled by the Western model of economic development, put the country's material, human and financial capacities under severe strain. The State, however, was determined, against all reason and despite the social circumstances, to impose its technocratic vision of things. Though the network of co-operatives expanded and the free-market economy continued to develop throughout the 1960s and 1970s, both led in fact to bitter disappointment. Agriculture continued to deteriorate and the food deficit to worsen while the allegedly miraculous industrial sector failed to absorb young school-leavers.

Faced with this situation, planners and economists, riding on the crest of a wave of fashion, were surprised to discover a 'non-structured' sector. They had previously been oblivious of it because there were no descriptive statistics and information available on the activities and functions of the small businesses of the sector. Immediately, surveys were commissioned, with all the fervour of the newly converted. The planners and economists discovered that, while the State was groping around in the dark trying to impose its views, society at large was putting down the roots of an endogenous economy in small spaces of freedom, centred on real human needs, using the means to hand, adopting techniques that were easy to assimilate and preserving the social fabric.

Definition and typology

The sector initially became the object of study in 1976 through the good offices of the National Statistics Institute in the Planning Ministry in collaboration with the Office of Overseas Scientific and Technical Research, represented by the economist, Jacques Charmes.

The objective was clear — to situate the 'non-structured' sector in the economy as a whole. The following three definitions were put forward by J. Charmes in different surveys and publications:

The non-structured sector is made up of all ventures with workforces of less than 10 in the secondary sector and in the services, of less than 3 in commerce, and by the totality of moonlighters, working at home or in the street.[2]
The non-structured sector is made up of all monetary activity not taken into account by official statistics and the accounts of the nation.[3]
The non-structured sector is made up of all activities that fall outside the ambit of periodic business statistics.[4]

The theory outlined above acknowledges that conventional economic wisdom is ill-equipped to deal with this field; statisticians do not possess the conceptual framework or an adequate methodology, whence the need to revise prevalent notions about the economy so as to collect data in a rigorously scientific manner.

Activities break down into two categories depending on whether they are pursued on single, fixed, purpose-built premises (the localized sector) or in a variety of other locations, in the street or in the home (the non-localized sector).

The non-structured sector, in the widest sense, is made up of categories 1 to 7 below, although *strictu sensu,* it is composed of only categories 3 to 7.

1. Ventures whose economic function makes them indistinguishable from the modern capitalist sector from which they are differentiated only by their size and the number of people they employ.

2. Ventures characterized by a greater number of apprentices and of home helps in the workforce, or by their structure and economic functioning.

3. Ventures operating outside the labour code and regulations and competing with 2 above.

4. Ventures characterized by the mobility of the employees and the precariousness of their situation.

5. Ventures offering goods and services rather than labour.

6. Underground workshops, in the home, which distort competition.

7. Recognized activities (weaving), especially for women.

The present study is confined to the first three categories and takes no account of shops, services, ancillary activities and the non-agricultural rural sector. It includes an exhaustive survey of the totality of city-based economic sectors but does not cover home-based work.[5] (See Tables 1 and 2 below.)

Thus, between 1966 and 1975, apprentices increased from 0.5 per cent to 3.8 per cent in rural employment and each employer employed 1.5 apprentices in 1975. The 1980 population-employment survey confirmed that the extent and significance of the phenomenon had changed. The rate of apprentices and home helps had continued to increase (8.1 per cent) while there had been a drop in salaried employment as a whole. Apprentices are to be found mainly in manufacturing industry (textiles, shoemaking, woodwork, metalwork and engineering) in the services (repair shops, garages) and in shops. It should also be noted that there is a tendency for the apprentice-home help/worker ratio to increase in areas where it is already quite high.

There would also seem to be a general increase in employment, particularly in the highly competitive informal sector (textiles, shoemaking, woodwork and furniture, repair shops) where the proportion of apprentices and home helps exceeds 50 per cent.

TRAINING

The increasing proportion of apprentices in the workforce has highlighted the problem of training in the non-structured sector. It ought to be remembered that 75 per cent of apprentices who receive training in the private sector do so in the non-structured sector and in small concerns with workforces of less than 10.

The most widespread form of training in rural areas remains unchanged — watching and listening, the transmission of knowledge through observation and practical application. It is a kind of rite of initiation in which the apprentice is expected to show interest and docility, obedience and daring. Nothing is free. What apprentices have to do is to conquer, to 'steal by looking'[6] the secrets of the trade.

TABLE 1

PROPORTION OF THE NON-STRUCTURED SECTOR IN NON-AGRICULTURAL EMPLOYMENT

Localization / Sector of activity	Non-structured sector Localized		Non-structured sector Non-localized		Total non-struc-tured sector	Including		Including		Propor tion of n.-s.s in the sector as a whole
	Urban	Rural	Urban	Rural		Urban	%	Local-ized	%	
Woodwork/ Furniture	11,526	2,760	2,001	180	16,770	13,550	80.7	14,286	85.2	70.2
Engineering/ Garages	8,750	2,379	4,862	1,321	17,312	13,612	78.6	11,129	64.3	74.3
Metalwork/ Blacksmith	4,785	860	-	-	5,645	4,785	84.8	5,645	100.0	54.8
Textiles/Garments	11,928	-	47,676	41,619	101,223	59,604	58.9	11,928	11.8	72.3
Leather/Shoes	3,317	630	207	-	4,154	3,524	84.8	3,947	95.0	54.2
Bread/Pastries	4,810	1,161	-	-	5,471	4,310	78.8	5,471	100.0	63.7
Miscellaneous (Rubber, ceramics, beads, jewellry)	3,545	-	-	-	3,545	3,545	100	3,545	100.0	27.1
Construction	1,255	625	25,445	12,675	40,000	26,790	66.8	1,880	4.7	28.4
Road transport	-	-	11,740	4,787	16,527	11,740	71.0	-	0.0	53.3
Retail trades	37,505	17,390	7,380	-	62,275	44,885	72.1	54,895	88.2	75.5
Hotels/ Restaurants	10,359	1,554	-	-	11,913	10,359	87.0	11,913	100.0	38.2
Repairs	3,653	774	2,547	516	7,490	6,200	82.8	4,427	58.1	97.8
Other services	7,434	5,763	18,212	1,537	30,946	25,646	82.9	11,197	36.2	98.0
Secondary sector (s.s. Construction)	48,161	7,790	54,749	43,420	154,120	120,910	66.8	55,951	36.3	68.4
Services sector (s.s. Transport)	21,446	6,090	20,759	2,053	50,349	42,205	83.8	27,537	54.7	71.5
Secondary and tertiary sectors together	107,112	31,271	82,888	45,473	266,744	190,000	72.1	138,383	51.9	72.2
Total sectors II and III	108,367	31,896	120,075	62,035	323,271	228,440	70.7	140,263	43.4	58.8

Source: Recensement des établissements en milieu urbain. INS. 1980.

TABLE 2

BREAKDOWN AND GROWTH OF NON-AGRICULTURAL WORKING MANPOWER BETWEEN
1966 AND 1980 BY STATUS IN THE PROFESSION (CATEGORY AND POSITION)

Year	1966		1975		1980		Total annual growth		
Status in the profession	Numbers	%	Numbers	%	Numbers	%			
Associated employers	11,425	1.9	20,600	2.4	19,240	1.9	3.8	6.7	−1.4
Independents	75,429	12.5	153,190	17.9	188,020	18.8	6.7	8.2	42
Wage-earners	443,403	73.3	614,540	71.7	704,330	70.4	3.4	2.4	2.8
Apprentices	2.971	0.5	32,680	3.8	48.290	4.8	22.0	30.5	8.1
Family helps	6,603	1.1	22,240	2.6	30,370	3.0	11.5	14.5	6.4
Apprentices and family helps	9,574	1.6	54,920	6.4	78,660	7.8	16.2	21.4	7.4
Total	604,595	100.00	857,590	100.00	999,910	100.00	3.7	4.0	3.1

Source: CNRS, *Apprentissage sur le tas dans le secteur non structuré en Tunisie.*
Annuaire de l'Afrique du Nord, Paris, 1980.

The employers' objective is to reduce wage costs in order to remain
competitive by making the apprentice as productive as actual workers.
They take on more and more apprentices because a job allocated to two
apprentices costs less than if it were done by one skilled worker. They try
to dissuade their best apprentices from leaving because if this happens,
they will lose the premium of their training and risk their secrets being
revealed. Training in intermediary units (workforce of eight) is more specialized and uses the apprentice more productively and more cost-effec-
tively. There is considerable rotation of employees.

Some criticize this type of training, saying that it is too long and
ends up sending under-qualified producers onto the market, thus distort-
ing competition (moonlighters, blacklegs). The truth is that it provides
better training for a trade than the excessively theoretical training
courses in conventional centres of education and training which last almost as long but provide inadequate preparation for a job and at best,
equip the trainee for the first few days on the shop floor. The merit of on-
the-job training is that it challenges the hyper-institutionalized model of
training, often so far removed from the realities of economic life. At the
very least, it never eliminates anybody while at the same time selecting
the best and allowing everybody to develop at his or her own rhythm.

INCREASING PRODUCTIVITY

It emerges from two surveys by sector (woodwork and engineering) and the country-wide survey on economic activity conducted in 1981[7] that added value in the Tunisian manufacturing industry was underassessed by a factor of 46 per cent and that inclusion of the non-structured sector would lead to a 10 per cent upward re-evaluation of GDP. The results of a comparison between the industrial and non-structured woodwork sectors showed that the non-structured sector accounted for:
- 1.9 per cent of jobs in industry
- 1.1 per cent of turnover
- 1.5 per cent of added value (with 31 per cent apprentices)
- 4.3 per cent of profits.

However, productivity, turnover and profit per employee were lower in the non-structured sector. Also noteworthy are the high production costs in the industrial sector where the wage bill and taxes can reach 74.4 per cent of added value. Average wage costs in the industrial sector were 648 Tunisian Dinars compared to 229 TD in the non-structured sector. In should also be noted that revenue in the non-structured manufacturing area break down as follows:
- 23 per cent for labour
- 2 per cent for the State
- 75 per cent for the employer.

An economy adapted to human needs

A series of microscopic units of production which disregard the labour code and regulations are now emerging in opposition to centrally-dictated State development policies inspired by a desire for all-out industrialization. The State adopts a free-market economy, encourages capital-intensive projects, seeks to improve productivity by introducing advanced and sophisticated new technology facilitated by international loans. But in so doing, it neglects the social and financial aspects of the problem. The smaller units, on the other hand, anxious to establish their independence and aware that their financial means are limited, set out to invent new and original models in an attempt to ensure survival and development. The modern sector moves forward like a bulldozer intent on submitting nature and humanity to its exigencies while, alongside, the non-structured sector, like some latter-day David, makes do, settles for less, makes the best of what it has, and seeks to adapt rather than to conquer.

It would be a mistake, however, to consider the sector as an embryonic form of the modern system and even less so as a negative phenomenon. It simply heralds an alternative style and other avenues of development, just as the counter-culture revealed the latent crisis deep within society and the need for new organizations. The non-official sector is, then, at the very least a symptom. Could it be a panacea? It has been praised for its high employment rate, its low capital requirement and distributed income, the low-cost quality training it offers and its potential technical autonomy. The fact remains that its productivity has often been considered feeble and the techniques it uses are mid-way between the archaic and the sophisticated. The question is a legitimate one — beneath the praise, is it not possible to detect a deep contempt for a sector occupied by the destitute, accepted and respected as were 'traditions' and 'particular features' in colonial times? It deserves better. It needs to be studied for and in itself with appropriate concepts and specific, pertinent analytical tools. It is to conventional economy what Michelson and Morley's experiments were to conventional physics — the first step towards a new theory.

Women and the informal economy

Towards a new exclusion

Whether we examine the corn fields of the north, the steppes of the central region or the oases of the south one fact is clear: women today, like those of previous generations, continue to slave at agricultural tasks. Has their work been recognized and given its just value in economic statistics? In an economy dominated by agriculture, in which subsistence production, domestic and family labour persist, the double esteem accorded to commercial production and salaried employment leads inevitably to a marked depreciation of female agricultural production or activity — a devaluation all the more easy to make when reinforced by the sexist prejudice of traditional society. In short, men have taken a dominant position in traditional agriculture and have appropriated for themselves the nobler aspects and rewards.

A recent survey of three hundred and five farmers in the region of Siliana in the centre of Tunisia has shown that wives are systematically excluded from ploughing, a task reserved to the head of the household. Standing upright, the husband leads the team, ploughs and sows; stooped, his wife reaps and gleans. In the olive grove, the husband digs, prunes the trees and — perched on a ladder — picks the olives; his wife, crouched below, prepares the bowls, gathers the branches and sorts the olives.

The male stands at both ends of the process; he is the alpha and omega. His activity as a farmer is prolonged by social and public life whereas his wife leaves her work in the fields to apply herself to domestic and subsistence tasks: the vegetable garden, animal husbandry, weaving.

Yet in the censuses, in statistical tables, it is he who is the bread-winner while she is simply a housewife. She merely assists.

The city woman is no better off. Far away from the fields, she prepares the *couscous,* makes bread, cooks the meals and thus fulfils a duty considered natural. But in the *souk,* the man who cooks for clients is a restaurateur, just as the man who bakes and sells bread is considered a baker. In short, women's work is either domestic or free of charge while a man's is remunerated and counts as economic activity.

What of the city woman who participates in artisanal activities? She cards the wool and spins the thread while men have the task of weaving it on their power-looms. She knits for the *chechia* and the male gives it its definitive form. Once more, a woman looks after the preparatory tasks while a man retains the surplus value: he is an artisan while she is only a helper.

The process is repeated everywhere without end. Through her own efforts, a woman weaves her carpet on the loom and keeps busy at her tasks. Her husband sells the carpet. Though she ensures a supplementary wage for the family by knitting, sewing and embroidering for her clients, the stealing of her contribution is justified by such phrases as 'natural role', 'secondary activity', 'supplementary wage'. Seemingly rational norms are conceived to quantify her work as a simple share in a man's economic activity. Inequality is thus given a scientific basis. In brief, the 'scientific' approach of classical economics, both in its concepts and methods, is rooted in sexual prejudice and continues to occult the informal work provided by women. The modern development project simply perpetuates, even aggravates her situation.

Exclusion redoubled: women in agriculture

An evaluation[8] of an integrated development project in the irrigated areas around Sidi Bouzid has shown how the participation of women in economic development is hidden and devalued. This region of the Tunisian High Steppe — which has known successively an agro-pastoral economy, a subsistence agriculture and now a market-oriented farming economy — illustrates well the evolution of women's work in a changing society.

WOMEN IN AN AGRO-PASTORAL ECONOMY

At the beginning of the century, the inhabitants of Sidi Bouzid lived from sheep-rearing and occasional cereal crops. The grazing territory belonged to the tribe while flocks, the only private property, differentiated families socially. Transhumance gave rhythm to life. In summer, entire families including women and children would go with their flocks to the plains of the north to take part in the cutting of the corn. They received in return a tenth part of the harvest. In autumn, they moved towards the oases of the south to take part in the date harvest and to sell their wool to the textile artisans of Jerid. Finally, in winter, they set off for Sfax to participate in the olive picking. In this way, essential reserves of grain, dates and olive oil were built up and animal products such as butter, dried meat and wool were sold.

During the periods of intense activity such as the harvesting of grain or fruits, women worked side by side with the men, while during prolonged halts or on their return to Sidi Bouzid, they would devote themselves to weaving. This was not a pastime but a production activity vital to the survival of the group. The tents and all their equipment were the fruit of such weaving while the men needed burnouses as clothing. In addition, coverings, carpets and *mergoums* were, in effect, savings and could eventually be sold to cover the expenses of, for example, a wedding.

WOMEN AND SUBSISTENCE AGRICULTURE

Under the pressure of a strong colonial regime, the traditional structures of Tunisian society weakened and the complementary exchanges between groups and regions came to an end. Grazing land shrank with the aggrandizement of both colonial farms in the North and the olive groves at Sfax. With the coming of combine-harvesters, seasonal employment opportunities decreased. In addition, the introduction of manufactured products led to the ruin of the artisanal woolen industry of the oases. It was then that the migratory herdsmen experienced both lack of employment and misery. They fell back on their homelands to become dry-land farmers while reducing both their flocks and the extent of their grazing. Their traditional economy thus undermined, the population entered into a long process of sedentarization characterized by an unbroken struggle against extreme poverty.

The women continued to engage in weaving and harvesting. They participated also in caring for the animals, all the more so as some of the men were obliged to look for work away from home. Even the collecting of alpha and its sale, formerly reserved to the poorest families, became an essential activity. In groups, women would climb the steep slopes in search of alpha. It was pulled by hand, and the work lasted from six in the morning to the end of the afternoon during a fairly long season stretching from March to August. Men did not take part in this work but were content to supervise the women, or at the end of the day, they would load the donkey or cart with the alpha bundles in order to take them to the collection depot and pocket the money from the sale. Sometimes even, they would simply wait at the depot where a young girl would bring them the fruit of the day's labour.

WOMEN AND IRRIGATED CROPS

In the 1950s, the population began to dig surface wells, and in the 1960s, the State started to develop irrigated commonlands. In fact, however, these agro-industrial farms were producing only 10 per cent to 20 per cent of their real capacity. Following some international development assistance by PAM, AID and FAO, a development project embracing both irrigated commonlands and private farms established the following aims of: increasing production; increasing productivity and the revenues of the poorer categories; and favouring the passage from a subsistence-type agriculture to a market-oriented farming economy.

Technical assistance from FAO and SIDA was to have enabled the country to achieve those objectives and to begin the process of rural development. The dividing up of the irrigated lands was to have begun a move towards private ownership, towards the seeking of profit and accumulation of wealth. In fact, however, kinship remained the dominant social model. The extended family composed of the father, his children, his brothers and sometimes even nephews and cousins (up to 150 people) remained the dominant social and production unit. Thus, the distinction between property ownership (a juridical category) and actual cultivation (an economic notion) was more formal than real, and financial transactions within the extended family did not replace kinship relationships but simply served to strengthen and reinforce them.

With these transformations, women experienced an extension and intensification of their activities. Under the authority and responsibility of the patriarch, seconded by some sons and brothers, they became accountable for agricultural tasks. Together, and without distinction, they carried out the same tasks, played the same production roles and acquired an equal status with the men. Eighty per cent of the active female population made up the bulk of the labour force, while men devoted themselves to specific tasks. In addition, women's work, traditionally seasonal, became continuous, each day having its own programme and chores. Today, women's work may be placed in one of three categories: (a) market-related agricultural work; (b) household work to ensure either the family's subsistence or a 'supplement' to its revenue; (c) paid agricultural work carried out for private or state landowners.

Market-related agricultural work

In order to evaluate accurately women's work and compare it to the work done by men, S. Ferichiou has drawn up the tables below: Table 3: areas irrigated by surface wells (cereal production); Table 4: irrigated public areas (mixed farming, market-gardening, fodder and arboriculture); Table 5: arboricultural areas.

TABLE 3
FARMING CALENDAR (IRRIGATION BY SURFACE WELLS)

Bold: Work performed by women; Roman: Work performed by men; *Italics:* Work performed by machine.

Operations	Sept.	Oct.	Nov.	Dec.	Jan.	Feb.	March	April	May	June	July	August
Market Gardening												
New potatoes	—	—	—	**Preparing the soil**	—	—	**Planting**	**Fertiliser, hoeing, earthing**	—	—	**Harvesting**	—
Late potatoes	**Planting**	**2 Fertiliser, 2hoeing, weeding, earthing**		**Harvesting**	—	—	—	—	—	—	—	**Preparing the soil**
Tomatoes	—	**Harvesting**	**Preparing the soil**	—	Seed-bed	—	**Transplanting**	—	**Weeding**	—	—	**Harvesting**
Pimientos	—	**Harvesting**	—	**Preparing the soil**	—	**Preparing the soil**	—	**Transplanting**	—	Replanting	—	Hoeing-weeding
Watermelons	—	—	—	**Preparing the soil**	—	—	**Sowing**	—	**Dressing**	—	**Harvesting**	Prepar. the soil
Turnips, carrots	Sowing	—	—	—	**Harvesting**	—	—	—	—	—	—	Prepar. the soil
Scallions	**Transplanting**	—	—	**Harvesting**	—	**Transplanting**	—	—	—	—	—	—
Onions	Harvest	—	—	—	Seed-bed	—	—	—	—	—	**Harvesting**	—
Beans	**Sowing**	—	Picking	—	—	—	**Hoeing**	—	—	Harvest Thresh.	—	**Sowing**
Forage												
Luzerne	*Prepar. the soil*	Sowing	—	—	—	*Prepar. the soil*	Sowing	—	—	Cutting		—
Vetch, oats	*Prepar. the soil*	Sowing	—	—	—	—	—	—	**Cutting**	*Binding*	—	—
Millet	**Cutting**	**Cutting**	—	—	—	—	—	—	—	Sowing	—	Cutting
Barley	Sowing	—	—	Cutting or pasture		—	—	—	—	—	—	*Prepar.*
Cereals												
Wheat	*Prepar. the soil*	Sowing	—	—	—	—	—	—	—	**Harvesting and threshing**	—	—
Barley	*Prepar. the soil*	Sowing	—	—	—	—	—	—	—	Harvesting and threshing	—	—

TABLE 4
IRRIGATED AREAS MIXED PRODUCTION (TREES, LEGUMES, FODDER, CEREALS)

Bold: Work performed by women; Roman: Work performed by men; *Italics:* Work performed by machine.

Operations	Sept.	Oct.	Nov.	Dec.	Jan.	Feb.	March	April	May	June	July	August
Arboriculture												
Olive Trees	Care	**Preparing basins**	—	Harvesting	—	—	Pruning	—	—	—	M' Haoha	—
Pomegranate	—	**Harvesting**	—	—	—	—	Care	—	—	—	Care	—
Peach	Care	—	—	Care	Prun.	—	—	—	Crates	Harvesting	—	—
Apricot	—	Care **Crates**	—	—	Care	—	—	—	—	—	Harvesting	Prun.
Market Gardening												
New potatoes	**Plant.**	—	—	Preparing the soil	—	—	Planting	Care-hoeing	Fertiliz.-earthing	—	—	—
Late Potatoes	**Planting**	**Fertilizing-hoeing**	**weeding-earthing**	**Harvesting**	—	—	—	—	—	—	—	Preparing the soil
Tomatoes	—	—	—	—	**Harvesting**	Seed-bed	Transplanting	—	**Weeding**	—	**Harvesting**	—
Pimientos	—	**Harvesting**	—	Preparing the soil	—	—	—	—	**Replanting**	—	**Hoeing-weeding**	—
Cucurbits (melon, pumpkins)	—	—	—	—	—	Preparing the soil	Sowing	Dressing	—	—	Harvesting	—
Turnips, carrots	Sowing	—	—	—	**Harvesting**	—	—	—	—	—	—	**Prepar.**
Scallions	—	**Transplanting**	—	**Harvesting**	—	—	—	—	—	—	—	**Prepar.**
Onions	**Harvest.**	—	—	—	Seed-bed	**Transplanting**	—	—	—	—	**Harvesting**	—
Beans	**Sowing**	—	**Picking**	—	—	**Dress.**	—	—	—	Thresh.	—	**Sowing**
Forage												
Luzerne	*Prepar.*	**Cutting**	—	—	*Cutting or pasture*	—	Sowing	—	—	—	—	—
Vetch, oats	*Prepar.*	**Sowing**	—	—	—	—	—	—	Cutting-binding	—	—	—
Millet	—	**Cutting**	—	—	—	—	—	—	*Prepar.*	**Sowing**	—	**Cutting**
Barley	**Sowing**	—	—	—	—	—	—	—	—	—	—	*Prepar.*

TABLE 4 (CONT'D)
IRRIGATED AREAS MIXED PRODUCTION (TREES, LEGUMES, FODDER, CEREALS)

Bold: Work performed by women; Roman: Work performed by men; *Italics:* Work performed by machine.

Operations	Sept.	Oct.	Nov.	Dec.	Jan.	Feb.	March	April	May	June	July	August
Cereals												
Wheat	*Prepar.*	Sowing		—	—	—	—	—	—	Harvest. - thresh.		—
Barley	*Prepar.*	Sowing	—	—	—	—	—	—	—	Harvest. - thresh.		—

TABLE 5
IRRIGATED ARBORICULTURAL AREAS

Bold: Work performed by women; Roman: Work performed by men; *Italics:* Work performed by machine.

Operations	Sept.	Oct.	Nov.	Dec.	Jan.	Feb.	March	April	May	June	July	August
Arboriculture												
Olive Trees	Care	**Preparing basins**		Harvesting			Pruning				M' Haoha	—
Pomegranate		**Harvesting**		Care Crates		—	Care Crates	—	—	—	Care	—
Peach	Care Crates	—	—	—	Prun.	—	—	—	Crates	**Harvesting**	**Harvesting**	
Apricot	—	Care Crates	—	—	Care	—	—	—		**Harvesting**		Prun.

Domestic tasks

A woman's workday includes both the washing of fruit and vegetables before they are marketed, and the weeding and the gathering of fodder for the animals and wild herbs for the preparation of certain dishes. These tasks are not entered into the family production record but are considered as cleaning, that is, as 'simple domestic chores'. Even stock-rearing, formerly an important resource for these people, has become — for it is now taken in charge by the women — a 'domestic activity' despite the revenue it brings. Likewise the weaving performed by women — the products of which are not only destined for family use — also provides an important source of revenue and allows the family to accumulate savings which are often reinvested in farming. A realistic taking into account of such activities would give a truer picture of women's share in agricultural work and their contribution to the real family income.

Salaried work

Seasonal work (harvesting, olive-picking) provides a good earning opportunity for families. Thus, money for piecework performed by women is paid to the family group. It is the head of the household who receives the global sum and the family unit becomes the purveyor of goods and services.

CONCLUSION

Within the development project, productivity appraisals made with the purpose of attributing financial or service aids to families tend to occult and underestimate the contribution of women. Such appraisals imply a distinction between customary usage and market values whereas in the case of the women of Sidi Bouzid, the two types of production — whether weaving or stock-rearing — are intrinsically interdependent. Likewise, reference to salary has little meaning in the context of family employment where remuneration is not individual but collective.

Again, the application of the ILO international workforce scale is abusive. According to this scale, a work unit is represented by a man between the ages of 20 and 59 years, working 8 hours per day for 300 days per annum. A woman of the same age whatever the volume of work completed is not considered to have achieved more than 67 per cent of a work unit. This does not correspond to reality. In the irrigated areas of Sidi Bouzid, women provide the major part of the labour force, are more present on the farms than men and do not cease to work even when pregnant or when breast-feeding their babies. On the contrary, further education, military service or temporary emigration are all opportunities for men to leave the farms.

A similarly erroneous point of view attributes only 50 per cent of a work unit to young girls aged from 15 to 19 while young men of the same age are attributed 67 per cent. In fact, young women from Sidi Bouzid receive little formal education and in consequence, work full time on the farm. They should therefore be attributed a full work unit.

The application of the ILO or similar scales encourages heads of household who wish to increase their productivity to mobilize female labour to the maximum — all the more so as the scale attributes only a feeble coefficient to the women's contribution. Thus, production policy leads to the exploitation of women and a significant devaluation of their work. Unaware of their true interlocutors, the project managers deal with the family patriarchs and the men. Hence, the irrigation wells are equipped with electric pumps but not the wells that serve the household. Later on, it is true, two co-operatives run exclusively by women — one for weaving, the other for stock-rearing — were integrated into the project, but one can affirm without exaggeration that the basis of family capital is the non-remunerated work of women. It is women who have paid the price for the integration of subsistence farming into the market economy.

For how long will women accept this situation? Will not future generations of women be disheartened by such work? Will the patriarchal family succeed in holding out against market forces? Unless women are formally involved and true recognition given to their work, the risk exists that farming in these irrigated areas will experience profound social and domestic upheavals.

Women in the food sector

Not so long ago, there existed a well-rooted and sacred custom that all urban and rural households should prepare and store essential food supplies. The activity covered various commodities — cereals, grains, vegetables, olives, fruit, meat, fish — and met the basic needs of the family. *Couscous,* the national dish, was prepared and stored for the year as well as other cereal products such as wheat, ground barley or spiced barley flour typical of certain regions and consumed at certain periods of the year. Spices, an essential ingredient in cooking, were prepared and put aside, as were also stocks of olive oil.

A basic aim in all this was to ensure and strengthen family autonomy in the context of a subsistence economy which privileged customary usage and avoided market considerations. If a product could not be stored, its basic ingredients were preserved, e.g. honey, semolina, flour, salted butter, dried fruits for traditional cakes etc. This activity was entrusted to women and it rhythmed their lives during the summer months. In the family homestead, they gave themselves to the task collectively within the context of the extended family without distinction of age or status. This sexual division of labour seems to have given to women the role of ensuring the passage of things from a primary to an elaborated state, as from the raw state to the cooked. Through this added value, they fulfilled their economic role, in its true etymological sense of managing the household.

Economic and social transformations were, however, to change and diminish respect for female work. In the modern economy, domestic activities were be supplemented by informal work. Major alterations were the passage from the extended to the nuclear family; the exodus of populations from the countryside in the search for work; galloping urbanization and western-style architecture such as high buildings; the introduction of new consumer models and the direction given by the State.

The case of Arbia

For several years now, a new 'small job' has grown up on the roads of Tunisia: at the exits of the cities and villages, children from the age of 10 to 15 years proffer to car occupants tabouna *bread — a type of pancake much appreciated by Tunisians.*

In the Tunisian countryside, every household has a tabouna, *that is, a cylindrical,* terra cotta *domestic oven in which wood is burned. The* tabouna *dough is cooked against the inner walls of the oven — an ancient technique which gives a golden, crusty bread.*

Arbia is one of those mothers who has found, through this job, a means of feeding her family. She is an illiterate, 54-year-old woman with five children aged from 6 to 16 years. She lives very close to the market at Radès, a suburb of Tunis, in a very large house recently extended and furnished traditionally. She owns a video recorder. Her husband is a worker of the national railways but his salary is insufficient to meet family needs. Arbia has decided to help him make ends meet, and as she would not dream of working outside her home, she had the idea of baking her own pancakes. But she does not consider this as real work: 'It is' she says, 'just a few tabounas *to help'. She sees her work as a domestic task and not as a commercial activity.*

Yet she does the baking while her husband and 12-year-old daughter sell her pancakes on the market. It is out of the question for her husband to allow her to sell her own produce. He is adamant on this point: it is not work for a woman! This did not prevent her, however, from going to the market in person to sell her pancakes for there is a large demand for tabouna *especially in summer and on market days.*

The proceeds are banked by her husband but Arbia finds this natural for the husband 'represents the honour of the family.' When she needs to buy something, she sends someone to him, for he is never far.

Arbia always manages to hide some savings from her husband, but in fact he is really happy with this arrangement for when in need, she is able to offer him some money. She hopes to continue this job until her children are grown. Then she will stop working as it is a tiring job. She hopes that one day her daughter will find a job commanding more respect.

A STAPLE PRODUCT: COUSCOUS

Preparing the *couscous* mobilized the whole family. It was a real event. The wheat was selected, ground, sifted and the *couscous* made, dried in the sun and then stored in jars. Parents, relatives, neighbours and friends were invited to help and none refused. Mutual aid was a duty and strengthened the sense of belonging to the same entity, the same group. It was doubly important to be there in that this task had both an economic and a social function: to ensure the nutritional needs of the family and to acknowledge the grain as a gift and blessing from God.

Under the combined influence of, on the one hand, modern living and, on the other, the nuclear family and salaried employment, traditions are destined to change. Family work and mutual aid will increasingly be supplemented by recourse to salaried help, until in the end, the latter will ensure the major part of the work. The mistress of the house will then be content merely to supervise the work. Already, certain helpers prefer to work from home and will become independent workers and execute orders from private or commercial clients, their networks of acquaintances and relations helping to make them known. However, the extension of the market will encourage the food industries to take over this niche. Already, they are equipping themselves gradually in order to become market leaders.

A SEASONAL PRODUCT: MALSOUKA

This dough which is used to prepare *briks,* a cake much appreciated during the Ramadan months, used to form an appreciable source of revenue for the womenfolk of underprivileged families in the towns and cities. Children and husbands would sell *malsouka* around the marketplaces. Production and trading costs were, of course, negligible. The business grew, however, because of tourist demand for the batter, which led to large orders from restaurants and hotels, and because of a change in the eating habits of families who turned more and more to this type of crêpe all during the year.

Such a growth in the market encourages entrepreneurs to establish industrial production. In such an instance, the informal sector suffers from the competition, and instead of being able to expand and organize itself throughout the year is obliged to confine its production to the period of intense consumption during Ramadan. Once more, 'domestic' paid work reaches the industrial stage and is taken out of the hands of women. It would perhaps have been better to have helped such women to organize and expand, thus ensuring a revenue to the poorest among them, rather than to have made financial investments from national savings, particularly for the import of machines.

A RARE PRODUCT: TRADITIONAL CAKES

Traditionally, every family bakes for the *aïd*, the feast that follows the sacred month of Ramadan, cakes that are offered to relatives, friends and neighbours. These gifts have a religious and social connotation, and are prepared also for great occasions such as marriage or circumcision. The tradition also offers the opportunity to women to distinguish themselves both by respecting tradition and innovating through the recipes they invent. As an activity, it has experienced the same evolution: salaried help, independent workers, small family production units and then industrialization. Thus, in urban milieu dominated by crowded collective dwellings, female employment and small families, the supplying of traditional cakes has changed. The independent workers who filled orders have been succeeded by family production units owned by middle-class women. The latter employ young apprenticed girls or female labour and work from apartments or rooms in villas situated in middle-class areas. They exercise their ingenuity in making cakes according to old regional recipes, which are bought by well-to-do families not only for the feasts but also for soirées and receptions. They sell their wares directly, receiving quite large orders and even enlarge their sales by selling their products to the up-market department stores. This strategy cannot, of course, be adopted by poor women who must fall back on making less refined cakes.

However, very soon, medium-sized industrial enterprises entered the field, aiming to respond to the needs of a normal clientele, especially during periods of increased consumption such as during the *aïd* or the summer, the season of marriages and tourism. Finally, larger industrial units were created by the chain store pastry shops who were already commercializing a large range of products — ice-cream, European pastries, croissants, etc. — and could adapt best to market variations.

The same scenario is therefore repeated. The informal sector detects the market, helps to develop it and then, in the final analysis, sees it taken over by the formal industrialized sector. Poor women must then confine themselves to low profit, seasonal products and are obliged to vary their wares unceasingly. But what should be noted above all is that female, 'domestic' work, is overlooked and devalued until market development revalues it — and the industrial sector appropriates it, taking it out of the hands of women.

The case of Cherifa

Mme Cherifa, descended from a bourgeois family related to the Bey who had reigned in Tunisia before independence, is 66 years old. She has three daughters and an adopted son and lives in a large, old Arab house in a middle-class quarter in Tunis. In former times, the daughters of well-to-do families learned to cook and make Tunisian pastries. Cherifa had benefited from this teaching, liked it and had acquired a certain talent. She married at the age of 15 a frivolous husband who quickly squandered her inherited fortune. Through some sacrifices, they managed, however, to retain the family home.

Cherifa then decided to help redress the disastrous economic situation by offering to make traditional pastries for relatives, neighbours and friends on the occasion of religious feasts, betrothals, marriages and circumcisions. The making of such cakes requires much knowledge, preparation and work, but Cherifa was very talented and the pastries she would offer her friends and acquaintances were much appreciated. People began to ask her help in preparing quantities of cakes for diverse occasions, for which she received for her work what people were inclined to give. Progressively, she began to make cakes in advance and build up a small stock of baklawas, kaaks and makrouds. In the meantime, her husband attempted to look after the lands that still belonged to the family but no longer sufficed to provide a living. In fact, it was the mother who made ends meet though, through respect for her husband, in a discreet manner. On his death, Cherifa found herself the sole breadwinner for her four children.

In order to preserve the intimacy of her home and prevent commotion in the precincts, Cherifa preferred to deliver her wares at the homes of her clients. Her son, who was not very interested in pursuing his studies, took over the task. He began by opening a first shop where the family production is sold, and now owns two shops which work totally independently of each over. He is well off and pays taxes, both local and on his income. As for Cherifa, she continues to make and sell her own wares outside the formal commercial circuit. As she works from within her own home, she considers that she is not subject to paying tax.

For a long time, she made do with three ovens installed in her own home. Nowadays, she has part of her production baked twice every week by a neighbouring baker in order to meet increased demand. She takes in her money but 'has never learned to count' thus expressing a certain contempt for money. She is happy with what people give her, which in fact is largely sufficient. She considers herself happy, sheltered now from need and to have succeeded in restoring the family's economic situation. Living between 'her platters and her ovens' she has no dealings with the municipality. One of her daughters, married and with grand-children, lives with her and intends to continue her mother's occupation.

Women in the textile industry

Nomadic women, no less than the women of town and village, have devoted themselves traditionally to wool production. They card, spin and weave the wool by day and by night. This activity goes beyond autarchy, and has become part of a system of exchange, earning for the family substantial financial resources. Even more, it has become a vital element in the regional economy, as for example, in the oases of the South.

In the beginning, women were independent producers and owned the raw material itself, their tools and looms. Their families were their clients or else, through their husbands, they disposed of their products directly on the market. But this independence was gradually undermined by artisans and traders. Little by little, women were induced to prepare work for the artisans. They would card and spin the wool which would then be brought to the weaver who would then produce the woolen blankets on his power loom. Again, they would knit and deliver to the weaver the *kabous*, which he would transform into the *chechia*, or they would weave *burnouses* (woolen capes for men) which the artisans would finish by sowing on the fringe. Thus, the greater added value would be appropriated by the artisans while the women's work tended to be underestimated and their remuneration low. The traditional sexual order in which women are subject to men rests firmly in place.

Women who did wish to preserve their independence vis-à-vis the artisan and who wished to continue producing ended most often by falling into the grasp of the wholesalers. Their lack of capital, the infrequency of orders and the organization of the commercial networks induced them to work for wholesalers who provided them with the raw wool. They became simple, domestic piece-workers, in particular as the market became dominated by industrially produced woolen products. Above all, women carpet weavers suffered under the iron law of the wholesalers, owners of vast networks of domestic piece-workers who were remunerated according to the quality (first or second choice) attributed to their work. In a market that was expanding owing to exports and tourism, women — the source of added value — were dispossessed by the wholesalers of both surplus value and their profit margin. One is led to believe that competitivity in the carpet trade has been acquired at the expense of women and their work.

City women prefer hand embroidery to weaving and many dream of providing sheets, table cloths and hand embroidered place mats for the marriage trousseaus of their daughters. But competition from industry is keen and tends to confine hand embroidery to the fine craft market. Hand embroidered pieces are sold therefore through contacts or ordered specially by luxury shops frequented by the well-to-do classes or by couples preparing to marry.

Of old, preparations for the bride's wedding dress — embroidered in gold, silver, paillettes and pearls — used to start at a very young age. Today, girls who still wear wedding dresses simply hire them from shops, which in fact are rarely owned by lacemakers. In brief, the artisanal activities of women have been taken over by artisans and shopkeepers, and have thus become marginal. Their downgrading is reflected in the domestic piece-work activities.

In previous times, poorer women would hire out their services to families on a daily basis, doing sewing work. Those women who owned a sewing machine would work at home and fill orders from customers who would provide the cloth. Dresses, skirts and pinafores made up the greater part of their work. The more talented seamstresses who had had some professional training specialized in ceremonial wear, evening dresses and coats. They would draw their models from specialized revues or from patterns bought from abroad. However, competition from local industry or imports frequently forced these women to accept subcontract work from factories: ironing, making button holes, etc. They became a labour reservoir for the clothing factories which would pay them the lowest rates or take them on as trainees or temporary staff. After a few months, they would be laid off and then recruited again by the same factories at the same level.

The case of Nejiba

Nejiba is 48 years old and lives at Marsa in the North Suburb of Tunis. She has two student daughters and a son who is an employee at the Tunisian Electricity and Gas Board. She hails from the village of Kbiset Mediouni.

In her childhood, girls were taught carpet-making and weaving before being taught how to cook. She considers that she has always done such work. At first, she used to weave blankets and rugs for family members or friends in preparation of their marriages. Remuneration was left to the appreciation of the clients.

For several years now, Nejiba has been making rugs and decorative carpets as well as woolen blankets.She has equipped her garage as her workshop, and receives her clients there. Her daughters help her with the orders, calculations etc. She dreams of taking on a young girl able to read, write and answer the telephone. She herself has no formal education, for in her time children in the village did not attend school. However, she does not give the impression of being illiterate. She is a fervent Muslim and wears the veil but that does not prevent her from being tolerant and open.

Nejiba has exhibited her work at the Artcrafts Salon, an important exhibition organized each year at the Conference Centre in Tunis. She likewise participated in an exhibition organized by the Tunisian National Women's Union. Her daughters had encouraged her to show her products

at such fairs. She did not hesitate as she is aware of the quality of her work. In addition, it gives her confidence.
Nejiba's husband died four years ago, leaving her some property. Her weaving and carpet-making gives her, she thinks, an added security in face of life's unforeseen events. She lives fairly well from her work and thanks God. She gives the impression of knowing what she wants, of being a good and efficient businesswoman.

Initiatives for today and tomorrow

A new approach

The economies of developing countries used to depend on a metropolitan centre that regulated how they functioned within the overall framework of an empire. After independence, the young states were faced with a series of urgent social demands in education, health, and training, but they were also anxious to establish an economy that would generate high employment, revenue and wealth. To these ends, they made a clean sweep and took society on a forced march towards modernism. Industrialization, the mechanization of agriculture and urban development would, it was thought, produce enough wealth to provide balanced exchange with the developed world. Developing countries unanimously adopted the free-market model with its twin articles of faith — growth and productivity. Unfortunately, they forgot that confrontation is the heart of exchange and that their struggle was ridiculously unequal.

The upshot was inevitable and swift: unbalanced exchanges, increasing debt, a disjointed economy, conflictual industrial relations and imbalance between the regions. The free-market economy operates best in economies whose producers are ensured of a surplus capable of satisfying immediate, necessary and indeed superfluous demands. It can only flourish in a society in which the individual, ensured of the minimum needed for survival, dares break through the organic bonds of the group. The norm of competition supersedes those of solidarity and the ideals of individual accomplishment and personal achievement are given priority. It is a specific, historical phenomenon, not a universal absolute and to have overlooked this fact was a costly mistake.

In reality, developing societies have not yet reached that stage of development. Capital is scarce, the individual still needs the group's protection against certain risks, a role that an embryonic State is powerless to assume. Furthermore, this type of society values harmony and complementarity between its members above all else; the blood ties of the group take precedence over the individual. Differentiation by wealth is undesirable. The community spirit is deep-rooted and commercial exchange is neither the only nor the predominant type of exchange. Relations between the members of a tribe or a group and the rules by which they function tend to empty of sense the concepts and practices of conventional economic discourse. For example, the distinction between title to property and the economic exploitation of that property does not exist in a society where the extended family still predominates. For although the land may belong legally to an individual, those that work on it, the members of the same family, share its fruits. The social structure and economy of a developing society are specific and differ — in kind, not in degree — from those of a developed society. To overlook this specificity, to apply conventional economic theories, national accounting plans and statistical instruments to these societies under the pretext of rationality, scientific investigation and standardization inevitably leads to confusion and failure. To take another example: if GNP in industrialized countries is underestimated by between 20 per cent and 40 per cent as a result of including only commercial production in statistics, the error may easily be compounded in economies where home-based and non-commercial production are of such considerable importance. To confine work to salaried employment in societies where mutual aid and family work form such an integral part of production leads to serious misapprehension of their economies. The distinction between production and consumption established by national accounting is not always pertinent. Indeed, the general application of conventional economic models to developing countries is both a logical error and an ideological prejudice.

The first thing to be done to understand these societies and their economies is to observe and listen attentively. Scientific observation, group interviews, assessment of internal and external exchanges, the search for meaning through personal investigation and surveys of the individuals and populations concerned ought to make it possible to put forward a series of hypotheses and concepts, to draw up questionnaires for specific fields of activity and/or regions. The results of these may subsequently be compared to actual conditions on the ground. While fully scientific (observation, hypothesis, experimentation, evaluation), this procedure may appear cumbersome. But how is one to proceed otherwise? Irrigated crops condition the farmer's work and daily round far differently from, say, wheat or lumbering in mountain areas. The same is true of regional differences; there is a greater difference between the peasants of North and South Tunisia than between the latter and their Libyan counterparts. Any attempt to study these economies without referring to their social structures, norms and values will fail to produce programmes for positive change. In an initial phase, qualitative methods will have to be used to identify the difficulties of these societies and the internal obstacles to self-development.

In a second stage, a quantitative data base will be required to elaborate action programmes for local communities in ways that circumvent dependence on the international system and intervention by the state. After all, etymologically, economy means the management of the affairs of a group who by interacting equip themselves with the means for livelihood. Each society tolerates a certain level of production determined by its repercussions on the equilibrium of that society. In this connection, statistics ought to cease to be a state privilege and become an objective system of assessment to be used for self-evaluation by groups, sectors or regions. The State ought to resume its role as catalyst of development by, for a start, involving university institutes and pluridisciplinary research institutions in regional and sectorial study programmes and by removing responsibility for the National Statistics Institute from the Ministry for Planning which represents the interests of the State, whose centripetal tendencies are obvious and which never has to pay the price of its errors of appreciation. The Minister for Social Affairs is a more suitable Ministry for the Institute. Regarding university researchers, while they do not work in the service of the State, there would seem to be no reason why they should not be more available to the population at large, especially as community service would help to integrate the university in the region where it is located. In conclusion, society and its economy would be all the better known and respected if studies were pluridisciplinary and based on observation in the field. Locally-based researchers might be in charge of training in the sector under investigation. Their reports would first be sent to the region or sector which would then be free to make choices, clarify objectives and define a strategy — with the assistance of the researchers if so desired — to be defended subsequently at local, regional or national level.

If the area of study is precisely defined in this way, the resulting programme will have a correspondingly high chance of success. The totality of experiments and initiatives of this sort will eventually form the outline of a development policy for consideration by the State. The informal sector can only be enhanced by field investigation. Its real value will then appear clearly. It challenges the State's blithe and dangerous ignorance of real social needs but it also transcends an infinity of obstacles — inadequate financing, lack of training facilities, scarcity or unavailability of proper equipment, fussy regulations and administrative procedures. In short, the informal sector is the quintessence of freedom of initiative and is all the more extraordinary in that the State system effectively tries to place it out of economic bounds.

The case of Hadda

Mellassine is a working-class suburb of Tunis located on the banks of an insalubrious sebkha. It used to be a Jewish ghetto, a centre of pottery-making, whence its name Mellassine, meaning potters.

Hadda has been making canounes[9] since she arrived there 40 years ago. She is a robust 60-year-old, clad in a bedouin melia *and she still speaks with a country accent. Her husband went off one evening 30 years ago, without a word, leaving her with 5 daughters and 3 sons to raise. The elder is 'a real bandit' who has two wives but is a real stickler where his sisters' morality is concerned. 'He could easily kill them, says Hadda, if he heard that they were out at night'. The second son has withdrawn into himself since he was injured in an accident at work. The youngest is mentally handicapped. Hadda seems to accept all these misfortunes without much complaint. 'It's fate', she says.*

She originally left her small poverty-ridden village in Central Tunisia along with ten other families at the end of the war. They all squatted on the sebkha *in Mellassine and have had problems with the authorities who have vainly been trying to expel them ever since. Hadda used to make tapestries in her village but did not know how to sell them and never thought of working outside the home on account of the indignant opposition of the menfolk. She learned how to make canounes and sold them locally. She had no choice. 'We have had to put up with poverty ever since we were young. Our men have never been able to do anything here. One day in ten they peddle things in the street, trying to dodge the city police. Some are petty criminals, others are sick. And as if that wasn't enough we have our children to feed and there are lots of them. Thank God that we found a trade that we can carry on here with dignity and honour'.*

Curiously enough, it was a European who first taught her how to make canounes. Very quickly, her sisters and female cousins began to make them as well — but not the men; it is an exclusively female activity. The different families make the canounes in rudimentary huts they built themselves, with bits and pieces of scrap iron, wood and plastic. They are protected from the sun and rain and also from the eyes of the men, for they have kept that age-old sense of modesty in relations with the opposite sex. The huts are a strictly female preserve in which the women spend the day, having entrusted the household chores to one of their daughters. The men appear, as if by accident, only when the product is ready for sale. According to Hadda : 'Men take no part in production. That is a woman's job. The only thing men know about the canoune is that you use it to make tea!' Men are unwelcome in the huts. The women prefer to be alone together. Each 'workshop' is occupied by 4 or 5 women, the mother, her daughters and daughters-in-law. Production is a family affair and daughters continue to take part after marriage.

Work begins at 5 or 6 in the morning in summer and towards 7 in winter. Hadda begins her day by baking tabouna bread, a traditional flat bread baked in a small cylindrical clay oven. After breakfast, she goes to the workshop, a mere few metres distant, where she is joined by her daughters. They make tea and start work. At noon, the daughter who stayed at home brings lunch. Work then resumes until nightfall. The raw material is mainly clay that they get at Djebel Lahmar, another working-

class estate right beside the Hilton Hotel. Digging for clay is prohibited by the authorities who pursue offenders. Hadda does not understand why since the clay belongs to everybody. She wonders whether 'they consider us as Tunisians or whether we are foreigners in our own country'. Clay extraction has become an illicit act, preferably performed by night. The women generally call on the services of drivers who also belong to the Ouled Ayyar tribe and accompany them on these risky expeditions. They use a covered Peugeot 404 van to fill up on raw material once a week or once every two weeks. The trip costs 50 Dinars. The men of the family do not usually take part in the operation. 'If we had to depend on the men, we'd have a meal once every ten days', says Hadda.

They sort through the clay, sift it and mix it with another kind of clay before kneading it. The resulting paste is shaped into canounes which are then left out to dry before being fired. They wait until they have collected between 100 and 150 canounes before they arrange them around a fire made of tyres and discarded shoes and other inflammable refuse gathered from the streets and waste lots. Firing lasts a day and a night and, as may easily be imagined, causes a certain amount of pollution. The retailers drive around in their trucks to pick up the canounes. Hadda's price, in 1989, was 0.120 Dinars (approximately 8 canounes for $1). There is tacit agreement about the price and some women charge more and pocket the difference. The income is used directly by the women. They send off the young male children to do the shopping. For more important errands, they give the money to the men. Some of the young women prefer to get the money themselves; they count the number of canounes they produced and use the money for personal purchases. As a general rule, the money earned suffices for daily subsistence and even for unforeseen expenses and the young women's dowries. In theory, the men do not have direct access to the money because, says Hadda, 'we'd die of starvation if we let them near it'. The work is dirty. The hut is makeshift, there is mud underfoot and smoke billows in from the burning rubber and plastic. Despite all of this, Hadda and her fellow-workers obviously enjoy the work, because it earns them their daily bread and, to a certain extent, their independence. 'I like the work', says Hadda, 'although it is dirty. I have always dreamt of this kind of work. It is a sign from heaven. Our marabout is happy with our work. It has kept us alive for 40 years, it has fed and reared my children. Without it, I'd be dead of starvation.' The younger generation, however, find the work difficult and irksome. They would prefer a cleaner job. There is no guarantee that they will continue on after their parents.

The idea of building more functional premises and of working in better conditions is, of course, mooted but remains unrealisable. In the same way, the idea of a producers' association or organization is welcomed but seems to come up against a series of obstacles — illiteracy, force of habit, the precariousness of the situation, the danger of closure by the authorities. Following complaints about the pollution caused by firing in

1986, the authorities suddenly decided to close down the kilns. Bulldozers were sent in to level the huts. The women resisted and threatened to throw themselves under the bulldozers, while the men looked idly on. After the League of the Rights of Man intervened, Hadda was received by the Governor, as her group's spokeswoman. This was the first time that she had been in the city centre and she found the experience distressing. Yet in the Governor's presence, she recovered her energy and told him : 'Just as you would not allow anybody to deprive you of your livelihood, because then you'd be nothing, so we are attached to our work. It is our life. If you take it away from us, you will kill us!'

Hadda's case is a fairly accurate reflection of the situation of women from the disadvantaged classes who involve themselves in informal activities to uphold their dignity and ensure the survival of their families. With little or no resources, these women have to struggle against an economic system from which they are excluded and against a social role that effectively places them on the sidelines of society. Yet they are gifted with a remarkable spirit of enterprise, an innate sense of the market and a marvellous capacity to adapt. They procure their raw materials and meagre tools in their immediate environment. Fiercely independent, they keep men away from their work but are obliged to entrust them with the sale of the product since they themselves are forbidden to have contact with others. Thus, Hadda and the other members of her group have had to call upon the services of the menfolk to sell her wares. The parallel with Charipa is striking. Though she is the source of the pastry business, it is her son who opens a shop and becomes a person of substance in the community.

Again, if women are to enjoy complete control over their product, women must come to a realization of their status as producers and stop looking on their activities as secondary. The least that can be said, however, is that the marginalization of the informal sector by the central authorities does not help them to do so. If Hadda and the others had obtained recognition as fully-fledged producers, they would not have encountered such difficulty. They have two main problems — ensuring a steady supply of clay and finding fuel. Because the anarchic housing on the site at Jebel Lahmar is being renovated, the authorities have prohibited the extraction of clay there. In an effort to stabilize the population and to prevent further building, a complete infrastructure (roads, electricity, running water, sewerage) is being installed and the unoccupied area is being landscaped. Since the plants and trees would be threatened by extraction of clay — which is not, in any case, an officially recognized activity, — all such extraction is now forbidden. Had these women's activity been recognized as a source of production, the central authorities would have striven to organize the clay extraction in such a way as to protect the environment, or would have directed the women towards neighbouring clay-rich zones or, failing that, would have advised on the use of a natural substitute and would have trained the women in how to utilize it. Instead of blindly dictating production goals, the State would have thus played its proper role of support and assistance. Similarly, the authorities saw repression as the only way of dealing with the fuel problem, alleging that the area was already bedevilled by water pollution. Yet had there been a real desire to integrate these women in the production process, had they been recognized for what they are, producers, the State would have sought to safeguard their means of livelihood at the same time as it tried to protect the environment. The problem was to find the most efficient firing technique to ensure both the competivity of this low-capital business and the protection of the environment. A solar energy kiln or a butane gas kiln are possible solutions. The technicians in the Energy Office might have given their attention to the problem from both the technical and financial angles. Moreover, these women are entitled to assistance and subsidies for job creation in the same way as the structured sector and also to government-subsidized loans. State aid would, however, have to be limited in duration to forestall any impression of automatic support, but provided it revises its conception of the economy from top to bottom, there is no reason why the state should not promote the participation of women in the informal sector.

The informal sector and planning

Is the informal sector of interest to planners? It is possible that the State may wish to encourage this successful sector by opening credit lines or waiving certain taxes and levies — in short, by legalising a de facto situation. But by forcefully integrating it or dictating to it, the State will merely deprive the sector of its flexibility and the sense of risk that results from keen competition. The sector will then gradually decline from attention of the wrong sort and be obliged to join the 'modern sector' or die. In fact, the State ought to seek inspiration in the informal sector to review the extravagant subsidies it awards to the coddled private sector. Easy, cheap credit has brought forth capitalist businesses that are over-equipped and voracious consumers of foreign currency. Their exports more or less cover their imports of raw materials and spare parts. But to repay the foreign loans contracted for investment, money has to be taken from tourism, from agriculture when the harvest is good, from mining (petrol, phosphates, etc.) when the market is buoyant, from the money sent home by the emigrant population when Europe is not in the doldrums and emigrants forced to return home. In short, a public sector designed and developed to drive the economy forward has become a parasite and a burden on the balance of payments and on the economy as a whole.

It would be wiser to vary credit by activity, allocating investment according to a strict productivity/employee ratio and to modulate interest rates accordingly. Account will naturally be taken of the annual import/export report to calculate tax rates and interest rebates, thus rewarding initiative, success and respect for the broader interests of the community. The State will not assist or subsidise any new business seeking to supersede an informal network which already satisfies local needs in conditions of normal competition. However, assistance ought to be made available to new concerns set up with an exclusive view to exporting, because the informal sector is not at present in a position to cover the international market.

Enhancing the role of women

If the State were to reassess its role in this way, it would then be possible to maximize the economic role of women in Tunisian society by including home manufacture and production in national and regional development plans. If the two major problems of the rural milieu — transporting water and collecting fuel — were solved, women would be free to devote more time to production such as weaving or pottery-making. Rain-water tanks, for example, built of locally available stone and using traditional binding materials would solve the problem of drinking water and also initiate local masons in the techniques of stone-building. But producing is not enough. The product also has to be brought to public attention and advertised. What has happened is that the most promising areas of food processing occupied by female producers, such as spices and traditional pastries, have been taken over by 'modern' companies. These then proceed to employ independent women at a minimum wage or on a temporary basis, replacing them in due course by machines. It goes without saying that the companies in question receive assistance from the State and describe their products as 'traditional'.

A more efficient approach would set up a system of quality control and a special label for production by women, to include, for example, farm produce such as poultry, eggs, butter and cheese, and weaving in the form of *kelims,* rugs and *mergoums.* Products would be advertised on radio and television. Trade fairs would be organized and the women themselves could form associations to protect them against encroachment from large industry. Instead of competing with women, the central institutions — essentially the Arts and Crafts Office — would be transformed into support and marketing organizations. They could provide training for young people in crafts threatened with extinction or oblivion by the tourist industry and publicize new techniques for improving quality. Village fairs with several products on offer would have an important role to play because it would enable women to accede to marketing, previously a male domain.

The parties concerned

The informal sector has always served to show up the defects in the official system and always will, just as it heralds new tendencies because it is forced to adapt so quickly to market forces. Given the small scale and the heterogeneous nature of the sector, each business or activity almost requires to be treated separately and on its own. Short of that, however, it seems obvious that study and support programmes ought to be undertaken at regional and local level (where, incidentally, twinning between towns and regions may have a certain role to play). Unlike the State, the region has modest pretensions and has to compete with other regions. It has, or ought to have, precise knowledge of the available talents and can put the different target groups in contact with their future partners. Its programmes will bear fruit, however, only if there is an openness to innovation and flexibility in regulation and taxation and if it is careful not to become a sort of miniature welfare state. The least that can be said is that the State's role needs to be radically revised, to leave far greater areas of freedom to local and regional authorities who have more intimate knowledge of the needs and capacities of the communities they serve. The best initiatives filter upwards from the base and are never imposed from above.

Notes

1. J. Charmes, *Méthodes et résultats d'une meilleure évaluation des ressources humaines dans le SNS d'une économie en voie de développement en Tunisie. Le secteur non structuré, quelles technologies, quel développement?* Salambo, Tunis, 1983.

2. J. Charmes, *Le secteur non structuré, son importance, ses caractéristiques et ses possibilités de promotion,* INS, Tunis, 1981.

3. J. Charmes, *Le secteur non structuré et l'économie du développement. Nécessité de sa prise en compte et d'une reconsidération subséquente des théories et des politiques de développement,* in *Séminaire sur l'économie et le développement; l'analyse en termes réels et monétaires,* FSEG, 27–28 April 1983.

4. J. Charmes, A. Sanaa, *Promotion de l'artisanat et des petits métiers en Tunisie: une politique compréhensive à l'égard du secteur non structuré,* Ministry of Social Affairs, Tunis, 1985.

5. INS, *Recensement des établissements en milieu urbain, 1976, Tunisie entière,* Tunis, 1980.

6. A popular saying constantly repeated throughout the artisan class. It means that knowledge is never given freely, that it is an opportunity not to be missed.

7. INS, *Premiers résultats de l'enquête sur le secteur industriel non structuré,* Tunis, 1984.

8. Sophie Ferichiou, *Les femmes dans l'agriculture tunisienne,* Edisud, Cerès Production, 1985.

9. A *canoune* is a baked clay pan in which charcoal is burned for the purposes of cooking or boiling water for tea and coffee, etc.

Chapter III

The survival strategies of poor families in Ghana and the role of women therein

Vicky Okine

Introduction

It is now widely accepted that informal economic activities are a key source of income earnings as a means of survival for poor families, particularly women in underprivileged households. The informal economy of Ghana, as in other Third World countries, consists of different components. Subsistence agriculture is the most important sector. It accounts for about 80 per cent of the working population and nearly 90 per cent of women. Petty trading in both locally produced commodities and imported consumer items is the second largest sector. Trading is probably the most diversified of informal economic activities. It however, tends to be dominated by foodstuff and consumer items purchased by low-income groups. The third important informal economic activity is manufacturing and services. Manufacturing consists mainly of two components — traditional industrial activities such as metalworking and basketry, based essentially on indigenous technology, and other light industrial activities based on skill and acquired from the modern sector. Much of the manufacturing activities are heavily dependent on imported inputs, and tend to be male-dominated. There are, however, few important manufacturing activities that engage the attention of women. They include soap-making and food processing. These will be one of the areas of our detailed analysis of the current situation of the informal sector.

The increase in the economic activities have imposed heavy demands on their time and health. For example, it is estimated that their new economic roles take up to sixteen hours of their working day. Further aggravating the situation, is the little or no access to modern technology.

Study areas

Ghana if a comparatively small country with a population of some 14 million people occupying an area of 239,460 sq km (1984 population census). Informal economic activities in the country as indicated earlier are diverse. The categories engaged in it also vary. They include persons who own their enterprises and have people working for them, individual workers, apprentices, unpaid family workers, agricultural workers etc. Informal sector incomes also differ. Within such diversity, it is difficult to get an overall uniform view of the sector.

Two villages in southern Ghana and an urban market were selected to present a sample of the group and type of informal sector workers and economic activities which are relevant to this study. They were selected to show women in subsistence agriculture, trading and food processing. The study areas are Kabob, a village in the Central Region and Azalea Bootee in the Greater Accra Region where the capital city is located. Both villages give a sample of rural economies which have been transformed by colonial capitalist penetration. The women in the study areas also typify the classic roles women play and the informal economic activities they engage in.

A third area was the Canals Market Complex in Accra where women traders predominate. A few Government employees engaged in petty trading to supplement their income were also selected for this study.

KABOB

Kabob is a small village in the Central region. It is a typically rural community located in the heart of the forest zone within the Mfantsiman District, some 130 km from Accra. The village has a population of some 500 people living in 40 compound houses. There is a total of 70 households of which 48 are headed by men and 22 by women.

The houses were built of mud, and plastered over with cement and roofed with either corrugated iron sheets or bamboo. It appears that the quality of the materials used in building each house varies according to status.

The village is linked by one untried road which runs through the centre of the community. The women sell cooked foods as well as soap and cigarettes by the sides of this road. The village gets its water supply from a nearby stream and rain water. There are two public conveniences; one for men and one for women.

Electricity is provided by a community generator run by diesel oil when available, particularly when there are visitors in the village. The inhabitants otherwise rely on hurricane lamps.

The major occupation of the people in the village is farming. Men are engaged in cash crop farming whilst women cultivate food crops for subsistence and for sale at the nearest market — Amnesia, about 35 km away. The journey to Amnesia takes over one hour as the road is very bad and full of pot-holes. Apart from farming, other economic activities include food processing, livestock and petty trading.

The socio-economic groupings identified in the village are as follows:

* a privileged group represented by educated people who are teachers and civil servants. They also farm but are usually farm managers because they are able to hire farm labourers.
* a group made up of farmers (both cash crop and subsistence food farmers) and food processors.
* a lower stratum of poorer people made up of those who do not have easy access to or cannot maintain access to productive resources. They usually sell their labour on other peoples' farms and are paid in kind, receiving a third of the proceeds of the farm. Other members of this group who do not or cannot work as farm labourers sell foods and popular consumer items like kerosine and sugar.

AZALEA BOOTEE

Azalea Bootee is also a small village. It is located in the Accra Plains. It has a population of 384, occupying 49 houses. Though it looks isolated, it is joined to Madonna, a suburb of Accra which is only 7 km away.

The inhabitants are of mixed ethnic origin. The largest group are Gas. Next to the Gas are the Fouling who migrated from the Northern savannah region of the country. The Foulings are cattle herders by occupation. Agriculture (farming and livestock) as well as trading are the main economic activities.

The village is composed of poor people engaged in farming, charcoal making and petty trading in food and other basic consumer items.

All the women in the village are excluded from one or a combination of these activities:

* males working as masons, electricians, blacksmiths, stockmen, etc.
* cattle herders who work for the cattle owners; and
* cattle owners, who constitute about 5 per cent of the population. The village draws its water from a public stand-pipe which is connected to the water supply system for Madonna. There are public latrines in the village but no electricity. Hurricane lamps, firewood and charcoal are their main sources of energy.

The farmers in this community are increasingly being deprived of their farm lands, as the region is continually selling off land to members of the Accra-based middle class for real estate development.

CHANTEUSE MARKET COMPLEX

The third study area chosen for the study was the Chanteuse Market Complex, the second-largest market in the city of Accra. It is a centre of brisk business and is comparatively well organized.

Methodology

Preliminary contacts were made with the local elders and members of the Committee for the Defence of the Revolution (CDR). The women in both study villages were briefed at a gathering about the research design and methodology. During the preliminary meetings; discussions were held with the women to prepare a report. At Azalea Bootee, three educated residents were selected to administer the questionnaires after an interview explaining the aim and purpose of the research. At Kabob, the questionnaires were administered by the researcher and two others who served both as translators and interviewers.

After the administration of the questionnaire, the researcher stayed in the village for one week during which three families were closely observed. The aim of this was to arrive at an analysis of their way of life. The households were selected on a random basis. Twenty per cent of the women and 5 per cent of the men in both villages were interviewed. At the Chanteuse Market Complex, the researcher employed the random sampling technique. Three women were selected and observed on an afternoon each week over a period of three weeks. Initial interviews were conducted. These developed into conversations after the researcher had won the confidence of the respondents. This familiarization was a strategy to get the women to talk freely. Civil servants were also interviewed as part of the third study area/group.

Unit of analysis

This will be the household comprising head of household, spouse (if any), children and other relations who eat from the same cooking pot.

Problems encountered

Various problems were encountered. Respondents were unwilling to spare time from their activities to answer questions because of previous disappointing experiences with researchers. For example, a large survey was planned for the third study area, but the identified groups expressed lack of interest or said they had no time.

The selected study areas by no means represent a general overview of informal sector activities in Ghana. However, due to financial and logistical constraints, it was not possible to make a detailed survey as this would have entailed recruiting additional personnel and giving them some training, and the necessary support services.

It would have been timely to relate this study directly to the Economic Recovery Programme and Structural Adjustment Programme which the Ghana government is currently implementing. However, to do this in detail would have stretched this study beyond manageable limits.

The role of the informal sector in the Ghanaian economy

Since the 1970s, informal economic activities in urban and rural areas have emerged as key sources from which a sizeable proportion of the Ghanaian population generate subsistence income for themselves and their families. Adult female members of low-income households have undoubtedly been the most involved in and dependent on informal economic activities.

Before the establishment of British Colonial rule in Ghana, the then Gold Coast, production was communally organized. The dominant social economic activity was agriculture where men and women produced food for consumption.

Next to agricultural production, was a robust petty trading sector made up of the various ethnic groups, people from neighbouring African States and Europe. These trading activities, unlike agricultural production, tended to be male-dominated and used slave labour. Minerals (i.e. gold) and grains used were some of the commonest objects of trade.

With the arrival of British colonial rule, the Ghanaian economy underwent significant structural transformation. British merchant capital qualitatively transformed the nature of trade. Ghana became an important source of essential raw materials for feeding England's industries, especially in Manchester and Liverpool. Gold, rubber, palm products, ivory and scores of other tropical products were exported in large quantities. It was during this period that women emerged as the dominant actors in internal trading which at present constitutes one of the most important informal sector activities.

Apart from greater trade, colonial agricultural development policy advocated cash crop production. The types of commercial crops produced were raw materials required by the industries of the British Empire. Cocoa became the principal cash crop and export commodity.

The process of economic and social transformation, the basis of which was laid and perpetuated by British colonial capital, significantly af-

171

fected the economic roles and the social responsibilities of women. Since male labour was mainly occupied in agricultural and waged activity, female labour was restricted essentially to home-based enterprises. The communally-oriented household production system, where both men and women produced for consumption was undermined. This was profoundly felt in the Northern Territory (the colonial name for present day Northern Ghana) where males were recruited to work on the cocoa plantations and in the mines as unskilled labour.

Under this emerging social division of labour, women assumed greater responsibility for the maintenance of the household. For example, women gradually became solely responsible for production and marketing of food for the household.

Secondly, petty trading by women in both urban and rural centres emerged as a significant component of the economy. Engaging in trade became an important means of securing an income for working-class households in the cities where various items such as rice, yams, plantains, fish, vegetables, cooking oil etc. were sold. The now-popular roadside selling points for prepared foods evolved as a way of making an income and meeting the demands of poor workers — mostly of unskilled and semi-skilled labourers working in the modern sector.

The economic structure that was bequeathed to modern Ghana was characterized by this dualism. There was the modern sector, dominated by the production and export of primary commodities, and a non-modern sector dominated by small independent economic activities of the poor — mainly women.

The processes of economic deterioration in more recent times, accompanied by worsening poverty, especially in the rural areas gave rise to what one might describe as a female labour response. Female labour in the 1970s was not only devoted to informal economic activities as a supplement to family income earned by those engaged in the modern sector, particularly men; it was above all the means of subsistence for the entire household. Without the wife, sister or grandmother's involvement in petty food production or petty trading, low-income households, especially those in the urban areas could hardly have survived under the harsh economic conditions. The significance of the intensification of women's informal economic activities in the 1970s was eloquently emphasized by a female researcher when she made the following observation:

Inflation has soared to unprecedented heights and consumer goods have disappeared from markets; yet the basic market structures remain unchanged. The market trader has proved herself more resilient and resourceful and the consumer is finding himself more and more dependent on the services of the woman trader. (NCWD, 1978, p. 266)

Another female researcher who did an analysis of 'how men spend their time' concluded that the total time spent on trading ranked first. She showed that economic activity was by far the biggest demand on a woman's time (NCWD, op. cit., p. 38). These developments illustrate the fact ʰat for a developing and dependent economy, astronomical rates of un-   ᵐent, low-incomes, a rising cost of living and increased poverty   ᵢfy reliance on informal economic activities. This important role shows, yet again, why the informal sector should engage the serious attention of policy-makers.

The importance of the informal sector and role of women in it

During the economic crisis of the 1970s and the early 1980s, and current attempts to revitalize the economy, informal sector activities have become a source of sustenance to many families. The urban and rural poor have been most affected by the slump and therefore constitute the majority in the informal sector. Among these, women are the most burdened.

Since the informal sector plays a crucial role in the economy, and since about 80 per cent of people engaged in it are women, their role and contribution as independent entrepreneurs needs to be assessed. Therefore we will examine the structure and organization of informal sector activities particularly those of women or those which are dominated by women. Our focus will be on the role of women in agriculture as food producers, food distributors, food processors and petty traders; and the conditions under which they work, highlights the major constraints which face them in the various areas of production.

Women in subsistence agriculture

Subsistence agriculture essentially refers to the cultivation of food crops on a small-scale to satisfy the survival needs of those engaged in it. This type of agriculture is characterized by marginal returns; income, when derived, is very small and goes into meeting the consumption needs of the household.

In 1974, small-scale agricultural production accounted for 95 per cent of the country's overall production and 96 per cent of total land cultivated. Subsistence agriculture is the mainstay of agricultural production within the country.

Women, particularly those in southern Ghana, dominate in the cultivation of food crops. They are involved in nearly all stages of production and yet are missing from agricultural statistics. They receive no special attention in the planning process. As already indicated, the commercialization of agriculture has increased women's workload. They have been left with more and more responsibility to produce for subsistence as men moved into cash crop production. Nonetheless, they account for a much greater percentage of total output. The share of small-scale food producers in total output for 1984 is compared with that of large-scale farmers in Table 1.

TABLE 1

SHARE AND PRODUCTIVITY OF SMALL-SCALE AND LARGE-SCALE CROP PRODUCTION

Crop	Total production (in tonnes = 1)	Small-scale production			Large-scale production		
		Tonnes	Share in 40%	Yield/ hectare (tonnes)	Tonnes	Share in 10%	Yield/ hectare (tonnes)
Maize	488,000	414 300	97.2	1.26	13,700	2.8	1.21
Sorghum	177,300	176,300	99.3	0.83	1,000	0.7	0.77
Millet	155,100	154,800	99.8	0.71	300	0.2	0.60
Rice	74,300	36,700	49.4	1.56	31,600	50.4	1.59
Yam	852,300	849,700	99.7	6.52	2,600	0.3	6.50
Cocoyam	1,516,900	1,513,700	99.8	6.00	3,200	0.2	5.33
Cassava	3,520,200	3,587,200	99.1	10.54	32,900	0.9	14.03
Plaintain	2,031,700	2,018,600	99.4	7.17	13,100	0.6	6.89
Groundnuts	157,200	156,000	99.3	1.43	1,200	0.7	1.12

Source: Republic of Ghana. Agricultural Statistics 1984.

METHODS OF CULTIVATION IN SUBSISTENCE FARMING

The farming methods employed by women engaged in subsistence farming are still largely primitive. Shifting cultivation is the usual practice. This is the rotation of fields after a period of cultivation. The portion of land that was cultivated is left to fallow while a new one is cultivated. Bush burning is generally used to clear the land. The vegetation is cut and burned. The land is then cropped for a period of between two and four years during which its fertility is known to have diminished. Tractor service for clearing the land is now available. But it is too expensive for small farmers whose incomes are extremely low. For example, at Akobima, the women simply did not have access to the services of a tractor. At Ashale Botwe they did: but it was too expensive and therefore only a small minority could afford to hire it during the planting season.

The bulk of women farmers interviewed were subsistence farmers. They had neither the chance nor the means to adopt new farming methods. They cannot afford to take the risks involved because a smaller than expected yield would not simply mean a reduction in their income, but hunger for the whole family. They tend to farm less than one-and-a-half acres; and seldom not more than 6–8 acres. They must feed their family and provide income for other needs from the proceeds of these small farms.

Below is a table indicating the average size of farm holdings per house in the survey areas:

TABLE 2
SIZE OF FARM HOLDINGS OF FEMALES

Average Farm Size	Frequency	%
1–2	12	20
2–4	18	30
4–6	10	16.7
6–8	8	18.3
8–10	6	10
Above 10	3	5

Source: Field Survey 1988.

Women engaged in subsistence farming depend on locally-produced seeds usually stored from the previous year's harvest. Because of poor storage facilities such seeds are often damaged by insects. Very few innovations have been introduced into the farming system. They are still strongly guided by local custom and depend heavily on the weather.

ACCESS TO FACTORS OF PRODUCTION

Land

Throughout rural Ghana women enjoy free rights in communal land only through their male relatives — either father, brother, uncle or husband. Every village compound has some land allotted to it. Each compound contains land for the family head, who parcels plots out to his wife or wives, as the case may be, upon marriage. The family farm is cultivated by the men, wives and children. This male-centred system of access to land creates problems for women in certain parts of Ghana. Bukh in her study of Tsito in the Volta Region of Ghana, observed that unmarried women often have difficulty in obtaining land from male relations because of it (1979, p. 54).

Fifty-six per cent of the women interviewed inherited their farm lands from their grandfathers; 30 per cent from their fathers and 14 per cent from their uncles. Those who do not enjoy these privileges often beg for a piece of land from friends. These latter often concentrate on other areas of activity, notably petty trading and sale of cooked foods; because the plot is often too small even for subsistence farming.

Labour

The ability of women to sustain food production is, however, dependent on the availability of labour. Women in the sector often rely on their own labour and that of family members. Very few of them can afford to hire labour. A majority depend on an informally organized system of labour — the nnobua system. Under this system, a group of friends come together to work on the farm of one person after another until they have gone round the farms of all members of the group. The availability of labour strongly influenced the type of crop produced and the size of land cultivated. Most of the women cultivate cassava, cocoyam and vegetables because these are relatively easier to cultivate than for example oil palm, yams, etc. Crops like these are therefore often left to men to cultivate.

Capital

Capital for production is usually hard to come by. Some farmers borrow from richer farmers and money lenders. Occasionally a few lucky ones are able to obtain some credits from the banking institutions. But in general, institutional credit to subsistence farmers is minimal because of their low annual income and high rate of default. For example, out of the total credit provided in three regions in 1973 (305.5 thousand dollars) only 3.6 per cent was for the food sector (IFAD, 1988).

The study however revealed that a majority of the women are unable to secure credit. At Akobima, for example, they once tried to make use of the nearby Rural Bank at Dominase; but they were disappointed. They are compelled to depend on their own resources and therefore tend to engage in other vocations to generate capital for their businesses. Normally they supplement this with whatever they can get from their parents, and from their husbands upon marriage.

DIVISION OF LABOUR IN SUBSISTENCE AGRICULTURE

In the survey area, men, women and children all play important roles in the initial phase of the farming season — especially in the preparation of food farms. The specific roles played are outlined in Table 3.

TABLE 3

ACTIVITIES OF MEN AND WOMEN IN SUBSISTENCE AGRICULTURE

Activity	Men	Women
Land clearing	Fell big trees; cut them into logs	Clear undergrowth; gather and pile up logs, headload logs to the village
Land preparation	Dig out tree stumps and deep roots	Gather
Planting	Dig holes for seed planting	Women put seeds in the dug out holes
Weeding		Weed round the plants
Harvesting	Cut stalks; assist in harvesting vegetables	Harvest vegetables, root crops, pluck corn off stalks, cut by men,i.e. corn, plantain
Transportation of foodstuffs		Solely done by women in the form of headloading in baskets to the village
Marketing		Solely performed by women

Source: Field Survey 1988.

Women work on their husband's farm. After completing work on these farms they would attend to their own farms. Proceeds from their farms are usually sold to purchase kerosine, matches and other household requirements.

Women are also responsible for the marketing of farm produce from their husband's farms. They start very early in the morning by headloading the produce from the farms to the village for transportation to the markets on market days. They are helped by their children. The average weight of headload of cassava, maize or plantain is about 30 kg.

Table 4 gives estimates of the person-days required to headload produce for one hectare of various crops from the farm to the village. Estimates were adapted from a report of a Special Programming Mission to Ghana undertaken by the International Fund for Agricultural Development and are based on carrying two loads of approximately 30 kg each over an average distance of 5 km a day.

Since women have such little or no access to the essential factors of production, including improved technology, it is no wonder that efforts aimed at increasing food production to feed the ever-growing population have proved futile. More often than not, they are by-passed in the distribution of material assistance designed to increase food output.

TABLE 4

ESTIMATED PERSON-DAYS REQUIRED TO HEADLOAD VARIOUS CROPS
FROM FARM TO VILLAGE

Crop	Yield (with traditional technology) kg/ha	Persons-Days required to headload produce from one's farm
Cassava	3000	50
Maize	700	12
Palm Fruits	5000	83
Plantain	1725	29
Cocoyam	900	15
Yams	3250	54

Source: IFAD, 1988, p. 87.

Women as petty traders

Next to subsistence agriculture, petty trading (the hub of the commercial sector) is the most important activity that engages the energies of women in Ghana. In fact, women make up about 86 per cent of employment in the commercial sector.

Women traders are generally responsible for buying food from farming villages, transporting it to market centres and other points of distribution, and selling it at the markets. They also provide warehouse services. Their involvement at the various stages of food distribution effectively brings almost the entire network in the country under the control of women.

Ardayfio in her study of Urban Market Systems (1981) categorized women traders into three — the wholesaler, wholesaler-retailer and retailer depending on the level of operation. Together, all these groups act as agents in the transfer of food from farms to the consumers.

The wholesalers occupy the top echelon in the hierarchy and are a very powerful group usually operating on a large scale. They are able to and to exert tremendous influence in the distribution, availability and prices of food sold in markets. However, they constitute only a small fraction of the total population of women traders. In 1980, they made up under 2 per cent of women engaged in petty trading.

Ninsin (1972) notes that these wholesalers provide credit facilities to farmers. At harvest, they collect the produce and sell in bulk to other traders. Only a small fraction of the farmer's total output is retained for consumption. Some own trucks or have access to trucks which they use to haul the foodstuffs to the marketing points.

The retailers are less influential than the wholesalers. In 1984, 97.9

per cent of those engaged in the commercial sector were retailers engaged in petty trading, hawking and peddling. Only a minute fraction of the retailers are also wholesalers. While the retailers tend to operate within the immediate locality, wholesalers are generally long-distance traders.

The women of Akobima usually sell palm oil, cassava, plantain and cocoyam at the nearby market centre. On market days, that is Wednesdays and Saturdays a truck, which comes to the village on market days only, arrives in the village around 11.00 pm on the eve of market days. The truck is then fully loaded with their produce for transport to the village, some 35 km distant.

The procurement of farm produce and its distribution sometimes take days. All those involved in going into the interior to buy farm produce spend days (about 2–3) away from home. They often use extremely bad roads and have to sleep in the forest or by the roadside. Ardayfio, in her study cited above, found that most of the vegetables sold at the Accra market are obtained from 212 different locations, mainly Ga villages. However, bulky staples such as cassava and plantains are brought in from more distant places — from the Eastern Region, Ashanti and Brong Ahafo Regions and even as far as Bawku in the Upper East Region. This shows the extent and nature of movements of women in their relentless drive to secure and distribute to urban food consumers. Table 5 shows the sources (by region) of the flow of foodstuff into the Kaneshie market in Accra. It is important to note that no foodstuff is produced in the city of Accra. Everything sold at the market has to be brought in by rail or by road.

The table indicates the places from which foodstuff are brought into markets in Accra. So much is the involvement of women in making food items available to consumers that Ardayfio notes: 'There is evidence that the creditable performance of the women traders in this respect is unrivalled by the efforts of the government's Food Distribution Corporation'(1981, p. 3).

It is noted elsewhere that the crucial contributions of traders mean that 'they fill an important gap in the marketing system' (IFAD, 1988, p. 90).

Quite apart from the sale of agricultural produce in the markets etc. a myriad of other everyday trading activities exists in the country. It comprises children selling imported commodities such as apples, sweets, handkerchiefs, and office workers, mostly women who sell clothes, food items etc. in their offices as well as women in the rural and urban areas selling cooked corn, rice and beans, kenkey and a wide range of fast foods in lorry parks, gas stations and by the roadsides to various consumers.

TABLES 5
FLOW OF GOODS TO ACCRA MARKETS

Commodity	Main Source	Region
Plantain	Nkawkaw	Eastern
	Asamankese	Eastern
	Konongo	Ashanti
	Dedescaba	Brong Ahafo
	Sunyani	Brong Ahafo
Cassava	Suhum	Eastern
Yam	Kete Krachi	Brong Ahafo
	Ejura	Ashanti
Vegetables	Bortianor	Greater Accra
(tomatoes	Ga Rural (Ofankor)	Greater Accra
garden eggs	Afuaman	Greater Accra
pepper etc.)	Ashale Botwe	Greater Accra
	Ada	Greater Accra
	Adieso	Eastern
	Bawku	Upper
	Keta	Volta
Grain	Ga Rural	Greater Accra
	Techiman	Brong Ahafo
	Tamale	Northern
	Bolgatanga	Upper East
Fruits	Suhum	Eastern
	Obas Krowa	Greater Accra
Fish	Accra	Greater Accra
	Salaga	Greater Accra
	Tema	Greater Accra
	Akosombo	Eastern
	Kwami Krom	Eastern
	Apam	Central
	Ada	Greater Accra
	Aflao	Volta
	Kpandu	Volta

Source: Ardayfio; Urban market system (1981, p. 42).

Key problems within the informal economy

Although women contribute crucially to the national economy through active involvement in the informal sector, they are denied the resources and interventions necessary to enhance their productivity. Therefore they continue to encounter age-old problems. These problems may be classified as follows:

ACCESS TO LAND

The most significant productive resource for subsistence agricultural workers is land for farming. This resource is however controlled by male-dominated institutions and the state. Women can have access to land only through their male relatives. This has often restricted their access to land.

ACCESS TO CAPITAL

In theory, both rural and urban women should have access to credit from banks such as the Agricultural Development Bank (ADB) and Rural Banks. Practical experiences of women however revealed the contrary. The ADB has specific loan schemes, e.g. Agribusiness Individual loan for farmers, and a commodity credit scheme for traders, etc. The latter is a group lending programme. Illiteracy however, prevents women from even knowing what facilities are available. This is compounded by the collateral requirements of the banks, which explains why women in the informal sector are compelled to resort to informal credit arrangement.

LABOUR

Traditional farming and food processing methods are labour intensive. The fact that they use primitive techniques forces them to resort to the intensive use of family labour.

TRANSPORTATION

The bulk of activities carried out by women especially in the rural areas is undertaken without any reliable means of transport. Farms are usually located far away from the village where the few laterite roads do not extend. Two problems arise from this. The women have to divide their labour time between actual production work on the farms and carting the farm produce to either the village or the nearest road. If they have to send their produce to the market they become victims of transport operators who charge exorbitant rates. At Akobima, for example, about 60 per cent of the women interviewed remarked that they retailed only to surrender what they earned to transport owners.

STORAGE

The lack of reliable storage facilities affects the turnover of the traders and manufacturers adversely. A lot of food items go bad and out of season within a short time. Those engaged in palm oil production are forced by this and the lack of capital to sell off their stocks when they could make a little more if they could withhold it from the market and release it during the off seasons.

EXTENSION SERVICES

Women, especially those in rural areas, are hardly ever reached by male extension officers. Accordingly, they have remained ignorant of new techniques etc., and their needs are under-represented due to lack of proper evidence.

Conclusion

The foregoing discussion has shown the important role of women in the nation's economy through their leading role in the informal sector. The analysis has drawn attention to their role in subsistence agriculture food trading, and the manufacture of food and other household necessities. Without them many households, especially the poor ones in both rural and urban communities could not survive. Women produce, distribute, market and manufacture a greater portion of foods consumed in the country by even wealthy households.

The majority of them are small-holders producing on a very small scale and relatively unaffected by developments in the use of improved tools and seeds. Their involvement in agricultural production is often a continuing struggle to provide enough just for their households. This does not encourage savings against future consumption, against economic shocks and other hazards. Yields are low and highly determined by the weather, yet women are denied necessary support by the state. Modern inputs, where available, are too expensive for them. The uncertainties in their environment make it too risky to try new methods of production. They are caught up in a typically 'no exit situation in which poor people, especially women, are trapped' (Jain, 1987, p. 3).

Despite the enormous contributions made by women through production and commercial activities, they are not acknowledged in official statistics. Neither are they given official support. Rather, they are often harassed by tax collectors and other law enforcement agents of the state.

Some survival strategies of poor families within the household economy

Having emphasized the contributions of women within the informal sector in both rural and urban areas, we will now discuss how poor families cope with the perennial situation of recurrent poverty.

Information from the villages surveyed will be used to show how families in rural communities survive. Following that, evidence from selected female wage workers we interviewed will be used to show how women in urban centres cope with poverty.

Some of the questions to be answered are:

- How do women acquire the start-up capital for their work or business?
- In the villages how do they cope with the problem of labour shortage and primitive technology?
- How do they solve the problem of access to markets?
- How do they cope with the problem of inadequate accommodation facilities?

The discussion will also point up the dominant attitudes in their communities, and which have become determinants and rationalizations for their behaviour.

Coping with poverty in rural Ghana

It was observed from the two villages that a majority of the women started their income-earning occupations (farming and food processing) without any working capital. Most of them were in fact born into farming and accumulated just a small income from farming with their parents.

Land is inherited from either their grandfathers, fathers, or is given to them by their husbands upon marriage. The land is not bought. Neither are the seeds purchased. As stated previously, the seeds are acquired from the previous harvest. It is only hoes and cutlasses which they have to buy occasionally.

Labour often poses a problem. Because of the very simple technology (tools) being used in farming, labour has come to play an important role in determining how much land a household can develop, and therefore how much they can produce. At Akobima labour was 'hired' on small scale and paid in kind with one-third of the harvest. This is the abusua system that has been employed extensively in the cocoa industry.

However, because farms are generally small and parting with a third of the harvest affects a household's overall income, a number of supplementary practices have developed as a way of coping with the need for additional labour. A few of these may be identified. One is the tendency to have many children who then assist on the farm when they are of age. The other is the use of the informal organization and circulation of labour called *nnoboa*.

Nnoboa

This is an informal network of friends who come together in groups of not less than three. They work on each other's farm until the cycle is completed. Oftentimes, the sons of farmers or the women constitute themselves into the group.

Susu

A *susu* group consists of people closely associated in a village or family members engaged in the same occupation. A group could consist of any number of people. The size usually ranges between 10 and 50 people. Each member of the group undertakes to pay a specified amount of money on a periodic basis. The period of payment varies from one group to another. It could be on a daily, weekly or monthly basis. Contributions are pooled together and given to each member on a rotating basis until everyone has received a pool of the contributions. At the end of the distribution, that is after each member has received a contribution, any member of the group who wishes to discontinue may do so. Those who wish to continue begin another round.

The contributions are usually collected by an agent, appointed by the group who is paid a fee from what he collects.

The *susu* credit system requires no fixed capital and written records. It is thus very vulnerable to abuse by the collectors.

It has been observed that this type of credit system is comparatively better organized in the rural areas than in the urban centres.

On the whole, we noticed that the rural poor did not like to borrow money from money lenders etc. primarily because they knew no one would risk lending them any money. One respondent remarked that since she is a mother no one would think of giving her a loan because they will say that she will use the money in buying fish to eat.

At Akobima, it was found that women did not belong to any organized credit association such as the *susu* group that prevailed in the second village Ashale Botwe. The reason for this difference is however due to the fact that farmers at Ashale Botwe needed to hire labour and pay for tractor services in cash. They seemed to be more integrated into the money economy than the Akobima village which is still very rural.

Posnausky's study of the village of Hani in the Brong Ahafo appears to suggest that the pattern is characteristic of small villages trying to cope with socio-economic distress. He observed that the focus of agricultural production shifted noticeably from an emphasis on export crop to growing foodstuffs particularly yams and tomatoes mainly for consumption. Crafts that had been abandoned were revived and blacksmiths began to make hoes and cutlasses which had become scarce at the time. Bukh in her study of Tsito in the Volta region also noted that women in the village stopped cultivating yams. Instead, they went into the cultivation of cassava, a less nutritious but easy to cultivate root crop.

The significance of this pattern of reaction — towards self-sufficiency and autonomy — for our study, stems from the role of women in the village economy. As the group solely responsible for farming and satisfying the food needs of the household, the burden of the village economy fell squarely on them. They had to provide the extra labour required on the farm both directly by themselves and indirectly by bearing more children and also by working long hours.

Coping with poverty in urban Ghana

Urban women, like their rural counterpart are also faced with similar challenges and the need to evolve appropriate strategies to meet them. The difference between the poor urban women and their rural counterpart is that the demands on the former are far greater than anything the latter could contemplate. They have to pay taxes, spend money on transportation, pay rent and other bills for utility services, etc. Unlike women in the rural areas, these are largely immigrants who have to pay a price for every facility or service they use.

The principal economic activity of women in the towns and cities is petty trading and hawking. By definition, petty trading and hawking are very small-scale operations which qualify as informal sector activities. Most women operate in this sector also because they lack capital to engage in any large-scale economic enterprise. The problem of financing economic activity therefore faces poor urban women as well.

Various ways of securing necessary capital to start petty trading have been developed. A few lucky women are able to raise a small amount of money from their husbands, and others from relations. Among the women we interviewed, very few of them obtained credit from the banks.

Outside these groups we identified two tendencies. One concerned women who were determined to overcome their poverty and yet lacked the finances for starting a trade. In the food trading sector, it was possible for women of this category to buy on credit from market mammies who mediate between producers and the markets.

That is they would usually buy in small quantities, sell and pay on the next market day when they would procure fresh food items to sell and pay on the following occasion. The financial nexus that bound the two together survived purely on trust. But ultimately this means enabled some women food sellers to get established however small their operations continued to be. A similar nexus existed between women-traders or hawkers of manufactured consumer goods and shop owners.

The other tendency is equally innovative. Women engaged in that practice were not desperate, however. They had normally started off as traders. However, due to difficulty in making adequate profit, they resorted to the *susu* savings system as a less painful way of increasing their meagre income so that they could discharge their numerous financial commitments and responsibilities.

Unlike the rural environment the need for money is very strong. Working women are therefore always exploring new avenues by which to supplement their income. Below is a profile of a few urban-based women. They comprise two junior civil servants and three traders. Their profiles show how they endeavour to cope with what appears to be a perpetual shortage of money for maintaining a minimum standard of living. Their stories also give a picture of their attitudes and life styles which are not very different from those of many poor urban women. We will identify them as Mabel, Mercy, Madam Cecilia, Auntie Donkor and Madam Faustina respectively.

Mabel

Mabel is employed as a typist in the civil service. She is 27 years old. She was married; but is now divorced and has one child from that marriage living with her.

She earns a monthly income of 8,000 cedis out of which she must meet all her expenses, i.e. accommodation, transportation, food, clothing and medical care for herself and her daughter. She spends between 3,000 and 4,000 cedis on transportation alone. The balance is usually not enough to take her through two weeks. She therefore borrows money from those she stays with (in a compound house), and pays at the end of the month. However, when she 'is very tight' she hawks with the help of a friend. This friend is a full-time petty trader in cooking utensils and other household accessories. She would give Mabel an allocation of utensils to sell and keep the profit. She gives this allocation to Mabel on credit who then sells them to friends and other co-workers.

Mabel's customers are equally short on cash. They therefore agree to pay for the utensils over a period of two to three months. The defect rate is often alarming. When they pay for the items she takes out her profit and pays the rest to her friend. When her friend left town, she lost this facility for making supplementary income outside her formal employment. She became heavily indebted to all manner of people. Sometimes when she could not raise a loan from the usual source she would just sit down and as she puts it, 'look up to God for help'.

Mercy

Like Mabel, Mercy thinks her job as a clerk is preferable to staying at home, although it does not earn her enough income. At the end of every month she is lucky to get money as 'Chop money' from her husband. This is inadequate however, though she considers it better than nothing. She believes that in the final analysis, 'it is God who take care of them'.

In spite of her faith, she prepares and sells doughnuts and other pastries for sale in front of her house. The children in her household also assist in selling her pastries at their schools.

Unfortunately, she is constantly being molested by the police. When she is caught her basket of pastries is confiscated. Since selling pastries is a part-time and occasional occupation, she does not earn much and so cannot always afford to pay the usual tax.

Madam Cecilia

Madam Cecilia has been a trader for the last nine to ten years. She does not know her age because her mother was illiterate and could not recollect the year in which she was born. She is married with six children — five of whom are in school.

They all live together. She started trading in foodstuffs by travelling into the interior where oranges were abundant. These she sold to retailers or retailed herself in Accra. She had to stop because many of the oranges went bad, incurring great losses. Her husband helped by providing her with initial capital. It was not enough yet she had to depend on it to trade in plantains when she quit selling oranges.

About three years ago, her husband, who was working as a mason with a public corporation, lost his job. She was forced to use much of her working capital to maintain her family. Apart from this disaster, business has been bad for the past three years. She would travel long distances and pay exorbitant transportation costs that all but absorbed her profit margin. She therefore stopped going into the interior to buy foodstuffs to sell at the Kaneshie market.

She now goes to the market every morning to buy directly from the 'market mammies' and retail to consumers. She would for example pick load of cassava or kontomire and retail. She could make about 500 cedis in a day. On bad days she would borrow items such as pepper and tomatoes from her friends. She was confident that she would definitely get something before sunset each day — 'God will provide'.

Madam Cecilia prefers this to trekking with all its discomfort, perils and financial losses. Now all that she is concerned about is getting some money to feed the household.

Auntie Donkor

Auntie Donkor is a trader involved in long-distance trade for the past fourteen years.

She travels to villages in the interior to buy food items which she then sells at the Kaneshie market.

She leaves home at 4.00 am on Tuesdays and Thursdays together with a group of friends who have joined together to hire a haulage truck for these purchasing trips. The villagers bring the farm produce to the roadside where they are purchased by middlemen — also women. These middlemen resell the food to the group at expensive rates. They have a monopoly over the trade with the producers. It is therefore not permissible for Auntie Donkor and her group to purchase the items directly from the villagers. In any case it is a convenient arrangement since the middlemen go round all the collection points to buy and bring the items to the roadside.

Things were good when they started. But since 1983, prices of food, transportation, labour, etc. have soared. She thus barely makes a profit.

The taxes she has to pay are exorbitant. She therefore cannot rent a stall in the market. To avoid this additional expense she has been selling her foodstuffs after 4.00 pm and only on the pavement. This is when the police are off duty. Fortunately she has established a network of customers who depend on her for their supplies and know the days and times she comes to the market.

Madam Faustina

Madam Faustina, otherwise called Auntie Fausti is 35 years old and has had partial elementary school education. She lives with her second husband with whom she has one child. She had three children from her first marriage. Like Madam Cecilia, her husband lost his job and the whole family has since had to depend on her enterprise to survive.

She learnt how to sew but could afford neither a sewing machine nor rent a place for sewing because she could not find the necessary capital to start.

She initially started trading in plantain but had to stop because of financial difficulties. She now sells fish. It is not too profitable but at least she did not need much money to start; and at the end of the day she has money to buy food for her family.

She is well-known by the people from the village who supply her fish. She therefore buys on credit. She goes to buy the fish on Wednesdays and returns to Accra on Fridays to sell what she could procure. She in turn credits the fish to her customers. By the following Tuesday all those who bought some of her fish on credit will have paid. The cycle thus begins again with another journey to the fishing village. Auntie Fausti says she does not use any of the fish she sells because it is too expensive for her. They cost between 600 to 1,000 cedis each while she spends about 100 cedis on fish for her family.

From her sales she is able to obtain an average weekly income of 3,000 cedis. This is what she and her household live on. Apart from selling fish she has no other job.

Auntie Fausti does not have a stall and like Auntie Donkor she does not want to be arrested and to have her fish seized. Accordingly, she goes round the market in the evenings — after 4.00 pm to sell her fish on credit. She has to be extra careful about the way she organizes the sales.

She gets home quite late — sometimes after 8.00 pm. By this time, the elder child would have to take care of the younger ones.

Her situation is typically desperate. She sums up as follows: 'All the money I make I have to struggle really hard for'. She nevertheless believes that one day she can make it. 'God's time is the best', she said.

The foregoing profiles amply describe the difficulties that urban-based women go through to survive. Most of them are either illiterate or semi-literate. A growing number have broken marriages leaving them as the heads of their households.

Women's informal organizations and support networks

Several organizations operate in both the rural and urban environments in which women operate. In most instances, the organizations were created by the women themselves as an independent means for promoting solidarity and self-help measures.

We found evidence of self-help networks in our investigations in the two villages. The areas in which the women help each other included such domestic areas as fetching of water, cooking and child care. The services of the networks extended also to the economic sphere, particularly farming.

The networks usually comprise close friends. It has been observed that some of these networks involve women in the market economy and also facilitate their access to economic resources which otherwise may be scarce and beyond their reach. This may be true of certain women's associations. In my view the self-help networks enable the women to socialize household chores and economic activities. In this way the networks reduce the tedium of work and thereby the oppression of the kind of roles the sexual division of labour sometimes imposes on them.

In urban centres like Accra, co-operatives, social and religious associations, trading and other associations are common. They are also essentially self-help associations combining the provision of purely social support services with economic ones. Most of them are active mainly on social occasions. The trading associations are, however, based in the market and are active throughout the year. Their main concerns include the monitoring of food prices, availability and sale of the food items they sell, the allocation of market stalls, and the level of market levy which they have to pay.

In one of the two villages — Akobima — a co-operative association has been formed. The initiative had come from the villagers but was reinforced by the National Council on Women and Development (NCWD). It aimed specifically at introducing the women to new and more productive economic activities. In this way the NCWD could introduce the women to an improved technology for the processing of palm fruit into palm oil.

It would therefore appear that the level of organization of the social and economic life of women in both the rural and urban areas would depend on the level of social stress and type of economic activity. Thus informal self-help networks dominated at the two villages whereas formally organized associations were prevalent at the Kaneshie Market in Accra.

Conclusions and recommendations

Conclusions

The central issue addressed in this study is the role of women in the informal sector and their contribution to the national economy. Throughout the study we have emphasized that women have assumed far greater responsibilities in maintaining and sustaining their respective households because of the country's economic crisis during the last two decades. They have expended a greater portion of their time, labour and talent in exploring ways of coping with these unprecedented demands. Accordingly, the range and nature of strategies that have been evolved are impressive.

The implications of these metamorphoses are far-reaching. Three of them may be isolated by way of conclusion. First of all, they expose the effect that economic backwardness in countries like Ghana exerts on women.

Economic backwardness and the crisis it produces have transferred Ghanaian women from their traditional roles and in particular, from childbearing, to key economic sectors as their work assumes greater importance.

The difference between the Ghanaian working woman and her West European counterpart, is both striking and revealing. The working woman in a West European city, town or village, would probably see her new role as a worker as part of her liberation towards a new positive status of equality with men. Technological innovation and related benefits have considerably reduced the pain and tedium of work. And she, above all, has the benefit of leisure and, possibly, pleasure.

The experiences of the Ghanaian woman point to the contrary. She has to work out of dire necessity: it is a choice between survival and non-survival, a cruel and painful choice. She has to toil under extreme primitive conditions as well as material limitations. She has to invest extended time and labour in her work in order to ensure the survival of her household. All this and much more does not add to, or promote her liberation. They rather make her a slave in a different guise — this time subject to the relentless impersonal forces of the market. In short the backwardness of the economy has not freed Ghanaian women, especially those from poor backgrounds. It has rather compounded their situation.

That the economic roles of Ghanaian women has not liberated them is further confirmed by the extent to which policy-makers regard them. It should be recalled that Ghanaian women have been making enormous contributions to sustain the average Ghanaian household and the entire economy — in rural areas, towns and cities. Yet these strategic roles are not recognized. Hence, the lack of any meaningful state support.

We would deduce from this, not the usual explanation that it is because this is a male-dominated society. The persistent impoverishment of women should rather be attributed to their lack of political power. It is timely that women have been forming a number of self-help associations. But these have predominantly economic and social functions. The conspicuous lack of organized political concern and action to back up their growing economic role is bound to leave crucial decisions affecting the status and well-being of women in the hands of people who have entirely different sets of priorities.

Finally, the economic and political factors combine effectively to impose a peculiar cultural milieu on women. This milieu is pervaded by poverty, ignorance, powerlessness, illiteracy and lack of individual as well as collective autonomy. At this point, it is important to remark that the autonomy of the village from economic and political forces is a negative one and imposes a need to forge self-help associations of all sorts. Unless this is understood, all of us will be guilty of unnecessary fantasies and mystifications.

Recommendations

It should be emphasized that the informal sector is a heterogeneous entity: it has diverse characteristics, occupations and actors. It would therefore be unrealistic to pretend that specific solutions can be found for its component units. Any attempt in this direction is likely to be incoherent, self-contradictory, ineffective and, ultimately, useless.

Furthermore, the problems of the informal sector are closely linked to those of the formal sector (Ninsin, 1988). It would therefore seem logical that the problem of disarticulation of the formal sector will have to be solved as a precondition for effectively dealing with the problem of the informal sector. This is nonetheless a holistic as well as long-term solution. In the meantime, a number of general problems of a political and economic nature should be identified and dealt with.

SCARCITY OF CAPITAL

This is a problem that runs through the entire sector and undermines potential for expansion and improvements. It could be tackled at two related levels: the institution of a special credit scheme to be operated through the Agricultural Development Bank, Ghana Commercial Bank, the Cooperative Bank and the Rural Banks. To give it a mass base, the credit scheme should be linked with the susu system. That is, a conscious effort should be made by the state to promote this among women in the various trades. It will not only strengthen the 'savings consciousness', but more specifically it will formalize and integrate it into the banking system and thereby provide an effective channel of credit disbursement and guarantee.

COOPERATIVE MOVEMENT

The *susu system* is generally based on specific trades which are also the bases for quasi-co-operatives or trade associations. This latent co-operative spirit could be kindled into a strong co-operative movement with trade and financing as binding forces.

More especially, the co-operatives could link into a powerful network of political agents for promoting the interests of women.

The potential danger here is that the political élite may not tolerate such a potentially strong women's political movement, and they may therefore be indifferent to the idea. Fortunately, however, organizations like the National Council on Women and Development (NCWD), which have built up years of experience and expertise in dealing with women, could easily assume this organizational task.

A strong politically conscious women's co-operative movement can effectively press issues related to women in the informal sector and others for attention. Indeed the co-operative movement should be regarded as the only promising basis for spreading technological innovation, new ideas and methods, and various cultural and production practices in agriculture and industry to women, and also for facilitating access to and control over land, labour and transportation.

BASIC MANAGEMENT SKILLS

Quite often promising enterprises in the informal sector have been ruined by inexperience and inefficiency. A deliberate policy of identifying individuals and co-operative leaders for management training relevant to their specific industry will be necessary. This should take the form of workshops, short residential courses and similar training programmes.

NATIONAL COMMISSION ON WOMEN

There is the need to guarantee action on matters affecting women. The establishment of a National Commission on Women (NCW) may secure this. To avoid giving birth to another glorified monument, it is suggested that the NCW should come directly under the head of State. This alone will guarantee the political support and clout necessary for achieving progress on these proposals from the very start.

REFERENCES

Andad, C. *The Role of Women in Agriculture (The Case of Food Production).* Council of Women and Development. Accra, 1978.

Anheir, H.C., and Seibel, H.D. *Small Scale Industries and Economic Development in Ghana; Business Behaviors and Strategies in Informal Sector Economies,* Cologne Development Studies, 1987.

Ardayfio, E. *The Rural Energy Crisis in Ghana: It's Implications for Women's Work and Household Survival.* Rural Employment Programme Research Working Paper, 1986.

Ardayfio, S.E. *Urban Marketing System: An Analysis of Operational and Environmental Conditions of Markets in Ghana:* UN/ECA (Addis Ababa) 1981.

Brown, C.K., and Gyeke, D. *Women in Co-operatives. A Pilot Study of Women's Economic Associations in Ghana.* National Council on Women and Development Project Report, October 1979. Project Report, October 1979.

Bukh, J. *The Village Woman in Ghana,* Scandinavian Institute of African Studies. Upsala, 1979.

Hart, K. 'Informal Income Opportunity and Urban Employment in Ghana'. *Journal of Modern African Studies,* Vol. 77, No. 1, 1973.

IFAD. Report on Special Programming Mission to Ghana, 1988.

ILO. Employment, Incomes and Equality: A Strategy for Increasing Productivity Employment in Kenya. Geneva: ILO, 1972.

ISSAS. The Informal Sector: Issues and Concepts. Institute of Social Studies. The Hague, 1985.

Jain, D.Address to the Round Table on Development on the Theme Survival Strategies of the Poor and Traditional Wisdom — A Reflection, Bangalore, May 1987.

_____. Methods for the Integration of Women's Issues in Development Planning. Paper for UNESCO Symposium, Paris (Oct. 1987).

Kennedy, P. 'The Role and Position of Petty Producers in West African City'. *The Journal of Modern African Studies,* Vol. 19, No. 4, 1981, pp. 565–94.

NCWD. Proceedings of Seminar of Ghanaian Women in Development, Vol. 1, 1978.

Ninsin, K. *Economic Recovery, the Informal Sector and Social Equity: An Enquiry into Aspects of the Ghanaian Development Experience.* Essay submitted to the Rockefeller Foundation under its Reflections on Development Programme, 1988.

_____. Planning for the Growth of Small Scale Industries in the Informal Sector: The Realities and Challenges of the Ghana Situation. Institute of Statistical, Social and Economic Research (ISSER), University of Ghana, Legon, 1972.

Posnasky, M. 'How Ghana Crisis Affects a Village'. *West Africa,* 3306 (2nd Dec.) 1980.

Republic of Ghana. Agricultural Policy — Action Plans and Strategies 1984–1986, Ghana.

_____. Ghana in Figures 1987, Statistical Service.

_____. Economic and Financial Framework, July 1987–June 1990.

Reynolds, E. *Trade and Economic Change on the Gold Coast 1807–1874,* London, Longmans Publications.

Sethuraman, S.U. (ed). *The Urban Informal Sector in Developing Countries, Employment, Poverty and Environment,* Geneva, ILO, 1981.

Steel, W.F. *Empirical Measurement of the Relative Size and Productivity of Intermediate Sector Employment. Some Estimates from Ghana.* Canadian Journal of African Studies, Vol. 9, No. 1975.

Thomi, W.H., and Yankson, K. *Small Scale Industries and Decentralization in Ghana,* University of Ghana, 1978.

Trager, L. 'A Re-examination of the Urban Informal Sector in West Africa'. *Canadian Journal on African Studies* RCEA XXI: 2, 1987.

UNICEF. Ghana: Adjustment Policies and Programmes to Protect Children and Other Vulnerable Groups, Accra, 1975.

World Bank. *Ghana: Towards Structural Adjustment,* Vol. 1 (Main Report), No. 5854, 1985.

Yankson, P. The Planning Requirements for the Informal Sector in Development at the Local Levels in Ghana. ISSER, University of Ghana, 1989.

Chapter IV

Women's involvement in the urban economy in Colombia

Marie-Dominique de Suremain

The feminization of poverty

Colombia has a surface area of about 1 million sq km and a population of 30 million inhabitants (29.5 million at the last census in 1985).

In the course of two generations a series of major demographic, economic, social and political changes have left deep marks on the cultural, political, economic and social life of the country. Colombia has changed from a rural to a heavily urbanized society: a sharp drop in the death rate was followed by a drop in the birth rate the so-called 'demographic transition' a period of industrialization gave way to one of economic crisis; in the last ten years or so the underground drug economy first marijuana and later cocaine, has come to occupy an important place, the country has had problems in modernizing the State machinery, and there have been violent social conflicts.

These frequently sudden and even violent changes have profoundly affected the living conditions of women in every class of society. Though women may in general be said to have improved their living and working conditions in the course of two or three generations, this has only been at the price of renewed efforts that have involved increased responsibilities and a growing tension between their various activities.

Economic structure and employment

Since the 1950s Colombia has been transformed from an agricultural and rural economy to an urban economy with the emphasis on industry and services (see Tables 1 and 2).

TABLE 1
DISTRIBUTION OF THE URBAN POPULATION IN COLOMBIA
(1938–1985)

Year	Urban population		Rural population		Total	
	millions	%	millions	%	millions	%
1938	2.68	30	6.32	70	9.00	100
1951	5.10	43	6.86	57	11.96	100
1964	9.09	52	8.39	48	17.48	100
1973	13.55	60	9.31	40	22.86	100
1985	18.53	70	8.00	30	26.53	100

Source: DANE census returns.

TABLE 2
GROWTH OF THE PRINCIPAL CITIES IN COLOMBIA (1938–1985)
(IN THOUSANDS OF INHABITANTS)

City	1938	1951	1964	1973	1985	Growth 1983/1985
Bogotà	360	720	1,700	2,860	3,970	x11
Medellin	250	500	1,090	1,620	2,070	x8
Cali	110	300	660	1,030	1,400	x13
Barraquilla	117	300	540	770	1,200	x7
Manizales	100	140	240	260	400	x4
Cartagena	90	130	250	350	600	x9
Burcaramang	70	130	260	430	600	x9
Cucuta	60	100	190	330	500	x8
Pereira	60	120	190	280	400	x7
Urban population	2,680	5,100	9,090	13,550	18,530	x7

Source: DANE census returns.

In 1951 the population was mainly rural, with 70 per cent of the inhabitants living outside the towns and villages (municipal centres); by 1985 the proportions had been completely inverted, with 70 per cent of the population urbanized.

The role of agriculture (especially the growing of coffee) in the gross domestic product has dropped by half (40 per cent in 1945–1949 as against 22 per cent in 1980–1984) in favour of industry (up from 15 to 21 per cent in the same period), transport and services.

TABLE 3

GDP BY BRANCH OF ACTIVITY (1945–1984)

(PER CENT)

Branch	1950–1954	1965–69	1980–1984
Agricult./Fishing	33.6	26.6	22.5
Mining	3.2	3.0	1.4
Manufacturing industry	17.4	21.1	21.4
Construction	2.8	3.2	3.6
Communications	0.3	0.7	1.5
Electricity and gas	0.3	0.7	1.0
Shops and restaurant	10.4	9.9	9.8
Financial services	3.5	5.6	7.7
Transport	6.6	6.9	8.1
State services	7.3	7.0	8.2
Personal services	7.8	7.2	7.7
Renting of accommodation	6.7	8.0	7.0
TOTAL	100	100	100

Source: Employment Mission, Chapter I of the Final Report, cited by UNICEF.

The cause of the rural exodus towards the cities was the big drop in the traditional peasant economy in favour of a capitalist agriculture aimed primarily at exportation.

Industry is being modernized with a view to eliminating imports through the creation of heavily capitalized firms generally dependent on multinational companies.

The gross domestic product grew quite quickly between the 1950s and the mid–1970s with a new peak in 1978 (8.5 per cent overall and 6.4 per cent per inhabitant). From 1979 to 1983 the country felt the effects of the international recession, the rate of inflation rose (though not so much as in neighbouring countries), growth ran out of steam, the currency dropped more sharply in relation to the dollar, while wages and the social expenditure of the State rose more slowly than inflation.

From the beginning of the 1980s the deterioration of the terms of exchange and the growing foreign debt burden began to have an adverse effect on the Colombian economy. The increase in State expenditure, especially on military items, produced an endemic budgetary deficit.

The proportion of State expenditure in the budget devoted to education dropped from 25.2 per cent in 1984 to 21.5 per cent in 1985 and 19.6 per cent in 1986 and to public health from 6.3 per cent to 5.3 per cent to 5.1 per cent in the same years.

During the period 1975–1985 Colombia had an average growth rate of

3.6 per cent, lower than in the previous decade (6.9 per cent) and also than in the previous 50 years (Londoño, 1987).

In these cycles the different urban branches of activity did not progress at an even pace. The biggest fluctuations affected industry, which experienced a sharp recession between 1980 and 1983 followed by a moderate revival in 1983–1984. A similar ebb and flow seems to have characterized the years from 1985 to 1988.

The tertiary sector, in contrast, appears to have expanded more evenly, mainly on account of the public and private services, whereas trade has experienced ups and downs that are out of phase with the cycle in industry (in terms of volume of activity) especially during the most recent period.

During these periods the characteristics of the demand for employment and of the labour market changed radically. The average age of the urban population fell considerably in the 1960s and then rose slightly in the 1980s (from 23.7 years in 1976 to 25.3 years in 1984). The working-age population, i.e. those over 12 years old, is also young but gradually getting older (from 30.7 years in 1976 to 31.9 years in 1985).

The sharp drop in the population growth rate over the last decade (from 3.5 per cent in 1975 to 2.9 per cent in 1985) has resulted in a smaller average size of household and, in conjunction with a higher level of education, has made for increased participation by women in the urban labour market. However, the roots of this participation must be sought in the differential rates for migration by sex since the 1930s and 1940s.

The regional capitals and other cities have served as a pole of attraction for the migration of women and did so even before changes in the agrarian system led to major migratory flows that have provided the ba-

TABLE 4

NUMBER OF WOMEN PER 100 MEN IN THE URBAN POPULATION

City	1938	1951	1964	1973	1985
Bogotá	122	121	114	114	111
Cali	107	110	112	113	112
Medellin	120	118	114	114	112
Barranquilla	109	112	113	112	109
Bucaramanga	114	123	121	118	112
Caragena	115	116	115	115	110
Manizale	95	114	108	118	112
Cucuta	106	115	112	110	107
Pereira	98	112	115	117	112
National average (urban)	102	117	113	113	110

Source: DANE, census and calculations by author.

sic population of the cities since the 1950s.

Bogota and Medellin emerge as the cities which attract the most women migrants. It will be noted, however, that certain regional and local data make for a sharp rise in the index even for smaller cities such as Bucaramanga, Manizales and Pereira between 1938 and 1951. On the subject of these different migration rates, certain hypotheses suggest that rural areas tend to drive away more women than men (Castro, 1979). Possible reasons are that capitalism and the regression of the peasant economy resulted in insufficient opportunities for paid work in agriculture for women and that the rigidity of patriarchal relations and the harshness of living conditions for the wives and daughters of peasants made them look to life in the cities for freedom and better conditions of existence.

To this explanation must undoubtedly be added the needs of the cities, where there was a constant and growing demand for domestic staff. Recruitment was carried out through various channels and was often supported even by the families of the women concerned, who sought to place them as young as possible in an urban family as 'living-in' or full-time employees.

TABLE 5

ACTIVITY RATE OF THE POPULATION*

Age-group	1951	1964	1973	1978
Women				
10–14	6.53	4.20	11.45	5.39
15–19	25.79	21.74	27.68	20.64
20–29	23.07	24.08	32.88	42.55
30–39	19.67	19.68	23.96	37.35
40–49	17.16	19.55	20.09	31.62
50–59	14.23	17.38	16.34	27.56
60+	8.06	10.24	11.55	12.26
Total	17.7	17.3	22.3	26.1
Men				
10–14	17.11	15.59	22.49	16.76
15–19	85.32	66.51	58.70	55.27
20–29	97.45	92.63	87.49	90.10
30–39	98.03	97.35	92.83	98.64
40–49	96.16	97.08	91.46	97.66
50–59	95.22	93.94	84.77	91.01
60+	76.03	70.22	58.76	67.79
Total	79.7	72.8	67.9	69.4

* The age-limit given in the statistics has varied over the years. The statistics we have used concern the population over 10 years old.

Source: DANE, census returns, cited by the Employment Mission, Vol. 1, p. 139.

Between 1963 and 1973, the highest rate of female migration was for girls of about 15 years (more than double the rate for boys of the same age) but it was already high for girls of 10.

Analysis of the activity rate for the female workforce (economically active female population/female population of working age) in Table 5 shows that in 1951 the highest rates were those for the 15–19 years age-group and in the later years of reference for the 20–29 years age-group.

In the last decade the proportion of the female population seeking domestic employment has fallen owing to the decrease in migratory flows directed chiefly towards employment for women in domestic service.

The activity rate still plays a significant role in regulating the employment and unemployment of women, as we shall see in greater detail in the next section.

From 1951 to 1964, the activity rate dropped for women under 20 years owing to increased enrolment in education. The peak value, which had previously been located at 15 years, shifted to the 20–25 years age-group and then steadily fell until it reached in 1964 a level just a little higher than in 1951.

During the next decade the curve retained the same shape but the general level of activity rose. A different kind of change has taken place in the last ten years: considerably more young people have remained at school and the activity rate for young people over 20 years has risen more quickly and stayed high. However, the curve no longer displays a second peak after the age of 35 or 40, a common characteristic of developed countries that reflects the resumption of paid work after the children have been educated.

The average rates of economic activity for urban women, after a slight fall owing to greater enrolment in education, have steadily risen and, according to the Employment Mission (sometimes called the Chenery Mission,[1] reached 40 to 42 per cent in 1984–1985, i.e. nearly 10 points higher in the space of ten years in the main cities.

It is important to look more closely at the reasons underlying the increased participation of women in paid activities and the forms it has assumed in order to discover whether trend is a consequence of improved incomes and living conditions or of greater exploitation of women from the most disadvantaged social classes.

For this purpose we shall be referring to available information including comparison with the curves for male activity, the increased enrolment of women in education, changes in family structures and in fertility patterns, comparison with urbanization trends, the characteristics of each region and the relations of each region with its own labour market.

The first thing to be observed is that the activity rates for women increase more sharply than the rates for men, which have remained relatively stable over the last ten years. After falling to 80 per cent in 1951 and to 67 per cent in 1976, the activity rate for men rose slowly to 70 per cent in 1979 and 73 per cent in 1984. This rise is, however, in contrast to that for women, almost exclusively due to demographic factors, namely the arrival at adulthood (after the period of schooling) of those cohorts born during the population boom. In addition there has been a slight tendency in recent years for young people to enter the labour market at a slightly younger age while older men have tended to retire a little later. Women have been affected by the same demographic trend but in a much more marked fashion. Other factors influence this rate.

The first one that springs to mind is the higher enrolment rate, of which women have been the main beneficiaries. The illiteracy rate fell to 33.6 per cent in 1964, then to 16.8 per cent in 1978 and 12.5 per cent in 1985. It dropped even more in the cities: in 1978, 10.4 per cent of women were illiterate but only 7.8 per cent in 1985 (the rates for male city-dwellers are similar: 7.5 per cent in 1978 and 6.4 per cent in 1985).

In 1978 the activity rate for urban women was not closely correlated with their level of schooling, except in the case of those with higher education diplomas (see Table 6).

TABLE 6

STRUCTURE OF THE ACTIVE FEMALE URBAN POPULATION
BY LEVEL OF EDUCATION AND ACTIVITY RATE (1978)

	No education	Primary	Secondary	Higher	Total
	%	%	%	%	%
Urban EAP	10.4	46.6	36.8	6.2	100
Activity rate	31	27.5	30.3	54.2	

Source: Employment Mission.

The studies carried out by the Chenery Mission (Maldonado and Guerrero, 1987) reveal that for the period 1976–1984 the activity rates for women with secondary or higher education rise more quickly than the rates for women without education or with only a few years of primary schooling. This implies a change of attitude towards paid work expressed in a growing supply of female workers, at least in the case of young women with some or complete secondary schooling. In 1984, more than half the women between 20 and 40 years old with primary or secondary education and living in a large city were either engaged in a paid activity or in search of a job.

The increasing participation of women in paid activities does not necessarily imply their access to formal better-paid jobs, as we shall see later, but it does represent a structural trend.

There exist other reasons for this greater tendency to seek paid work, in particular a drop in fertility due in turn to urbanization and education.

TABLE 7

ACTIVITY RATES FOR WOMEN, BY AGE-GROUP
AND LEVEL OF EDUCATION (1976–1984)

Year	Age group 20–29 years	Age group 30–39 years	Level of education
1976	57.8	49.4	
1984	46	47.1	No education
1976	49.3	39.9	
1984	54.7	48.2	Primary
1976	52.4	42	
1984	58.7	54	Secondary
1976	57.6	66	
1984	55.6	76	Higher

Source: Surveys of households, DANE, cited by the Chenery Mission (Maldonado and Guerrero).

In Colombia, the demographic transition followed the country's rapid urbanization in spectacular fashion: in 1964, 48 children were born per 1,000 inhabitants but the figure had dropped to only 25 by 1985, corresponding to a fertility rate of three children per woman.

The complex relationship between the drop in fertility and paid employment for women will not be examined in detail as it does not come within the scope of this study.

It will be noted, however, that urban women have fewer children and are more likely to have a paid job than rural women. Urban women engaged in a paid activity, moreover, have fewer children than the others. Of the women engaged in a paid activity, those working at home have more children than those who work elsewhere (Prieto, 1968; Miro and Martens, 1969; Prada, 1972).

These relationships may be interpreted in different ways: on the one hand, the cities offer more information on birth control than rural areas but they also oblige women to be involved in the production of monetary income. On the other hand, the more educated women will tend to seek paid employment outside their homes and their personal aspirations will discourage the idea of a big family. Less educated women will be unfamiliar with birth control and will therefore have to devote more time to raising their children and find paid employment that enables them to combine their economic and domestic roles.

Paradoxically the women in families with the most dependants, owing to their numerous offspring, are unable to accede to the more highly paid jobs. We shall examine this question more closely when we consider the different forms of employment and income for women.

The aspiration to have a job and the need to supplement the family income fuse in a subtle dialectic in which economic pressures, changing patterns of behaviour and social changes all play important parts. In the last decade there have been some major changes in family structures, which are becoming less stable, less rigid and possibly less tightly knit. The number of separated women, widows or common-law wives is increasing considerably, as Table 8 shows.

TABLE 8

CIVIL STATUS OF URBAN WOMEN (1976–1985)

Civil status	1976	1985
	%	%
Unmarried	42.7	39.0
Cohabitating	5.3	9.8
Married	40.6	34.3
Separated	3.9	9.3
Widowed	7.5	7.5
Total	100	100

Source: Survey of households and census returns, from *The Chenery Mission.*

Owing to their economic responsibilities, the activity rate of these women was already much higher than that of married women and rose by ten percentage points during the decade to reach by 1985, in the case of separated women, a level comparable to the rate for men.

TABLE 9

EVOLUTION OF ACTIVITY RATES FOR URBAN WOMEN,
BY CIVIL STATUS (FOUR CITIES)

	Activity rate	
Civil status	1976	1985
	%	%
Unmarried	42.8	43.1
Cohabitating	30.7	37.4
Married	24.6	34.6
Separated	59.2	68.3
Widowed	22.3	23.9
Total	34.8	42.7

Source: Ibid.

Numerous studies (Ayala and Rey de Marulanda, 1982; Suremain, Dalmazzo and Cardona, 1988) draw attention to a rise in the number of female heads of family, particularly among low-income groups.

According to certain authors the proportion hovers around 10 per cent in the high-income classes while among the poorest social classes it is shown by surveys to lie between 20 and 30 per cent.

We should define what we mean by 'head of household'. In the traditional definition the man is generally regarded as the head of the household and it is only when he is absent that the woman is so referred to. Women heads of household would therefore be women who do not live with an adult male. According to a survey on households conducted in Bogota in 1982, only 1 per cent of 'spouses' were men and 99 per cent were women.

In our view, however, the growth of a woman's family responsibilities involves much more than simply finding herself 'without a man', through separation, through widowhood, or as an unmarried mother. The couple, whether married or living in cohabitation, is more precarious and more unstable than in the past. A survey dating from 1970 conducted in the working-class districts of 15 Colombian cities (Suremain, Dalmazzo and Cardona, 1988) found that 22 per cent of the women were mothers who were unmarried, separated or widows while the other 78 per cent were living with a spouse either in marriage or in a consensual union (48 and 30 per cent respectively).

The latter were asked if their spouses were absent from the home often or for long periods and 38 per cent of them answered 'yes'. It may therefore be assumed that these women have to cope alone with all levels of family responsibility during the absence of their spouses. These responsibilities are affective, material and probably economic in nature. Though it would take a more detailed study to prove that nearly 40 per cent of the women living with a spouse are in reality the head of the family, at least as far as stability and parental authority are concerned, it may be deduced that the moral and economic responsibilities of women, particularly in the working-class sectors, are much heavier than the conventional categories and usual statistics suggest. We are therefore justified in considering that the reasons which motivate women to seek a monetary income spring as much from these obligations as from new aspirations engendered by better education.

There exist few studies that explain the fundamental reason for the increase in separations in the working-class sectors. The impact of education, which has induced a radical change in the aspirations of a great many women, is much more marked in the working classes than among more advantaged groups. The breakdown of the traditional family structures on account of migration, and the consequent lessening of social constraints, is surely an important factor. It also seems to us that men under economic pressures and in search of better living and working conditions adopt a strategy of personal survival and mobility in spite of their family responsibilities. Women who act likewise during their years of youth change radically once they have children.

Certain sociological studies (Rico, 1986) draw attention to the dramatic increase in the number of adolescent unmarried mothers, especially in outlying working-class districts. More permissive moral attitudes lead to early sexual relations among the young. The absence of any sex education together with the lack of reference to or discussion of the subject in the family, itself in crisis, leads to an increase in unwanted pregnancies. Only a minority of unmarried mothers get married. The rest are abandoned by their companions, rejected by their parents and do not receive any aid from the State. They are unable to complete their schooling and in consequence are unable to provide for their own and their children's needs.

This study estimated at 500,000 the number of unmarried mothers in Colombia in 1985, 60 per cent of them having had their first child before the age of 20. In Bogota the number of unmarried mothers between 15 and 19 years old was said to be about 15,000.

Though precise figures are lacking, social and political violence is also contributing to a rise in the number of widows and separated women at an age that is steadily getting younger. Death by homicide has become the primary cause of male mortality. The rates range between three and 15 homicides a year per 1,000 inhabitants depending on the city, with an annual increase of 20 to 50 per cent.

Single-parent families have more difficulties than those which are able to unite the contributions of two or more adults for their economic or emotional equilibrium. These difficulties are further aggravated when the head of the family is a woman since in almost all cases her burden will be heavier (responsibility for her children, paid work in addition to work in the home) and her resources more limited (less well-paid jobs, more limited access to housing, credit, social security, etc.).

The increase in the number of women who are heads of household may therefore be regarded as an indicator of the impoverishment of the population and of the feminization of poverty.

This affirmation is corroborated by other worrying indicators. Household income is lower for homes headed by a woman. Infant mortality rates are also higher when the mother is head of the family and has a low educational level, when she works away from home or when she is the only female presence in the home (Ordoñez, 1987).

In the total or virtual absence of State help towards some of the child-related tasks that women have to perform, in particular the care and minding of young children, the extended family has ceased to play a significant role. The ever-increasing work-load of women adversely affects the physical and moral health of the children. Far from holding the mothers to blame for this situation, steps should be taken to work out appropriate solutions. We shall describe later how the women themselves are trying to find an answer to this problem by organizing themselves through community work.

Returning to Table 9, it will be noticed that the rise in activity rates is also notable for married women and women living in cohabitation.

The model in which the man is the sole economic support of the family is therefore becoming much less common. Whereas only 25 per cent of wives and female companions declared themselves to be 'economically active' in 1976, the proportion had reached 35 per cent by 1985.

At the same time the activity rate of unmarried children of working age rose during the same period from 34 to 43 per cent, revealing the abandonment of schooling and/or a rise in the number of student-workers.

For all these reasons we think that a difficult economic situation has prompted the various members of the family to join in the efforts of the head of the household to generate monetary income. Thus the breakdown of traditional models and changes in the distribution of responsibility for ensuring the survival of the family group have been accentuated by economic pressures.

Certain economists (Ayala and Rey de Marulanda, 1979 and 1982) have called this phenomenon 'intensive participation' in the labour market and shown that more and more members of the same family group are seeking jobs in the hope of increasing the family income.

In the survey mentioned above, conducted among 2,000 women in the working-class districts of 15 cities in Colombia, this 'intensive participation' emerges very clearly.

In half of the households there is only one source of income, which is provided in 73 per cent of cases by a man and in 27 per cent of cases by a woman. In 80 per cent of the households the men are still the principal (in number and probably in amount) providers of income, but the role of women, who make a contribution in 52 per cent of households, is far from negligible.

Gainful activities by women have not increased at the same rate in each city. In Colombia, the regions offer sharp contrasts in agriculture, industry and culture. Bogota, the capital, concentrates the majority of industrial activities and services while Medellin, also an industrial city, has a large female workforce in the textile industry. Cali goes in for intensive cropping on capitalist lines and for trade while Barranquilla is a port and business pole distinguished by its African culture and its hinterland of intensive stock-breeding.

The following table shows how the particular activities of each region affect the participation of women in the labour market.

TABLE 10

ECONOMICALLY ACTIVE FEMALE POPULATION, WORKING AGE POPULATION AND ACTIVITY
RATE (EAP/WAP) IN THE FOUR MAJOR CITIES IN 1984

City (metropolitan areas)	EAP (thousands)	WAP (thousands)	Activity rate %
Bogota	749	1,715	43.6
Medellin	271	756	35.8
Cali	226	548	41.2
Barranquilla	145	434	33.4
Total	1,391	3,453	40.3

Source: Survey of households, DANE, 1984.

The major differences revealed by the table suggest that it is the employment structure and cultural factors which encourage women to seek a paid activity.

We shall now examine the question by considering the various labour markets and the place of women in each case.

TABLE 11

CHARACTERISTICS OF THE FAMILIES OF WORKERS IN THE FORMAL AND INFORMAL
SECTORS BETWEEN 1974 AND 1984 (%)

	1974		1984	
	Informal	Formal	Informal	Formal
Men	53.5	70.4	60.7	64.9
Women	46.5	29.6	39.3	35.1
Total	100	100	100	100
Place in family				
Head of household	40.0	50.3	44.4	49.0
Spouse	8.5	7.5	13.2	11.3
Child	16.3	26.8	23.9	28.9
Others	35.1	15.4	18.5	10.7
Total	100	100	100	100

Source: Surveys of households in 1974 and 1984, cited by François Bourguignon (1979) and Hugo Lopez (1987) respectively.

In these studies, based on the DANE surveys of households, the informal sector is defined as independent workers (excluding the liberal professions), domestic employees, and the workers and heads of private enterprises with fewer than five persons (1974) or fewer than ten persons (1984) (in 1984 the difference between the two was insignificant).

A comparison over time brings out some apparent contradictions between the two surveys.

On the one hand we see an increase in the participation of spouses (99 per cent women) and children that is more marked in the informal than in the formal sector and thus confirms the previous hypothesis. But we also find an increase in the number of heads of household in the informal sector, which suggests that the expansion of the informal sector is not just the consequence of the arrival of 'secondary' workers (especially women).

This is confirmed by the figures by sex: the men/women ratio in each sector evolves in such a way as to suggest that women are able to find only informal jobs. The difference in 1984 is not so marked as in 1974, indicating that the difficulty experienced by women in gaining access to formal jobs is tending to become more general.

The proportion of women working in the informal sector rather than in salaried jobs is tending to grow. It rose from 55 per cent in 1974 to 60 per cent in 1984. At the same time the number of men in the informal sector increased sharply (40 per cent in 1974 and 54 per cent in 1984) with the result that the gap between the sexes has narrowed considerably in this sector.

This apparent return to a more balanced situation is due more to the loss of jobs for men in the formal sector, which has driven them into the informal sector, than to the access of women to paid jobs. This is borne out by the general recognition that women (and young people) are more affected by unemployment than adult men, as the following table shows.

TABLE 12

ACTIVITY AND UNEMPLOYMENT RATES FOR MEN AND WOMEN
IN BOGOTÁ IN 1978 AND 1984

	1978 %	1984 %
Men		
Activity rate	65.9	70.0
Unemployment rate	6.2	9.5
Women		
Activity rate	37.1	42.3
Unemployment rate	9.1	15.6

Source: Survey of households, DANE, cited by Ana Rico, 1985.

The gap has widened between the years in question, with unemployment rising by three percentage points in the case of men and by six and a half in the case of women.

It would therefore appear that the crisis is driving men towards self-employed occupations or small enterprises. Women, on the other hand,

are caught up in the same movement but are finding it increasingly difficult to create self-employed occupations with the result that their unemployment rate is rising.

It would be a mistake to think that the situation is static; there is in
fact considerable mobility between the two sectors that can be explained
by life cycles (Lopez, 1987): most of those under 20 years of age (70 per
cent) begin working life in the informal sector as family helps, employees
in small businesses or domestic staff. Between the ages of 20 and 30 they
find jobs in the formal sector and then, as they get older, an increasing
number return to the informal sector to set up on their own as self-employed persons or as the heads of small businesses. Table 13 allows us to
distinguish the cycle for men from that for women. It can be argued that,
owing to the lower participation of women in paid activities, their return
to the informal sector does not take place under the same conditions as
for men. For women the conditions are certainly less favourable since
they are unable to benefit to the same extent as men from the accumulation of a little capital, social benefits or practical experience, all of which
would make it much easier for them to establish their own businesses.
For women the opportunities for finding work in the formal sector generally arise between the age of 20 and 30, a period that is not long enough
for them to build up the same amount of capital and experience as men.

TABLE 13

DISTRIBUTION OF ACTIVE FEMALE POPULATION BY AGE BETWEEN FORMAL AND INFOR-
MAL SECTORS IN FOUR CITIES (1984)

Age-group	Bogotá		Medellin		Cali		Barran-quilla		Total		
	FS	IS	FS	IS	FS	IS	FS	IS	FS	IS	%
10–19 years	35	65	15	85	35	65	27	73	29	71	100
20–39 years	65	35	55	45	54	46	59	41	60	40	100
40 years & over	38	62	18	82	22	78	26	74	29	71	100
Total women	38	62	33	67	37	63	35	65	36	64	100
Total EAP	45	55	49	51	42	58	38	62	45	55	100

Source: Ana Rico, 1987, based on the 1984 DANE survey of households.

Though Table 12 shows that the informal sector has attracted a
larger proportion of men owing to the crisis in the formal sector, it nevertheless remains the principal source of paid work for women (65 per cent
of women are engaged in an 'informal' activity).

Table 13 shows regional differences; Medellin, for example, the city with the largest number of salaried jobs is also the city with the strongest discrimination against women: only 33 per cent of women obtain a formal job and the proportion reaches only 55 per cent even for the 20–39 years age-group. At Barranquilla, on the other hand, where the employment structure is more informal for both sexes, the situation of women hardly differs from that of men.

It would therefore appear that women are less discriminated against (in terms at least of fewer opportunities for paid work) in local contexts where the formal sector is less firmly established. This amounts to a levelling down: the more industry expands, the greater the difference between the sexes, and the more informal activities expand under the impact of the economic crisis the more women participate in them in the same conditions of poverty as men.

This hypothesis is based on the available figures and is therefore dependent on their reliability. However, other data prepared by the same author on the basis of the same survey of households appear to show that the reality in Medellin might be different. According to these data, the proportion of jobs for women in Medellin in 1984 was 51 per cent in the informal sector and 49 per cent in the formal sector (and not 67 and 33 per cent respectively as shown in Table 13). That would suggest that there is no discrimination between the sexes concerning the opportunities for salaried employment.

The UNICEF report on 'Poverty and Development' gives totally different figures even though it uses the same source: according to that report, informal jobs for women in Medellin came to only 36 per cent, i.e. essentially the same as the formal labour force.

As we are unable to consult the DANE's original magnetic tapes in order to check these contradictions for technical reasons, we shall not come down clearly on one side or the other, especially as the data in question are frequently utilized by various authors. All this illustrates the difficulty of understanding the dynamics of the employment market for women in the absence of relevant data.

More light is cast by an analysis of each branch of activity: the predominance of industry in Medellin makes it possible to absorb a large number of women workers, especially in the textile industry. However, our calculations based on the first set of figures (Ana Rico, 1985) show that although 62 per cent of the industrial jobs for women are of the formal type (and 38 per cent informal), women occupy only 30 per cent of the formal jobs in that branch.

When, in a particular branch, the productive sector appears to offer more opportunities for formal jobs to women, it is the men who derive the most benefit. The following table sums up the findings for Medellin.

TABLE 14

FORMAL AND INFORMAL EMPLOYMENT IN INDUSTRY

IN MEDELLIN 1984

Industry	Formal sector	% %	Informal sector	% %	Total	% %
Women	50,000	30 (62)	31,285	42 (38)	81,285	34 (100)
Men	116,580	70 (73)	43,020	58 (27)	59,600	66 (100)
Total	166,580	100 (69)	74,305	100 (31)	240,885	100 (100)
All employment						
Women	125,245	33 (49)	130,355	36 (51)	255,600	34 (100)
Men	257,350	67 (53)	230,050	64 (47)	487,400	66 (100)
Total	382,595	100 (52)	360,405	100 (48)	743,000	100 (100)

Source: Calculations by the author based on the DANE survey of households, cited by Rico, 1985.

We would recall that the previous figures gave the distribution of women in employment as 49 per cent in the informal sector and 51 per cent in salaried employment.

Table 15, next page, gives similar data for all branches of activity in the four main metropolitan areas.

The branches with the most female employees are industry, commerce and the hotel trade and public and private services; these branches account for between 75 and 82 per cent of all employment depending on the city. The branches with the highest proportion of women are public and private services (56 per cent women in Bogotá, 45 per cent in Cali, 53 per cent in Medellin and 48 per cent in Barranquilla), commerce and the hotel trade (44 per cent, 42 per cent, 36 per cent and 35 per cent respectively) and, in third position, industry with proportions in the vicinity of 35 per cent depending on the city.

The most highly feminized branches of the informal sector are not the ones with the highest proportion of informal occupations. For these four cities the informal sector accounts for 76 per cent of occupations in commerce and 58 per cent in construction. The informal sector branch that employs the most women, especially in the cities, is that of private services, which employs 64 per cent women in Bogotá, 51 per cent in Cali, 60 per cent in Medellin and 52 per cent in Barranquilla.

Industry comes in second position (except in Bogotá) and commerce in third. There is a high proportion of women in the micro-industry sector in Cali and Medellin. Available statistics are insufficient for a more thorough analysis of the industrial branches that rely on a female workforce. However, it may be assumed that the main branches concerned are food processing and textiles. The wood, paper, chemical, metal and mechanical

TABLE 15
DISTRIBUTION OF THE WORKING POPULATION BY BRANCH AND BY SECTOR IN FOUR METROPOLITAN AREAS (1984)

Branch	Bogotá			Cali			Medellín			Barranquilla			4 metrop areas % informal employ.
	Bogotá employ. struct.	Women in IS%	Women in branch %	Bogotá employ. struct.	Women in IS%	Women in branch %	Bogotá employ. struct.	Women in IS%	Women in branch %	Bogotá employ. struct.	Women in IS%	Women in branch %	
Agriculture	1.2	12.6	30.0	1.2	4.2	21.2	1.3	3.2	5.0	0.9	—	5.4	55.1
Mines and quarrying	0.4	—	22.0	0.2	—	11.0	0.2	—	—	1.0	—	19.5	13.4
Industry	23.1	40.5	36.0	27.0	42.6	35.5	32.2	42.3	33.6	18.8	36.0	34.1	42.3
Elec., gas and water	0.6	—	13.0	0.4	—	—	0.9	—	7.5	1.0	—	7.7	1.9
Consturction	7.2	3.0	6.0	5.6	2.9	3.3	7.2	1.7	4.2	4.8	5.5	8.2	58.4
Commerce and hotel trade	23.8	43.3	44.4	27.0	40.5	42.0	24.1	33.4	36.8	30.3	34.0	35.0	76.0
Transport and communic.	6.4	5.0	14.0	5.2	3.0	11.2	5.4	2.3	6.1	7.5	4.9	8.7	51.6
Financial services	8.9	36.3	35.0	45.9	37.2	29.1	5.5	29.5	32.8	5.1	24.1	35.3	27.8
State & priv. services	28.3	64.0	56.4	27.9	50.5	45.0	5.5	29.5	32.8	5.1	24.1	35.3	53.5
TOTAL	100	42	40	100	39	36	100	36	34	100	36	35	55

Source: 1984 DANE survey of households, cited by Ana Rico (1986). Figures for Bogotá calculated by author.

engineering industries involve activities dominated by men.

When we examine the proportion of informal occupations in the four cities we find that the branches with the largest informal sector are not the most feminized: food processing and drinks and textiles employ 39 per cent and 51 per cent of informal workers respectively as against 73 per cent in the furniture and wood industry.

We may therefore assume that certain branches recruit their formal workforce among the male population and their informal workforce among women. Certain others such as construction, mechanical engineering, wood products, etc. employ men only both in their formal sectors and in the 'informal' workshops and small businesses.

These relationships could be further illustrated by a detailed study by branch of activity, particularly in the case of the textile and food industries. In the textile industry, subcontracting arrangements are probably common and provide a great many women with home employment whereas formal and informal production in the food industry, in both cases on a small scale, are certainly interwoven to a much more limited extent.

A detailed look at the services branch shows that 93 per cent of personal services are of the informal type (Lopez, 1987), a large proportion of them being domestic service, which accounts for 6 per cent of total employment in the four cities, 40 per cent of jobs in the personal services branch and 21 per cent of all services. We shall examine later the characteristics of and current programmes for this type of job. It is important for our purposes because it is an activity which is 95 per cent exercised by women and plays a special role in regulating the level of employment and unemployment of the unskilled female labour force.

Lastly, one should note the influence of the commerce and hotel trade branch (24 to 30 per cent of total employment depending on the city) which, as we have already observed, is the branch containing the largest number of small enterprises. Both large and small businesses employ a high proportion of women. This branch does not reveal a big difference between the sexes with regard to participation in the informal sector and in total employment. On the contrary, it would appear that the proportion of women in informal occupations is one percentage point lower than in total employment, suggesting that their participation in the formal sector of that branch is likely to be at least four or five percentage points higher.

It may therefore be asserted that commerce is the most attractive branch of activity for women in both sectors. When it is realized that commerce is a branch in which 76 per cent of jobs are generated by enterprises employing up to ten persons (including 39 per cent working in enterprises of two to five persons and only 13 per cent working in enterprises of six to ten persons), the high proportion of women in this branch, in which activities are very scattered, hints at difficult negotiations and working conditions for women.

One also gets the impression that other branches are completely dominated by men whatever the type of employment relations. This hypothesis will be confirmed when we analyse the relative incomes, by branch and by category of job, of men and of women.

TABLE 16

INCOME DIFFERENCES BETWEEN MEN AND WOMEN IN THE PRINCIPAL BRANCHES OF ACTIVITY (%) IN FOUR METROPOLITAN AREAS (1984)

Branch	Bogotá	Cali	Medellin	Barranquilla
Industry	+42	+52	+40	+50
Commerce	+43	+54	+52	+49
State and personal services	+67	+65	+64	+83
Average all branches	+45	+51	+43	+61

Source: Based on DANE survey of households.

Unfortunately no figures by sector of activity exist that might explain in greater detail the mechanisms that bring about such differences in income. It will be noted that the services branch, in which women are in the majority, is the branch with the most notable differences (both in the formal and in the informal sectors); next comes commerce and the hotel trade which, as already stated, is three-quarters informal. In manufacturing industry the contrasts are not quite so sharp, with Medellin apparently the city with the least obvious differences in income between men and women working in that branch.

On the basis of prior observations concerning job opportunities in industry, it may be assumed that, despite the limitations mentioned, the impact of the formal sector is tending to narrow the gap between men and women as a result of regulations on minimum wages and social benefits. The differences are probably greater in the informal sector because of differences in attitude in its various segments, the different proportions of women in the various industries, and differences in level of education between the two sexes and the two sectors, as we shall see.

Table 17 shows the distribution of the different categories of employment for the four big cities.

This table shows that although 92 per cent of self-employment is regarded as informal, the same does not hold for wage-earners (37 per cent in the informal sector and 63 per cent in the formal sector). The formal sector is composed of 95 per cent wage-earners and 5 per cent self-employed persons as against 45 per cent wage-earners and 55 per cent self-employed persons in the informal sector.

The proportion of women in each category varies greatly according to

TABLE 17

DISTRIBUTION OF EMPLOYMENT CATEGORIES IN THE FOUR METROPOLITAN AREAS
(1984)

Category of employment	For-mal sector	Infor-mal sector	Total	% inf. sector	% women in info. sector			
					Bog.	Cali	Med.	B/Q
A.								
Self-employed	5.5	54.6	32.5	92	-	-	-	-
Independent	3.9	42.5	25.1	93	32	35	32	30
Bosses	1.6	6.9	4.5	84	19	20	15	12
Family help	0	5.2	2.8	100	62	65	59	52
B.								
Wage-earners	94.5	45.4	67.5	37	-	-	-	-
Workers & clerical staff	94.5	35.1	61.9	31	35	30	28	25
Domestic staff	0	10.2	5.6	100	97	96	97	96
C. Total	100	100	100	54.9	40	39.3	36.3	36.4

Source: Hugo Lopez, based on the 1984 DANE survey of households, and Ana Rico, who used the same survey.

the city: between 30 and 35 per cent of the independent workers (42 per cent of the informal sector) in the informal sector and a similar proportion of the workers and clerical staff (35 per cent of the informal sector). Women are more numerous in the family help category non-remunerated and especially in the domestic staff category (respectively 52 to 65 per cent and 96 to 97 per cent according to the city). On the other hand they are rather underrepresented in the category of heads of small businesses (12 to 20 per cent according to the city).

In terms of income, the biggest differences between the sexes are to be found in the categories with the highest proportion of women, thus confirming the separation of the two labour markets and the existence of jobs 'for women' and jobs 'for men' and of particular conditions, especially in regard to wages, in each case.

There are almost no women in the category of heads of small businesses but the difference is less marked in the case of independent workers and especially domestic staff: the few males in this category (doormen, guards) earn wages which are nearly double those of female domestic staff.

In the case of workers and clerical staff we may observe once again that, by virtue of the current regulations and the application of the minimum wage in respect of these categories, the difference is less marked: in Colombia in 1978 (Rico, 1987), 35 per cent of urban women and 47 per

TABLE 18

AVERAGE INCOME DIFFERENCES MEN/WOMEN BY CATEGORY OF EMPLOYMENT IN FOUR
METROPOLITAN AREAS (1989)

Category of employment	Bogotá Income men/women (%)	Cali Income men/women (%)	Medellin Income men/women (%)	Barranquilla Income men/women (%)
Independent workers	+72	+79	+117	+63
Bosses	+29	+16	+ 12	+ 7
Family helps	—	—	—	—
Workers and clerical staff	+19	+21	+ 16	+26
Domestic staff	+122	+89	+102	+30

cent of men earned the minimum wage (though 41 per cent of women had an income lower than the minimum wage as against 15 per cent of men).

As for the category of family helps, there are no statistics concerning their income since they are by definition persons who are unpaid. More than 60 per cent of this category is composed of women (spouses or relations of the owner of the small enterprise) while the remaining 35 to 40 per cent are male children or relations undergoing their apprenticeship. Here the most appropriate comparison to be made is between their lack of income and the income of the 'boss'. A survey carried out among women working in small businesses has revealed that the relationship is not the same in families running small businesses owned by a woman as in those running workshops owned by a man (Ramirez and Gomez, 1987).

The fact is, when the father of the family is the owner of a small business it frequently happens that the rest of the family, especially his wife, collaborate as family helps. When the wife is the owner, however, the rest of the family work at other occupations and she does not generally benefit from their assistance. In other words, it is more difficult for a woman to set up a family business and any workshop or business directed by her is necessarily small in size since it has to depend on her own efforts alone with, at the most, the assistance of her children.

The biggest obstacle to the creation by women of an activity of the informal type is their low level of education. In the informal sector the women have a lower level of education than the men whereas we find quite the opposite situation in the formal sector. With the knowledge that men have a slightly higher average level, it can be deduced that the formal sector is much more selective for women than for men. Women with little or no schooling are rejected towards the informal sector whereas men are distributed less selectively between the two sectors.

TABLE 19
LEVEL OF EDUCATION BY SEX AND BY SECTOR OF ACTIVITY
IN FOUR METROPOLITAN AREAS (1984)
(average number of years of schooling)

	Bogotá	*Cali*	*Medellin*	*Barranquilla*
Formal sector				
Men	8.7	6.8	6.2	7.2
Women	9.4	7.3	7.0	8.0
Informal sector				
Men	6.6	5.1	5.1	5.1
Women	5.9	4.8	4.6	4.5
*Per cent of illiterate persons**				
Men				
Formal sector	1.3	1.0	2.6	2.3
Informal sector	3.1	2.6	3.7	6.5
Women				
Formal sector	0.9	0.7	0.7	1.4
Informal sector	6.0	5.6	7.7	9.5

* Percentage of economically active population of the corresponding sex in the sector concerned.
Source: DANE survey of households, 1984, based on Rico, 1985.

The greater degree of selection in the case of women is probably related to the fact that the range of employment opportunities open to them is more limited than for men. A research worker (Alison MacEwen Scott) has shown in the case of Peru that the remunerated activities of women were confined to 13 out of 107 identified occupations, much fewer than in the case of men. It is easier for a man, even without any vocational qualifications, to get a job in the formal sector. By contrast, women have to 'merit' such a job or prove their capacity in accordance with more demanding standards. We shall return to this problem in our discussion of training programmes and their impact on the improvement of working conditions for women.

Though access to a job in the formal sector is selective and based on criteria of age, sex and level of education (these three criteria being interlinked), it is in fact no less restrictive in the informal sector.

We have already seen that women do not find it easy to achieve the status of a 'boss' and are to be found in the categories of wage-earning clerical staff, family helps or domestic staff.

Studies of the informal sector reveal that conditions of subsistence, work and income vary considerably according to status of each worker.

In various research papers, Hugo Lopez (Lopez et al., 1986) has used statistical series stretching over a decade or so to study the sensitivity to economic cycles of each category of worker. Unfortunately the statistics available did not distinguish between the formal and informal sectors regarding the labour market for workers and clerical staff; nor do there exist complete series on the employment of women. It is possible, however, to extrapolate a few conclusions in regard to women from the general data.

On the labour market for workers and clerical staff the gap between job offers and applications for employment is chiefly expressed in terms of open unemployment. Wages are determined on the basis of the general conditions of productivity but also take into account the regulations and collective agreements which fix the medium-term level of the minimum wage. Real wages may be held down by inflation and policies of austerity but do not act as an adjustment mechanism between supply and demand. Studies on the subject show that, in the informal sector and despite minimal social protection and implementation of standards, the wages of wage-earners are relatively inelastic in a downward direction and that the minimum wage serves at least nominally as a fairly general reference. The result is that in a period of economic crisis this market contracts and suffers from as much unemployment as the formal sector.

This does not apply, however, to the category of independent workers for whom there is no such thing as unemployment in the strict sense. Employment increases during periods of expansion but also during periods of crisis.

It increases when the demand from the formal sector for goods and services increases at a time of economic expansion but it also increases during periods of economic recession because it then becomes a refuge for wage-earners from the formal and informal sectors. However, when the crisis leads to a drop in the demand for consumer goods and services the incomes of this group of workers are affected immediately. Lopez states that in 1981, at the end of a period of expansion, the real income of an independent worker (excluding the liberal professions) was higher than the average wage of workers and clerical staff but that it dropped by 16 per cent during the recession that followed.

It may therefore be assumed that some of the women wage-earners in the informal sector (of which women, it will be remembered, form one-third) will find their jobs threatened by periods of crisis while others in independent occupations (another third of the informal sector) will find their incomes affected.

The study of independent workers by Fernando Ramirez Gomez (Ramirez, 1985) has shown them to be very numerous but also engaged in activities that had many links with the formal sector.

In the informal sector these workers represent some 53 per cent of the people engaged in commerce, 33 per cent in services, 39 per cent in industry, 47 per cent in construction and 56 per cent in transportation.

Their growth in number is the result of two types of socio-economic process:

- the persistence of precapitalist forms of labour relations, which have acquired a 'functional' pattern in the economic system;
- the development of work at home as a result of the trend to deconcentrate certain productive activities and services.

The survival of the structure and processes of precapitalist production can be seen chiefly in retail shopkeeping, particularly in the working-class districts and city centres, and in the services sector (electricians, plumbers, etc.).

In the case of retailing, the interrelationship with the formal sector is located at the level of distribution, since most goods are produced by large firms or by production of the formal type. The studies on local commerce and itinerant vendors, carried out by Lopez in 1988, distinguish two segments that operate in different ways. One of them reflects the consumer needs of the low-income working-class population and takes the form of local commerce and commerce in certain parts of the city centre where the shops selling cheaper products are concentrated; the other takes advantage of the intense circulation of pedestrians and motorists (in the city centre and at certain crossroads) to sell retail or even in single units common consumer goods such as cigarettes, fruit or sundry objects. This type of activity reflects the need for employment or self-employment of the least skilled persons. The prices charged are generally higher than those of the cheaper shops but these vendors benefit from being located on the consumer's route.

Informal distribution is rarely dovetailed with informal production since at least one link in the chain (particularly wholesalers for the produce of peasant farmers) is of the formal capitalist type.

Where women are concerned, independent work seems to be more closely related to the subsistence economy and to the lower and more fragile incomes in the commerce and services branches. In the case of small-scale industry, women appear to work at home to a greater extent and to depend on subcontractual relations, particularly in the clothing and shoe industries. It is very rare for them to be independent and the owners of their capital. In either case they are in a highly precarious and more dependent situation, even within the informal sector.

Moreover, when we examine the relationship between the various categories of informal workers, we see that over a quarter of independent workers make use of members of their family or salaried workers on a partial or temporary basis. As we know that two-thirds of non-remunerated family helps are women, it may be said that men who work independently receive the invisible assistance of their wives and children. On the other hand, women who are independent are able to count only on the assistance of their children. The work of children is therefore closely associated with the independent activities of their mother. These forms of

219

activity are to be found in particular in commerce and catering (66 per cent) and to a lesser extent in small-scale industry (20 per cent) and services (8 per cent).

The situation of domestic staff is highly complex: though subject to a steady long-term decline, the number of those in this category tends to increase again in pace with the alternating periods of growth and recession. In times of recession, household incomes fall and families employing a servant tend to cut out that expense. However, unemployment and the fall in income of women with poor vocational qualifications (the youngest and the oldest) cause these women to offer their services on the market for a lower wage. As labour regulations for this category of wage-earner are not properly applied, their wages are often reduced considerably. Those employed accept not only lower wages but also part-time work. As a result this category undergoes internal reorganization: the youngest women offer their services as 'living-in' employees with lower wages in an effort to resolve at the same time their problems of food and of accommodation. They therefore content themselves with a meagre income. The oldest women offer their services by the day and work for several employers, accepting a total number of hours that amounts to less than a week (calculation of the minimum daily wage requires that six days per week be worked in order to earn the monthly minimum).

In consequence unemployment hardly shows up at all for this category. The unemployment of women is underestimated, partly because domestic work is regarded as a non-skilled part-time occupation of a temporary nature done while waiting to find a regular job or to set up more profitably on one's own.

Owing to the absence of child care facilities, the large disparities in income between social groups, the very limited impact of modernization on household work and the little change in the roles played by the two sexes, women in the middle and upper classes will continue to employ a person to ease their work in the home.

As the most important driving force behind the rural exodus of women since the beginning of the century, domestic service is not about to become a thing of the past. So long as poverty persists, the women of the urban working classes will continue to offer the strength of their arms for next to nothing. In the next section we shall see how certain programmes have come into existence to protect this sector of activity.

On the basis of earlier observations showing that the informal sector is unlikely to absorb urban unemployment (and when it does, it does so under highly unfavourable social conditions), most economists distinguish in general two subsectors (cf. Lopez, 1987):

The first subsector sets up barriers to entry in the form of particular requirements in respect of technology, capital and experience. It offers goods and services of a higher quality to meet a demand that is elastic. It is often a product of the dynamics of the formal economy, which 'deregulates' or decentralizes its wage-earners while maintaining close relations with them. It constitutes an alternative not to unemployment but to salaried employment. Some people in this sector obtain a higher income then wage-earners with similar qualifications but this income is vulnerable and subject to ups and downs in the economic situation. The second subsector is characterized by the absence of barriers to entry (or very low barriers) and by the production of goods and services of lesser quality; it is therefore in a situation of stiff competition and great dependence. The activities of this subsector would appear to be motivated to a greater extent by the need to survive and offer less potential for capital accumulation. They tend to be connected with commerce and services more than with industrial production.

This internal division within the informal sector would appear, according to the evidence or direct information we have accumulated in the foregoing pages, to overlap with a division by sex.

There consequently seem to be more women engaged in subsistence activities that are less technical, less profitable and less 'functional' in regard to the system. The income they derive from these activities is therefore more vulnerable and more irregular yet the women concerned are not protected from overt unemployment.

On the other hand there are more men in the 'functional' subsector aimed at the production of goods with a higher value added and the demand for men is more stable. If a man loses his job in the formal sector despite his greater level of protection, and along with many others has to work in the informal sector, his working conditions in that sector are less unfavourable than in the case of women.

If the crisis leads to greater poverty among men the danger will be real because it does little to mitigate the differences between the sexes (as Hugo Lopez points out). The disparities tend to accentuate the internal division within the informal sector and force women towards activities unlikely to increase or consolidate their incomes or to encourage their participation in the development process.

We shall in fact see that this situation is partly due to a relationship between production and reproduction that differs according to sex.

The production–reproduction relationship or the role of women in the urban economy

The following thoughts are based on research in Colombia conducted by the author as a member of a multidisciplinary team. The main purpose of this research was to analyse the conditions of social reproduction in urban working-class districts with particular attention to the role of women in the invisible day-to-day running of urban services (Suremain, Cardona and Dalmazzo, 1988).

It is important to begin with the conclusions of this research. We shall then describe in more detail and by means of examples the activities of women in the informal sector. The data so far collected appear to suggest that women have more limited access than men to formal jobs and that they are disadvantaged in relation to men even within the informal sector. Our aim of course is to help them achieve working conditions similar to those of men.

This required reflection of an advanced order: all activities that are socially necessary for a better quality of life needed to be explored. We needed a new epistemology, that is to say, we needed to reconsider the basic concepts relating to productive and non-productive activities and even the concept of work itself.

The old traditional simplification according to which 'productive work' means remunerated work and the family is regarded as a unit of consumption is still dominant.

The expansion of remunerated labour relations, in the form of the wage-earning system in dependent capitalist societies, has separated the place of production from the place of reproduction. Although such has been the predominant trend, this separation has not become established in every sector and, as we have seen, major companies have even fostered a move in the opposite direction by again encouraging work at home.

In practice, working-class families are showing that they regard their homes not just as accommodation but as a potentially productive investment that can always be rented out or transformed into a 'shop' or workshop.

The term 'remunerated activities' automatically suggests an ideal of full wage-earning employment, as if the basic objective of development were to provide a regular job in a big company for eight hours a day for the entire population (both men and women) (cf. Neuma Aguiar, 1984). Any person who does not fit into this pattern is considered 'underemployed' or in 'disguised unemployment'.

One consequence of this view is that the remunerated activity of women is regarded as marginal, residual or in the best of cases a negligible complement to the activity of men.

The full range of family strategies aimed at improving living conditions, in particular those of women need to be reconsidered. These strategies are not confined to the economic sphere or even to social movements in the public eye; they develop essentially in the shadows of daily life, in the life of the district, in the networks of solidarity and in the monetary and non-monetary transfers between families that are related or friends.

For a poor urban family, access to housing does not depend only on the monetary contributions of its members. Such investment is but the starting-point of a period of consolidation that may last from eight to 15 years and in some cases even longer. In the big and medium-sized cities of Colombia the problem of housing gives rise to a wide variety of solutions, ranging from the most spontaneous and illegal to the most formal of methods: 'invasions' of building land that obviate payment for the plot, 'pirate developments' that presuppose payment for the plot and a minimal ground plan, serviced sites that include the basic infrastructure, and 'minimum units' that include basic sanitation and a single room, etc. Starting from the initial rudimentary accommodation and going on to a finished home in a district equipped with public and social services takes at least a generation and sometimes even longer. The lack of facilities and of a minimum of comfort during this long period of time means that much extra work for the women. If their home is not connected to the mains water supply, if there is a power cut, if the streets are muddy, if there is no fuel to cook with, no welfare centre, no sewers or rubbish collection, the women suffer the consequences. This adds considerably to their household work. The whole subject is covered in minute detail in the study mentioned above.

This extra effort on the part of women can be said to have served in the past to mitigate the effects of the urban crisis and rendered 'livable' districts that have sprung up spontaneously without water, electricity or any kind of infrastructure. It is also through their efforts that the purchasing power of the monetary income earned by the men is considerably augmented and the family's living standard improved.

Women add to the monetary inputs of the men in several ways:

* through unpaid housework;
* through extra housework to obtain basic services (water, fuel, electricity, health services, kindergartens, etc.);
* through production in the home of useful objects, particularly clothes;
* through monetary and non-monetary savings (e.g. repair of clothing, salvaging of objects, search for the cheapest places to buy things, etc.);
* through active participation in community activities and in organizations fighting for legal rights and problems of infrastructure, or to establish new services and socio-cultural facilities;
* through the construction and maintenance of informal networks of solidarity through which women exchange services or mobilize the solidarity of the community when disaster strikes a family;
* through monetary inputs from a paid job.

If one wishes to understand how people live and survive in the working-class districts when the family's resources do not cover even half of the 'housewife's shopping basket' as calculated by the official statistics, all these activities have to be taken into consideration.

The following table sums up all the monetary and non-monetary resources contributed by men and by women. It is not so much a guide as an effort to understand the situation. The strategies of certain families may differ from this model.

TABLE 20

MONETARY AND NON-MONETARY RESOURCES OF POOR URBAN FAMILIES

Resource	Monetary (M) or non-monetary (NM)	Provider
Wage or income	M	Men in higher proportion than women
Social benefits	M and NM	Men in higher proportion than women
Family or neighbourhood solidarity	M and NM	Women in higher proportion than men
Savings	M and NM	Chiefly women
Fetching water, fuel, etc.	NM	Women
Prod. useful objects at home	M and NM	Women more than men
Constr. & repair of housing	M and NM	Men more than women
Community construction work and social organization	NM, but includes fund-raising	Men and women depending on activities

Men play a major role for three types of resource and a minor one in six. Men predominate in the provision of monetary resources and women in non-monetary ones although some women, as we have seen in previous sections, also bring in money.

In reality, monetary and non-monetary contributions run largely parallel with the production of goods and human reproduction. As Louise Vandelac (1985, see selected reference nº34) states, these two worlds differ, partly because one dominates the other but also because the role of objects, the motivations, the internal logic and the value systems of one and the other differ substantially.

Men also engage in unpaid work, particularly in the building of their own homes and in the running of local community organizations but their work is visible, recognized and proudly assumed.

We wish to draw attention to this aspect of the question, i.e. to the importance for themselves, their families and the social and economic development of the country that unpaid work for women may represent at a particular juncture. However, the complex nature of all the forms of social work performed by women and the interrelationships between their different worlds cannot be overlooked. As they become more and more openly involved in the market economy, women are making their presence felt in several areas from which they had hitherto been excluded. Yet their increasingly varied activities rarely prompts a redefinition of the roles of the two sexes. Indeed, they may even disguise to an even greater extent the role and contribution of women as mothers.

The result, far from fostering a new distribution of tasks between men and women in (monetary and non-monetary) social work and enabling men to play a greater role in the case of children, may be to accentuate the contradiction between the two spheres and subject reproduction-related needs more closely to the requirements of commercial production. In fact the growing burden of women contrasts with the rising unemployment of men, though the full extent of the problem is not yet perceived.

At meetings where women and their problems are discussed, many women state that when they took a job outside the home and brought back their wages their husbands would reduce their own monetary contributions to the household and sometimes even stop them altogether. Such behaviour, sometimes a form of blackmail and sometimes pure selfishness, is encountered as a more or less hidden strategy in numerous classes of society.

We occasionally wonder whether the thing to do is to urge women more forcefully to conquer a more important position in the world of commerce, the preserve of men, at the price of a heavier work-load and increasing tension, or whether it would not be better to transform the situation and create a new balance for the relationships between the two worlds.

In the light of the foregoing, the following chapter examines a few projects aimed at helping to defend the rights of women engaged in remunerated activities.

Programmes in support of remunerated activities for women

Domestic service

Even though the figures for persons in domestic service (6 per cent of the urban active population and 15 per cent of the female active population) suggest that it plays a rather insignificant role we shall devote a few pages to the subject because the people who evaluate the support programmes for this sector give a different impression.

Domestic service represents 25 per cent of all informal employment for women. This is far from negligible; it is in fact the largest category of informal employment for women.

However, it would appear that the DANE statistics tend to underestimate work paid by the day which, as already mentioned, is tending to replace jobs that include board and lodging. The latter jobs are themselves underestimated because the questions in the surveys of households are answered by the householder rather than by the employee and because there exists a great deal of confusion between the definitions of housework and remunerated domestic service as well as between the work performed by family helps and that performed by domestic employees.

A survey on the work of women (Rey de Marulanda, 1981), conducted in 1979 among a representative sample of urban households, showed that 37 per cent of urban jobs for women were provided by domestic service on a 'living in' or 'day' basis.

In our own study of the urban crisis (Suremain, Cardona and Dalmazzo, 1988) in 15 cities of Colombia, we found that 47 per cent of the women interviewed had a remunerated activity and that 44 per cent of them worked as domestic employees.

The confusion referred to above also affected our survey in spite of the care we took with these types of question. At first we asked the interviewees if their work represented a monetary input for their families and, if so, what kind of remunerated activity was involved. It so happens that in Spanish the word for 'office' or 'function', 'el oficio', is used just as much to designate a profession or trade as it is for housework. A proportion of the women therefore replied that their 'function' was to 'wash and iron' even though the question included the word 'remunerated'.

By checking this answer against the answer to the previous question we managed to distinguish women who were referring to a remunerated activity (some women did washing at home and delivered it once or twice a week) from those referring to their own unpaid housework (for they made no mention of any monetary income).

The close relationship between housework and paid domestic employment explains why this form of employment for women is one of the jobs with the least social prestige. Housework is regarded by public opinion as non-work, as a natural service that women perform for their families.[2] Domestic employment suffers from the same ideological connotation. As a result, society regards such work as servitude, absolute dependence, without precisely fixed hours or tasks and hence does not assign it 'worker' status.

Working relations remain on a private basis within the family that employs the woman. The employee is cut off from other working women. Her activity is more like a way of life (Leon, 1988) in which the regulations on wages do not reflect an economic model. Other factors play a major role: 'being well treated' as the employees say, the degree of social segregation (i.e. what is permitted and what forbidden, the tone of voice demanded, the way they must dress, the distance maintained in the relationship) and the amount of personal freedom allowed. The physical and emotional isolation of employees 'living in', the fact that it is impossible for them to have a sex life or family life, the widespread non-recognition of their rights and social benefits and their low level of education all contribute to making such employment one of the most exploited and disadvantaged of occupations.

As mentioned in previously, however, domestic service is not about to disappear except perhaps in the case of the 'living-in' type. There are several reasons for this. This form of employment is perpetuated in part by the shortage of community services: lack of day nurseries; primary and secondary schools which operate for only half the day and do not provide the midday meal; the small extent to which housework is mechanized; conservative mental attitudes to the roles of men and women in the sharing of household tasks; unemployment and falling incomes in working-class districts; and the growing activity rate for women from the middle and most prosperous classes.

A project co-ordinated by a non-governmental organization ACEP (Asociación Colombiana para el Estudio de la Población Colombian Association for Population Studies) includes actions aimed at defending domestic employees in Bogotá, Bucaramanga, Medellin and Barranquilla.

To illustrate the work it is doing we shall draw upon a lecture given by Magdalena Leon and the report of an evaluation seminar attended by female project staff and domestic employees from different regional groups.

The project is organized as follows:
1. Direct actions
1.1 Support for employees in terms of labour legislation.
1.2 Support to foster the sense of identity and the independence of employees.
1.3 Reflection with employers on social questions and labour legislation.
2. Actions with a multiplier effect
2.1 Support and back-up for the organization of trade unions.
2.2 Dissemination of ideas regarding the employer/employee relationship with a view to changing the degree of subordination and exploitation involved.
2.3 Promotion of legal standards and of their implementation.
2.4 Promotion of changes in attitudes and in the law in the various State authorities.

It is clear that the assistance to obtain legal recognition of the rights of these working women, to lay the foundations for training and organization and to inculcate mental and social attitudes aimed at putting an end to the silence and isolation in which these women are imprisoned goes far beyond the mere provision of practical advice.

In concrete terms, some of the 'direct actions' involve consultations or personal contacts with both the employee and her employer. Others are concerned with analysing, interpreting and applying the legal standards regarding social benefits, wages and time off. Such assistance is particularly necessary since both parties are usually ignorant of the law, which is both complex and scattered through different chapters of the Labour Code. It therefore became necessary to include in the project detailed study and the reformulation in simpler and clearer language of the various articles of the Code. Particular attention had to be paid to persons employed by the day, a category not explicitly covered by the Code. The total value of the benefits (holidays, bonuses, allowances, etc.) to which domestic employees are entitled averages about half of what other workers receive. Their affiliation to the general social security scheme became compulsory only in 1988.

The length of the working day for those 'living in' is not fixed and Sunday is rarely respected as a day of rest. The minimum wage is seldom paid: those 'living in' receive a part of their wages in kind (accommodation, food, clothing) so it is difficult to estimate their entitlement in cash; as for day workers, who usually work for several employers, it is extremely difficult for them to negotiate regular employment and the amount of their wages.

There is practically no protection in regard to confinement and post-confinement leave of absence and arbitrary dismissal without compensation is common.

The project provides information on all these points for the two parties and, at the request of the people concerned, calculates wages and benefits and chooses the most suitable days and hours in the light of the needs of the employees (particularly in respect of Sunday afternoons). Between March 1981 and May 1985, 6,665 'final accounts' were calculated at the project's headquarters in Bogotá and nearly 1,200 others during a single year (1984) in its other branches.

Specialist lawyers and persons trained to perform these calculations worked tirelessly for several years to perfect a methodology and develop more simple procedures. Courses in labour law were organized on a regular basis and teaching materials (posters, leaflets, videos, games, workshops, etc.) were arranged to spread knowledge of legal standards. The courses also provided an opportunity to incite employees not to lose contact with each other and to continue participating in educational activities and in attempts to improve their conditions. Some workshops stimulate creativity and personal expression with the aim of developing the personality and self-respect of the women taking part.

As for the actions with a multiplier effect, their purpose was to encourage the establishment of a union (with varying success, depending on the city) and several other forms of organization. Some major constraints on this work are the isolation of domestic employees, psychological and ideological barriers to their forming an organization, lack of free time and considerable instability of employment.

The movement has nevertheless gathered momentum as a result of several meetings at the national and Latin American levels attended by groups, associations, unions and women registered with the labour exchanges of the National Employment Service.

After marches, petitions, radio broadcasts and negotiations with members of Parliament, the campaigns in favour of compulsory affiliation to the social security system resulted in the voting of a law in 1988. Relations with other groups and NGOs concerned with the health and work of women enabled attention to be brought to the seriousness of the problem. In 1988 some other NGOs adopted this project for various cities. As a result it became stronger and less centralized and now covers a larger area, provides more extensive legal services and is breaking new ground in the organization of local associations or unions for domestic employees.

We felt it important to mention this work as it is the most carefully thought out and organized effort in this particular area. Being focused on the living and working conditions of women in the informal sector it goes against the grain of public opinion, which does not like the idea of domestic employees standing up for themselves. It has chalked up a few successes and represents a courageous struggle.

Small businesses run by women

THE ABSENCE OF WOMEN AS A CATEGORY FROM SECTORAL STUDIES

We made a long search for information on small businesses or occupations headed by women in the sectoral monographs dealing with informal sector street trading, food production, subcontracting for the clothing or shoe industries, local grocery shops, as well as various service activities such as midwifery, hairdressing, and so forth.

To our knowledge there exists nothing at all on the subject. However, there may exist a few dissertations in certain universities.

The most well-known studies on itinerant trading in Bogotá, Cali and many other cities in Colombia, on the sale of fish in Medellin and on trading in household appliances, hi-fi equipment and smuggled goods (legalized in the districts or covered markets known as 'San Andresitos'), do not distinguish the traders by sex. When such a distinction is made, the studies do not analyse the characteristic features, working hours and relationships with other activities in the sector according to sex.

We have therefore decided to extract from available documents all information useful to our purpose. Several sources have been consulted:

• a study on the informal sector of a medium-sized city;
• a general study on informal trading;
• a report on activities in connection with an action-oriented research project focused on regional and national meetings of working-class women;
• articles from a work on credit schemes for small businesses in

Colombia and Latin America;
* interviews with women in charge of various small businesses or persons responsible for solidarity funds in working-class districts.

A frequently cited study of Pereira (a city of the interior with 350,000 inhabitants), based on a survey of 152 establishments, states that the proportion of women working in the 96 informal enterprises was only 9 per cent as against 41 per cent in the 56 formal ones (Uribe and Forero, 1986). An examination of the types of establishment and the structure of the sample reveals the following.

The salaried personnel of small enterprises and domestic staff had been excluded from the informal sector, while the minor occupations selected shoe-shiners, sellers of lottery tickets, wardens, repairers of various types, construction workers, etc. were engaged in mainly by men. In addition, the presence in Pereira of a textile industry of the formal type explains why so many formal jobs were available for women in the city.

The arguments developed in the study are intended as a criticism of the usual definition of the informal sector based on:
* rural poverty and mass migration towards the cities, which is thought to have a direct impact on the growth of 'marginal' activities;
* an insufficient number of new formal jobs in the cities, resulting in unemployment and underemployment;
* the uncontrolled growth of informal occupations, which develop into a 'marginal pole' of the economy and perpetuate poverty.

The authors show that, in the case of Pereira, empirical studies do not make it possible to bring out a real link between recent immigration and informal occupations, to determine the dividing line between the formal and informal markets, to emphasize the importance of 'secondary' workers (those not heads of a family) in the informal sector, or to show that incomes in the informal sector are much lower than in the formal sector.

On the other hand they tell us that 'if there is one thing that can be shown, it is the marked segmentation of the labour market between men and women'. There is a clear division between an 'élite' of workers with higher incomes, more experience and a higher level of education (mostly men) and a more disadvantaged group (mostly women). But the study in question makes no attempt at further refinement of the data collected in order to support this hypothesis.

The same observation could be made with respect to a document produced by the National Federation of Shopkeepers for their 37th National Congress at Cali in November 1982. This study on itinerant and non-itinerant street trading includes a series of proposals for action to help that sector. A single paragraph (in a report of about 100 pages)[3] alludes to the role of women:

There appears to exist a high percentage of women engaged in informal commercial activities, particularly street trading, which is higher than the percentage of women engaged in other economic activities. Informal trading, especially by itinerant vendors, appears to be an attractive activity for women, partly because it enables them to have their children with them and to keep an eye on them while they work, which is not possible with other jobs. Small-time trading based on the home also appears to attract many women because it can be combined with their housework. The population of itinerant vendors includes many women employed at home while most of those with stalls help their husbands or fathers. At the same time the head of the family is engaged in other informal activities or may even have a formal job. A great many of the itinerant vendors are abandoned women or unmarried mothers responsible for an entire family.

Other studies mention that when couples are engaged in itinerant trading they share the work. The man works in the morning while the woman does the housework. In the afternoon the woman takes over and keeps an eye on the children while the man turns to other activities.

All these observations have a common denominator the close combination with housework and care of the family and children. Such a combination is made possible by working at home whereas it would adversely affect the productivity of local small-scale commercial activities, for example.

In most cases the women attend to their homes early in the morning tidying up, washing, preparing the midday and evening meals, looking after the children, fetching water and fuel (in Bogotá, for example, in the districts where the cooking is done using subsidized petrol, a person may easily have to queue for a whole day in order to obtain a 5-gallon can and it is quite common for one neighbour to replace another in the queue), etc.

The afternoon is devoted to money-earning activities which may, in the case of home-based micro-industry, last eight to ten hours at a stretch, especially when the work is in the form of subcontracting and the product has to be delivered regularly in large numbers in order to achieve a significant income.

Generally speaking, it is not very easy to discover to what extent the analyses of small businesses from particular standpoints (the 'functional' system for the production and distribution of goods for the working-class population and/or poverty-induced subsistence activities) or in terms of the potential for organization (associations of itinerant vendors, local shopkeepers — the 'tenderos' —, and heads of small businesses) or for accumulating capital or increasing income can in fact be combined with an analysis based on type of activity and a gender-based division of labour.

Even though men are predominant in the most 'functional' sector, which is socially and economically structured, and women tend to be relegated to subsistence activities, it seems to us that detailed sectoral studies alone can clarify the existing relationship between big and small-scale industry, between big industry and small-scale trading, between large shops and small-scale trading, and the role played by each sex in this social division of labour.

These studies must also be set within the actual local context if we want to improve our understanding of how local job opportunities arise and develop. A methodology for this purpose developed by numerous French research workers makes it possible to identify the strategies of companies and the labour market by branch of activity in relation to local conditions regarding the education system, vocational training, the local and/or national economic fabric, housing, town planning and so on.

We have collected the testimony of a few women working in small companies which illustrates the fragility of their situations and the extent of their dependence. We also include some examples of informal allocations from solidarity funds.

The next subsection will be devoted to what was reported to us and the one after to the subject of credit.

FRAGILITY AND DEPENDENCE OF SMALL BUSINESSES

A survey of women in people's organizations and in small businesses run by individuals singly or in association, carried out on the occasion of regional or national meetings[4] in 1985, 1986 and 1987 (Ramirez and Gomez, 1987), sheds light on the ways in which 116 small businesses operate. Depending on the type of classification adopted, 79 of the small businesses had a rudimentary division of labour with some of them employing paid workers or members of the family; 37 others were of the artisanal type (no division of labour for the various types of operation). Some 43 of the 79 small businesses were run as associations or co-operatives which accounts for the circumstances in which the surveys and interviews were conducted.

Some 46 per cent of these enterprises owed their creation to individual initiative, 15 per cent had been helped by a husband, brother or uncle, and 39 per cent by a public or private (NGO) institution.

Over half of the total were small businesses producing clothing or knitwear, about 15 per cent were engaged in popular crafts (toys, baskets, cards, paintings, pottery, wooden objects, flower arrangements, etc.), 10 per cent produced or processed food, 5 per cent were retailers and 20 per cent were engaged in various activities such as the manufacture of brooms, printing, recycling, bookbinding and sundry services.

Some of the women engaged in making up clothes were working under subcontracting arrangements, as one participant at the meeting in Cali explained:

Around 90 per cent of the clothes produced in Cali are made up by women because, as you know, by tradition we are taught to sew at a very early age... The men who work do not work on the production side but nearly always in the marketing of what their wives make. We often accept work at piece rates because unfortunately it is the most profitable.

When they were asked if their activities were profitable, 46 per cent replied 'yes', 8 per cent 'no', 30 per cent 'moderately' and 15 per cent 'not yet'.

The problems mentioned were connected with all the stages of the production process and with the impact of their work on their household tasks and vice versa. The most critical problems were the lack of capital and the difficulty of finding outlets. Next in order of importance came problems related to the purchase of raw materials, the lack of internal organization in the case of the co-operatives and problems of administration.

The fixed capital in their possession is insignificant and they regard the accumulation of capital as impossible because of their difficulty in keeping the family budget separate from that of the enterprise, especially when the latter is of the individual type. Those organized in associations also have difficulty in increasing their capital but the co-operatives, when successfully consolidated, have a firmer structure and resist better over time.

Working capital is used for the purchase of raw materials; 80 per cent of the enterprise buy these from wholesalers and factories. Credit, even short-term credit, is almost never given, whereas the shops that provide the raw material pay for the finished product with post-dated cheques or bills of exchange cashable 20, 30 or 60 days later; private purchasers often ask for credit. Only 60 per cent of them market their own products, with the result that the sales techniques employed are very limited. Some of these enterprises succeed in establishing a name (without getting involved in legal procedures but by inventing a name and trademark), a style of packaging, a form of advertising and a stable outlet for sales.

Losses and uneven sales are common occurrences and together often cause stoppages in production, difficulties in servicing the machines, or a drop in income and capital.

There is very little control over administration and bookkeeping so that profitability is very difficult to calculate. When short of capital the women often turn to private backers and moneylenders. The working day is long and exhausting: half the women said they worked over 16 hours a day either in the small business or in doing their housework. One of them spoke as follows:

'I work all through the week. I get up at five o'clock in the morning and busy myself with my children, my house, the business and the association. During the weekends I study at the SENA.[5] There is no day of the week on which I take a rest'.

The impression we gather from what these women say is that the great efforts they make are poorly remunerated. If they had greater access to credit and to training they would be able to reach a sufficient level of productivity to build up savings, and to stabilize and increase their incomes and thus create jobs. Other examples reveal many other factors that must be taken into account.

Our first example is an actual case-history in one of the poorest areas in south Bogotá, where districts have sprung up on the hillsides following the invasion and 'pirate' sale of building land. The 'district' is divided into sectors and now contains over 100,000 inhabitants. In one of these districts, called Potosi, the Social Foundation, which is financed by the various Savings and Loans Banks of the Society of Jesus, organizes a large number of community activities.

After completing a knitting course attended by about 30 women, seven of them set up a small business. The following conditions were laid down: (a) manual dexterity; (b) agreement to join a permanent group; (c) payment of a monthly subscription of 100 pesos. Training in the manufacture of various articles and to improve administrative skills has continued. Subjects studied include bookkeeping, marketing, dealing with mail, group dynamics, human relations and community participation. The support needed to cope with the various problems encountered by the organization has been provided by once-weekly technical assistance. To underpin the application for a loan of 130,000 pesos,[6] for example, the Savings Bank drew up a two-year investment plan.

This loan was for the purchase of wool and a few tools. The women knitted clothes for children, women and men in their own homes. Certain patterns were copied from fashion magazines or made to order while others were designed by the women themselves. The products were marketed outside the local district through an advertising campaign in the form of a fashion show. For training, evaluation, analysis, deliveries and the distribution of work the group would meet in the home of one of its members.

The limitations of this type of initiative quickly became apparent. The technical training proved to be insufficient for the necessary quality of finishing and for the correct adaptation of patterns so as to keep up with the competition and guarantee regular outlets. Marketing was confined to very small circles of customers because the small business was unable to absorb the high transport costs to reach a wider market. The knitwear, too expensive for the local market and not good enough in quality to compete in the centre of the city, did not sell well.

These are the usual problems for a group of beginners. The role of technical assistance was therefore to help the group to overcome such difficulties by conducting market research and preparing new lines of knitwear. However, it was necessary to reduce the costs relating to this technical and social assistance until solutions had been found for the main problems.

Another factor emphasized by the group was the constant opposition of the husbands to their wives attending meetings, even in neighbouring houses. This opposition went in some cases as far as physical aggression or psychological persecution. All contacts outside the district for buying or selling purposes became a source of conflict and anxiety, especially when this meant leaving the children on their own or under the supervision of a neighbour for some time.

The fragility of the agreement among the women, owing to their fear of losing their husbands, their undervaluing of themselves as individuals and the blocking of their initiatives and creativity made it difficult to maintain group motivation and ensure economic growth despite success in keeping the capital intact.

The experiment had its positive side. In particular, it enabled the women to build up a productive capacity and new skills and to create a recognized sphere of their own in which they were able to pool their particular problems and experience of life, to help each other and to discover the importance of teamwork. They spoke of the impact of this experience on their daily lives, on its income-producing possibilities and on their trips outside the district to negotiate purchases and sales. Another important factor was the introduction to group life with its conflicts and compromises. At present, the group has contracted a little and is thinking about its future prospects.

This sort of thing is a common occurrence when small businesses, whether run as associations or on an individual basis, are given assistance. The results are never entirely negative but seldom exceed the level of providing a supplementary or marginal income because they had not been conceived from the start on more ambitious lines. Market studies do not cast doubt on the role of women in the economy and development. The possibilities open to small businesses are limited by markets that are saturated and dominated by large companies of the formal type, with the result that they have little chance of expanding. This may limit their future prospects from the start and prevent them from generating an income above the level of subsistence.

The other enterprise where we conducted interviews was a co-operative of 180 women in Patio Bonito, a district in south-west Bogotá that was hit in 1979 by the so-called Rio Bogotá flood. The water rose to 1.50 metres above the ground, forcing the population to evacuate the area for over three months and to take refuge in temporary shelters. Numerous public and private institutions took action as soon as the tragedy struck but did not make any medium-term proposals. AVOCOL, a body that coordinates voluntary work in Colombia, co-operated with the parish in organizing the collection of funds in the city of Bogotá in order to raise enough money to set up a community programme.

The solidarity of the women in coping with the disaster was the starting-point of the project. Nuns organized a course of 'family guidance' the purpose of which was to manufacture household linen (aprons, tablecloths, bedspreads, etc.) and this led to the formation of a group. The nuns then sold these goods and though sales went slowly they did at least provide a small source of income for the women.

AVOCOL then proposed other training courses, in particular a course based on educational brochures for children aged 2 to 6. In all, some 600 women followed these courses and about 100 of them became childminders. They not only passed on what they had learnt to the children but also shared their knowledge with their neighbours by talking over the new ideas and the problems encountered.

Once firmly established, this group was given a course on the running of co-operatives and decided to found a co-operative with 60 members. The women had to face the opposition not only of their spouses but also of the men who were running the district; the latter said that 'they had nothing to do at home, that they were mad and that they would be incapable of making a success of such a project. They themselves had already had some experience in that area with the "Junta de Acción Comunal" (Communal Action Committee) and had failed three times in their attempts to create a similar co-operative'.

A financing plan was submitted to the Interamerican Foundation, which initially approved it for a period of three years and later extended it for a further two.

Meanwhile the women began to raise the necessary funds by selling 'empanadas' (meat and rice pies), 'cocadas' (coconut candy), 'tamales' (a sort of meat and maize paste wrapped in banana leaves) and second-hand clothes. With these funds and a contribution from AVOCOL they opened a small grocery store in which they sold articles needed by schoolchildren, food and everyday household supplies.

The next stage (1982) was to give legal status to the organization and to open a kindergarten to look after young children while their mothers were working, still unpaid, at the co-operative. At the same time, with a view to broadening their productive activities and financing the kindergarten (the rent of the premises used was paid by AVOCOL), a workshop was opened to make clothes.

The women were therefore engaged in three occupations the kindergarten, the shop and the workshop. While the shop and workshop began to show a profit, a large deficit soon appeared because the kindergarten costs exceeded the amount coming in. The co-operative found itself in a serious crisis which almost led to bankruptcy.

When the Interamerican Foundation provided financial support, the members decided to close the shop and concentrate on production. Premises were constructed to serve as the co-operative's headquarters and AVOCOL staff members in company with the leaders of the co-operative tried to obtain contracts for subcontracting work in the clothing industry. Through certain contacts relations were eventually established with a company producing men's shoes for export. Training was given to the 50 members then affiliated. The workshop began to sew shoes on machines lent by the company (this is still the situation). There were only 20 jobs. At present the co-operative functions with 180 women employed as follows:

Clothing workshop: located in the premises of the kindergarten, where eight women design models and cut out the material; 12 other women do the sewing at home. The former group are paid a fixed wage (very slightly above the minimum wage, which in July 1989 was US$90) while the others are paid at piece rate.

Shoe workshop: installed at the headquarters of the co-operative, it has created a number of jobs, including eight for administrative duties and 33 workers divided into two teams which each works an eight-hour shift. They earn a fixed wage.

The 'special line' workshop: a new line in shoes requiring great dexterity and special machines has recently created ten extra jobs. The wages are the same.

Cardboard workshop: under a contract signed with a cardboard factory 18 women make boxes of various sizes by hand. They work directly for the company concerned but their wages, based on the minimum wage, are paid to the co-operative, which then remunerates its members.

Stitching of the uppers: the uppers of the shoe are stitched by hand. Each day 86 women receive 12 pairs of shoes to be stitched at home. They are given training at the beginning of each year for the particular line being manufactured and the quality of their work is checked by a supervisor. They are paid 1,000 pesos per batch received (US$2.6 in July 1989); in other words, by working 30 days a month they earn a little less than those with a regular job in the workshops. This work calls for great self-discipline, concentration and manual dexterity so as to ensure perfect consistency in production, failing which the shoes are refused by the factory. This obliges the women to be extremely strict in organizing their housework so as to be able to work without any interruption (not always easy when one works at home). The burden of housework is somewhat lightened by the existence of a kindergarten.

The co-operative has also established the following committees and services:

Education committee, which organizes training courses on vocational and non-vocational subjects.

Solidarity committee, which makes small personal loans in the event of problems at home; the repayments are deducted directly from earnings.

Social security committee, which administers medical services and provides daily health care in the kindergarten.

The kindergarten, which takes in 70 children of members of the co-operative. It is run by four mistresses who were trained via various types of course and workshop, with particular help from university trainees. It uses activity teaching methods based on play. The kindergarten is properly equipped and the mistresses are paid the same as the full-time workers.

The 'chain': this is a tontine organized among the members of the co-operative. The monthly subscription of each member is paid into a kitty for which lots are drawn. This small capital is often used for house-building or the purchase of household appliances. Each winner drops out of the draw until everyone has had their turn.

The 'pumpkin' festival: in the slang of leather-workers, 'pumpkins' are leftover scraps and substandard rejects. Every year the members of the co-operative invite the representatives of the companies and their quality controllers to a play, dance or series of satirical poems in which they express their criticisms or describe their successes.

Financial aspects:

Each member of the co-operative has to pay in a monthly sum, deducted from her earnings, which is used to finance their bonuses or 'cesantias' (unemployment relief).

The sales of the co-operative have reached a figure of some 5 million pesos a month (about US$13,000 in July 1989) and its assets, essentially its two buildings, are valued at 18 million pesos (nearly US$47,000). The annual profits are substantial (6 million pesos or US$15,600 in 1988), making it possible to improve the working conditions of members and to invest.

The co-operative is self-financing and pays its outside staff such as its accountant, its auditor and the 'assessor' (a woman previously remunerated by AVOCOL).

The overall results of this experiment are highly positive: it has created a large number of jobs and initiated an interesting process of capital accumulation and redistribution whereby the provision of assistance to the informal sector can lead to the establishment of associations or of a 'third' sector.

The project, moreover, has devised its own solutions in matters of social protection, health, childcare, leisure activities, reflection on the identity of women, social participation and the democratization of power in the community (the district).

The leaders have become reasonably independent of outside assistance, though there is clearly some distance and a relationship that still remains hierarchical between the workers and the leading members or assessor as well as some dependence on contracts (based on personal relationships) with the assessor. Where their personal lives are concerned they have undoubtedly gained autonomy, self-reliance and self-confidence.

The weak point is the dependent relationship between the co-operative and the firms that subcontract work to it. The experience it has built up and its solid administrative structure should in principle ensure the stability of contracts but the dependence of the industries concerned on external markets and the fact that the co-operative's contracts are almost exclusively with the footwear company may make for vulnerability. It would appear that, compared with other subcontractors, especially the rural workshops (an association-enterprise employing 700 women working at home in the Cali region), the Patio Bonito co-operative has succeeded in negotiating better prices and in obtaining recognition for the quality of its work.

True though it is that in eight years the co-operative has achieved considerable success, it could not have existed without constant outside support of a financial nature but also in social and administrative matters, in internal organization and in its relations with the local community, the co-operative movement, and the various social movements in Colombia.

The overall effort represents a cost and a convergence of separate actions that are not easy to achieve. In our view, such action should aim at the reappropriation of the entire production process, at promoting the sense of belonging and the dignity of women workers, at reducing their dependence on large companies, and at reducing the fragmentation of tasks and the consequent pressure on output. But that is a more long-term ambition.

In the light of this example we shall now study the various institutional schemes designed to improve the production conditions in small businesses in Colombia.

CREDIT SCHEMES FOR SMALL BUSINESSES

The discussion in this section is based on several articles on the subject published in Ecuador and Venezuela (Berger and Buvinic, 1988), on conversations with persons responsible for credit schemes for small businesses and on interviews with women involved in informal credit schemes (akin to tontines).

The main thrust of government policies aimed at the informal sector and of the programmes of NGOs and non-profit-making foundations is concentrated on the question of credit.

The people running small businesses regard the lack of fixed and working capital as the chief obstacle to the improvement of their living and working conditions. This was clearly emphasized in all the surveys and interviews we conducted and, in our view, served to highlight the state of poverty to which these male and female independent workers are reduced. In the end, lack of capital and lack of money come down to the same thing.

This somewhat limited diagnosis has provided the basis for a large number of policies designed to overcome this bottleneck which is universally regarded as the crux of the matter.

Once we have accepted this assumption, which we shall try to set in a broader context later, it becomes apparent that women suffer from many handicaps in this field.

Although there exist few statistics by sex to show that in Colombia women have less access to formal credit than men, the indications in other countries all suggest that this is the case. There is a set of reasons for this:

As women tend to have lower incomes and smaller businesses they would ask for smaller loans and make fewer applications than men.

Women find it more difficult to offer security since they have less personal property, whether movables or real estate (see next section on housing and self-help construction).

In many cases the banks require the head of the family, a man, to sign and hence authorize the loan, or even to act as guarantor. This may give extra support but it may just as easily prove to be an obstacle.

One undoubted limitation is the difficulty of access to information: besides their lower level of formal education, women go out from their homes less often than men.

The type of action that has to be taken, the forms to be completed, the time that has to be spent on such work and the intimidating relations with bank officials constitute another set of obstacles. To overcome such difficulties, women often enlist the help of a friend to accompany them in their applications whereas men generally act on their own.

From the point of view of the banks, small loans are not regarded as profitable because the proportion of administrative costs is too high.

In addition, it appears that the scattered nature of such small loans makes recovery of the sum more difficult, with the result that they present a higher risk of non-repayment.

When interest rates are set below the market rates in order to make credit more accessible to small producers, the demand leaps up to such an extent that it leads to the paradox of the rationing of loans. The most influential and the richest borrowers end up by grabbing most of the sum made available for such loans for themselves.

This problem could be overcome by means of a policy for subsidies in which the State would bear the cost of reducing interest rates by a few percentage points. The Latin American States, however, do not generally have the necessary resources, or do not use them in this way in order to guard against the unwanted effect mentioned above. In recent years, moreover, the adjustment policies that have been imposed with a view to curbing the foreign debt result almost everywhere in the abolition of subsidies.

In view of these restrictions the inhabitants of the working-class districts and small firms turn to informal sources of finance.

The most important of these informal sources is family, neighbours and friends. For small and sometimes even for large sums there are no special conditions that have to be met (apart from a good and if possible reciprocal relationship, but even this is not always necessary), no documents to be completed, a minimum of trips to be made and total flexibility as regards repayments. Interest rates are decided between the parties and range from zero to the market rate. The duration of the loan depends on the possibilities of the two parties and the loan is made immediately if the money is available.

The risks are low because the lender is aware of the repayment capacity of the borrower; if the borrower is a member of the family, he may tolerate a long delay or even losing the money.

Certain professional moneylenders lend money against a physical security (household appliance, jewellery, valuable objects) while others do so because they know the borrower or else they require a guarantor. The formalities are minimal but the interest rates are high. The sum of money needed is usually available immediately but repayment deadlines are less flexible. The lender himself recovers the money owed so it is difficult to dodge repayment.

Small shopkeepers also sometimes lend money to families in a crisis: physical proximity and personal acquaintance may allow certain families, depending on the nature of their relations with the shopkeeper, to run up a bill that is sometimes quite large. This credit is for consumer goods and not for productive investment, but the dividing line between the two is not at all rigid. A Bogotá milliner whom we interviewed told us that she had obtained from a co-operative (after filling in all the necessary papers and attending compulsory courses) a loan to purchase a more efficient machine. She was just about to buy it when the Armero disaster occurred and her surviving cousins came to live with her. She had to buy furniture and linen and to use her loan to help the family group to survive. The use of loans for the purpose for which they were requested is never entirely certain unless the lending institution keeps a close watch. In the case of informal loans, the use to which the money is put is not a criterion for acceptance or refusal. The lender may be swayed by the borrower's reasons but in reality the question is of little importance to him.

Another source of informal credit is the tontines or 'chains' which women form, generally with other women, in order to meet their borrowing needs.

We have already come across one example in the Patio Bonito co-operative and we shall now describe two others, the first of which concerns a district called Comuneros in south Bogotá.

Comuneros is a district of 600 families in the southernmost part of Bogotá created at the beginning of 1982 by means of community self-management self-help housing. After buying the land the families installed the electricity, laid temporary water-piping and sewers, and built a meeting-room, classrooms, a Red Cross station, an office for the community's association and a large hangar inside which production workshops were set up.

A tipper lorry was purchased as well as shares in a bulldozer bought in association with other districts united in a 'citizens' movement'. The various projects subsequently came up against numerous problems of management and organization but the initial spirit of the pioneers, who wanted to build up a 'full community enterprise' rather than a mere 'barrio', made it possible to develop numerous other projects.

The Latin American ENDA, and NGO seeking to encourage the use of appropriate technologies and community organization received a request from the inhabitants of this district for help in reorganizing their production workshops for carpentry, clothing and shoes. After several attempts, some brief and others longer, it was concluded that the conflicts within the association made it impossible to reorganize the workshops and hence to reap the profits that could then have been used for the creation of other community projects as the leaders of the overall scheme had initially hoped. This diagnosis made it possible to design a new form of support for the economic activities and to constitute a revolving savings fund with the purpose of stimulating small businesses in the district.

In 1987, therefore, a savings and loan group was established among 12 persons. Each received from ENDA a loan that enabled them to set up, re-establish or expand their small business. The group was not initially intended to be composed solely of women but they formed the majority (ten members out of 12).

The loans, of a duration ranging from three to six months and at 3 per cent interest per month, were adapted to each case. At the same time each member was asked to pay in a monthly sum in order to constitute a self-financing fund. At the end of six months the savings of the group amounted to 100,000 pesos. ENDA, which had promised to give 1 peso for every peso saved, added the same amount. In November 1987 the 'Friendship' group was established. It was given training in the management and repayment of loans.

A special set of rules was devised for the group:
* the group, composed of heads of small businesses, promised to save 500 pesos each per week;
* the interest on loans was fixed at 3 per cent per month, 4 per cent in the case of overdue repayments;
* the only security was a bill of exchange under the terms of which each borrower undertook to repay the loan in one or more instalments, depending on his or her possibilities;
* in the case of repayment in instalments, capital plus interest would be paid back on a monthly basis;
* all members were entitled to loans up to a maximum amount of three times their savings;
* the administration and supervision of the loans was under the re-

sponsibility of a co-ordinating committee made up of a co-ordinator, a treasurer and a comptroller. This loans committee accorded loans up to 20,000 pesos. For loans exceeding that amount it was the 12-member assembly that took the decision;

- the group held regular meetings every three months.

The small businesses concerned are at present engaged in the following production activities:

- the manufacture of mattresses and tailoring (the only two men);
- the women members make 'arepas' (maize griddle cakes), knitwear, furniture and wooden toys, sewn clothing and shoes, and one member sells clothing from door to door.

All have been accorded loans for the purchase of raw materials and machines, for improvements to their premises, for the servicing of their machines, for repairs to the vehicle used for marketing their products and for the constitution of a working capital fund to permit sales on credit. In 1988 (first year of operation) 35 loans were granted for a total of over 2 million pesos, representing an average loan of 58,500 pesos. The two men received larger loans and for a longer period of time but it was not possible to ascertain the exact figures.

During the first seven months of 1989 ten loans averaging 65,000 pesos brought the overall total to 45 loans in 19 months for a total outlay of 2,700,000 pesos.

Even though the group began with almost no knowledge of bookkeeping and administration it has managed its affairs responsibly. Only one member has had to withdraw owing to family and economic difficulties (an unmarried mother of 20 who produced good-quality knitwear but who had many problems with her family and had no capital in reserve to pay for the frequent repairs to her machine; she had landed a contract with a factory that bought her knitwear, until her second pregnancy).

The present state of the group's accounts may be summed up as follows:

Outstanding loans	650,000 pesos
Money in the bank	71,640
Total	721,640

Accumulated savings	516,000 pesos
ENDA contribution	100,000
Interest received	105,640
Total	721,640

This represents a very notable increase in the amount of money initially involved.

When we questioned members of the group about the fund's impact on their businesses and private lives, they gave the impression of being highly satisfied. They emphasized the strengthening of the bonds of solidarity and the moral support that this provided even in the case of difficulties over repayments (as happened for one member, the only shopkeeper, who on several occasions had to interrupt her work because of problems with her teenage children). They also stressed the importance of the savings system, which enabled the group to continue to function even without the funds provided by ENDA.

Various problems have limited the scope of the experiment:

The group is not expanding in accordance with the rule it set for itself, namely, that any person wishing to join must be up to date in his or her subscriptions, i.e. have the same level of savings as the others; after two years of existence for the fund, this is virtually impossible. The rule was established out of a concern for fairness and equality and because of the difficulty of managing a multiple-track system. A little technical assistance in working out more flexible rules would help them overcome this difficulty, which could be fatal to the fund in the medium term.

From the management point of view, the accounts of the loans are not sufficiently maintained: the members rely on their memories rather than on the keeping of records. Given the limited number of members, that approach is still possible but it makes evaluation more difficult and will render management impossible after only a slight increase in the size of the group.

Activities have been limited to the granting and repayment of loans, whereas the original idea should have included a greater number of initiatives such as contact with other associations, the provision of social benefits for members, technical assistance in management, the keeping of accounts, marketing, advertising, etc.

The group, however, is at present asking itself questions along these lines and has taken the first steps to request technical assistance. It should be stressed that all members take an active part in community activities such as ensuring respect for the law in the neighbourhood, supporting the kindergarten and school, involvement in health groups, etc.

When ENDA first became involved in the district and people spoke only of revitalizing the community workshops and setting up a revolving fund, one of the leading women in the district (the treasurer, with a good level of formal education) decided on her own initiative to create a savings and loans group based on the system of tontines, of which she had already had some experience. The idea of savings was motivated by the fact that the start of the school year, illnesses and family events always take families by surprise and that they need to build up reserves to cope with the situation. However, day-to-day necessities and the opposing force of their husbands (who spend their money on drink and unnecessary objects for themselves when they notice that their wives have built up reserves) often prevent the women from keeping up the effort for more than a brief period.

The group began its activities in 1984 with 27 women making

monthly savings contributions according to what they could afford and not on a strictly regular basis. At the end of the first year the money saved was returned to each member to cover end-of-year expenses and the new school year, which begins in December–January.

It was then that the group decided to put itself on a more formal footing, to work out a set of rules and to appoint a management committee (president, vice-president, treasurer, secretary, auditor). The committee, which must always include two founding members, is appointed each year.

As the fund is liquidated each year it is possible for new members to join. The amount saved per month is 4,000 pesos (i.e. 12 per cent of the minimum wage); this sum is quite high and therefore selective, and it must be paid in before the fifth day of the month (when the scheme started, six years earlier, the subscription was 200 pesos and people paid in when they liked, but the rules have gradually become stricter). Loans are requested in a letter to the president; there is no loans committee if there is enough cash available the request is approved. The member who applies for a loan decides how much she needs (between 10,000 and 50,000 pesos) and the sum she is able to pay back each month or at the end of the period.

The amount of the loan depends on the accumulated savings, however, which serve to guarantee the debt. Interest is 4 per cent per month but more for overdue repayments.

Each member of the group is entitled to borrow at least once a year but may ask for a further loan each time she needs one if she is up to date in her subscriptions. No guarantee is required, simply a signed bill of exchange. Persons from outside the group have to submit a letter from one of its members, who acts as guarantor.

The group meets every three months to examine the accounts and plan activities to raise extra funds: lotteries, a dance, a fête, bus outings to leisure centres, etc. The bus outings are very popular and are organized two or three times a year. One of them filled four buses about 160 persons with families from the district.

The profits (interest on loans and sundry activities) are shared out each year among the members. It has recently been decided to retain part of the profits in order to recapitalize the fund.

Over the last six years the fund has granted an average of about 50 loans a year, representing a total annual investment of some 2 million pesos.

The use to which the loans are put varies: most of them are invested in self-help housing while others are intended for small family businesses, schooling expenses or family consumption.

The women interviewed expressed their satisfaction at belonging to the group. They emphasized how much easier it was to obtain loans and to plan family expenditure. They also spoke of their need to belong to a group, to exchange ideas, worries and joys, and of the opportunity to get to know their neighbours better and to help each other in times of difficulty. This completely spontaneous and well-organized fund is particularly striking for its dynamism, seriousness and discipline. The group has also introduced other services such as group purchases in quantity of certain staples such as rice, potatoes, flour, etc., but has been unable to continue for want of capital.

The special situation in this district, in which two clans are clashing over leadership of the community, the legislation of land ownership and the public services, has slowed down the expansion of property and initiatives in the common interest. But the creativity and seriousness of initiatives of this type show that it is often a mistake to design development projects of an unambitious or paternalistic nature.

By establishing rules that are more appropriate for each case and more flexible (which does not mean undisciplined, quite the contrary), existing resources are multiplied and serve to launch numerous activities. However, that in itself is not enough. The projects that become firmly established are generally those that are keyed to social dynamics, solidarity and community work. Women have a vital role here since it is through them that solidarity finds expression in everyday life.

In contrast to this type of initiative, the economic activities of public and private development programmes in the informal sector are often restricted to the purely economic and 'productive' aspects in accordance with a narrow conception based on an evaluation of such activities in monetary terms.

Schemes to assist small businesses are run by the national banks and by private non-profit-making institutions with international funding (for example, the Interamerican Development Bank finances the People's Bank and CORFAS, which is a corporation for the financing of business associations) or may be combined with national funding such as that provided by the Carvajal Foundation and, again, by CORFAS.

Under these various programmes, projects aimed specifically at women are generally undervalued and underfinanced. In programmes aimed at both sexes, women are seldom at an advantage except in the case of what are called 'solidarity groups' in which the group as a whole acts as security. These 'solidarity groups' function in a very similar way to the spontaneous or grass-roots groups we have been describing and are composed of a majority of women. In eight programmes run by private Latin American foundations and studied in an article on small businesses (MacKean, 1988), women comprised over 65 per cent of the members when the mechanism took the form of a 'solidarity group' but only 20 per cent in systems of the individual type.

When it comes to defending the interests of women from these working-class districts, this criterion is crucial and much more important than the other conditions pertaining to loans, such as duration, rate of interest, repayments, etc.

The programmes which offer appropriations for small businesses and negotiate with each applicant individually are generally aimed at that part of the informal sector we have termed 'functional', in which the separate units are bigger, the initial capital more firmly established and there is more assistance from other members of the family and a more favourable relationship with the formal market. It is easier for these small businesses to offer individual security and make medium-term commitments. They are enterprises in which men predominate and are more numerous in the micro-industrial sector than in commerce or services.

The programmes which offer loans to solidarity groups are concerned with the poorest and the most 'informal' of small business interests. It is here that women are the most numerous. By offering them a scheme that is based more on their needs than on what they possess, on solidarity rather than on saleable goods, they enable these women to show that they exist and have economic aspirations and to make use of their own monetary and non-monetary resources. For women, a greater obstacle to the obtaining of a loan than its cost or duration is the security that is required and all the formalities that have to be complied with in order to submit an application.

The insistence on training courses before the loan is granted is in reality a veiled selection mechanism that puts women at a disadvantage. The fact is that such courses require a lot of free time, especially during the day, which is well-nigh impossible for women who are barely surviving and have family responsibilities. Only those able to free themselves from their obligations and offset the economic impact of cutting down their activities for several weeks are able to complete the course and thus qualify for a loan.

In Colombia, a country that is described as one of the pioneers in this field (Lycette and White, 1988), the first private programmes on a fairly large scale (Carvajal in Cali, Corfabricato, later called Corsocial, and so on) employed this mechanism and concentrated on the most profitable small businesses. One example is the People's Bank.

In the 'solidarity group' system five to eight members engaged in manufacturing or shopkeeping, usually in a similar line, join together to form a group that will administer a loan and receive a course of training (Otero, 1988). The group may be composed of relations, friends, neighbours, acquaintances or of people who know each other well enough to stand as security for each other in regard to the collective loan. The group may be formed under the aegis of a promoter or come into being spontaneously. The loan application is assessed collectively and technical and social assistance begins with the first contact, focusing on the analysis of needs, the repayment capacity of each member and the collective responsibilities involved.

In some cases a brief feasibility study may be carried out in respect of each proposed investment through personal contacts or a visit. The loan may be granted to the co-ordinator of the group or to each of its members. The co-ordinator takes responsibility for collecting repayments and becomes the intermediary between the group and the lending institution for all problems that arise.

Apart from the document signed by all members of the group, no other guarantee is required. Provision is generally made for monitoring the activities developed as a result of the loan in the form of technical assistance, a programme of further training and in many cases complementary activities relating to trade unionism, health, literacy, housing, etc.

The first loans are small but may be increased in size after a repayment. In this way the group gains in self-confidence and the institution is able to assess its serious-mindedness. The cost of these small loans and the technical assistance is to some extent offset by delegating to the group and in particular to its co-ordinator the task of recovering the money and putting pressure on the bad debtors. The transaction is thus much less risky than in the case of loans to individuals, which makes it possible to grant loans to people with much lower incomes while at the same time requiring less security and fewer forms to be filled in, all of which is in different ways to the advantage of women.

An illustration of the system is provided by a study carried out on a branch of the Banco Mundial de la Mujer (World Bank for Women) at Cali (Guzman and Castro, 1988). The following tables are taken from an evaluation carried out at the end of 1986 on the basis of a representative sample of 217 people running small businesses (out of a total of 581 in 1988). Oddly enough, the Women's Bank does not lend money to women but, in its own words, 'to the family'. The beneficiaries are therefore of both sexes, though women predominate (68 per cent).

TABLE 21
COMPOSITION OF SOLIDARITY GROUPS, WOMEN'S BANK,
CALI (1986) (SAMPLE)

Producers) (35%)			Commercial activities (65%)			Total (100%)		
Men	Women	Total	Men	Women	Total	Men	Women	Total
18	57	75	51	91	142	69	148	217
24	76	100	36	64	100	32	68	100

Source: From 'Banco de la Mujer'; figures calculated by the author.

These statistics show that women are more numerous among the 'producers' (i.e. micro-industries) than among the 'commercial activities' (commerce and services) but that overall those engaged in commercial activities were granted more loans than producers. This tendency is even stronger in the case of programmes aimed solely at women but less so when the groups are mixed.

When we examine how this programme has evolved over time we find that the participation of women fluctuates. In November 1986, 75 per cent of the women had been members of a solidarity group for over a year, 88 per cent for between six and 12 months, and only 60 per cent for less than six months. These figures represent 60 per cent of the groups studied. This makes us wonder whether the drop in the participation of women, also apparent in the programme of the solidarity groups, is a consequence of the economic situation at the time or reflects a change in the programme in favour of small businesses run by men. The question is worth raising. Equally puzzling is the evolution of the income structure over time.

TABLE 22

INCOME DISTRIBUTION OF THE MEMBERS OF SOLIDARITY GROUPS ACCORDING TO PERIOD OF MEMBERSHIP (%)

Women's Bank, Cali (1986)

Income as% of minimum wage	Over 12 months		6–12 months		Under 6 months	
	Women	Men	Women	Men	Women	
0 to 0.5	70	52	50	63	43	44
0.6 to 1.8	30	33	50	23	43	33
1.9 and above	—	15	—	14	14	23
Total	100	100	100	100	100	100

Source: 'Banco Mundial de la Mujer'.

According to these figures the most long-standing members are the poorest and new members are distinctly richer. While it may be true that the loans serve as a means of increasing income, as announced, they do not enable recipients of more than a year's standing to benefit from the same advantages as the newcomers. The men who joined a year earlier were much poorer than the women while more recent male beneficiaries of the programme present roughly the same income structure as the women.

If the more recent structure is maintained, the programme could be said to favour men as much as women even though women are numerically in the majority.

Certain figures from this study are disturbing since they reveal that men apply for larger loans than women and that their monthly sales are greater.

This tendency may be the first sign that the programme is being diverted from its purpose, a fact of which its female promoters do not yet measure the importance in the article mentioned above. Another table shows that the small businesses run by women created a far higher total number of new jobs than those run by men. Taken individually, however, they created fewer jobs, as can be seen from the following table.

TABLE 23
JOBS CREATED IN SOLIDARITY GROUPS, WOMEN'S BANK, CALI (1986)

	Producers		Commercial activities		Total	
	Men	*Women*	*Men*	*Women*	*Men*	*Women*
Small businesses	18	57	51	91	69	148
No. of jobs created	37	87	91	128	128	215
Jobs, per small businesses	2.05	1.52	1.78	1.40	1.85	1.45

Source: From 'Banco de la Mujer'; figures calculated by the author.

The small businesses founded by men create proportionately more jobs than those founded by women, owing to the fact that 15 per cent of the jobs created in small businesses run by women are unpaid. The difference is slightly more marked in productive than in commercial activities.

When we analyse certain aspects of the programme, such as the indicators of improvement in the enterprise itself, we find big differences between men and women: men make a greater effort to improve their premises, to make purchases on credit from their suppliers and to buy machines, while women are noteworthy for keeping accounts, for a wider range of products and for resorting to supplementary loans from professional moneylenders. This information suggests that men invest to improve their economic performance and that women follow certain instructions about keeping their affairs in order but tend to be less successful economically; the fact that they often need to take out loans on less favourable terms suggests that the programme does not meet their needs.

These conclusions drawn from the analysis of the tables presented by the authors of the article show that all the findings must be examined with attention before it can be said that the programme is or is not really fulfilling its purpose. Simply taking the name of the Women's Bank is not enough to break the vicious circle which keeps women in a situation of inferiority or to contribute effectively to the improvement of their lot.

The findings usually presented are optimistic: the 12 programmes[7] studied by 'Acción Internacional AITEC' in 1986 (Maria Otero) included 540 solidarity groups and 2,194 beneficiaries, of which 60 per cent were women; 4,850 loans were granted, the average amount of each loan was US$520 and repayments on 12.2 per cent of the loans were in arrears.

From the economic point of view, the programmes aimed at solidarity groups included the monitoring of their activities, which make it possible to evaluate the impact of the loans on both the small business and family incomes. This was not possible in the case of ordinary bank loans or spontaneous revolving funds.

According to a study of 35 small businesses granted loans by the Cali branch of the Banco Mundial de la Mujer, sales increased by 53 per cent in some cases and profits by 35 per cent in others in the first year (Otero, 1988).

All the studies carried out in Colombia agree that these programmes have had a greater impact on incomes than on job creation (excluding the consolidation of existing jobs or more work for part timers) and a greater impact in the first than in subsequent years. This brings out the limitations of such programmes, whose sole aim is to maximize the individual potential of each small business without any attempt to change the macro-economic structure, which tends to restrict them and to make them dependent on production.

A study on the impact of these programmes in Peru (Reichmann, 1984, cited by Maria Otero, 1988) shows that this is particularly true for women. Some 72 per cent of the women questioned stated that their income had increased, with 40 per cent mentioning a rise of over 50 per cent. Almost all the women who had recorded the highest increases were engaged in activities not traditionally associated with women such as the manufacture of yeasts, spare parts for cookers and containers for soap.

The positive effects of these programmes lie more in the dissolution of relations of dependence and exploitation (unfavourable conditions in regard to subcontracting, marketing, division of labour by sex, etc.) than in the maximizing of individual potential.

Another myth to be treated with caution is the question of training and technical assistance, which are essential components of the more advanced loan schemes for small businesses. This is borne out by Cressida MacKean's observations on the subject (MacKean, 1988).

MacKean lists the main elements of the training programmes, basing her account on those run by the Carvajal Foundation in Cali, which in the last 15 years or so has initiated numerous programmes in Latin America.

In 1983 it was necessary to attend 13 courses in order to obtain a loan, including four compulsory courses bookkeeping, costing, investment planning and staff management. Before the loan was approved it was also necessary to pay several visits to a 'promoter' who would check that applicants were also able to put what they had learnt into practice.

The result was that 76 per cent of small businesses dropped out before the end. As already stated, this approach is a form of selection. For the small businesses that got over all the hurdles the results were highly positive: in one year the average number of jobs rose from 3.8 to 5.1 (thus exceeding the size of a small business if the upper limit is placed at fewer than five persons) and the monthly income of the family rose by 13 per cent in real terms.

Other assessments of the programmes with optional courses suggest that in themselves the courses have little impact on either income or the volume of business. They are too general in content, the practical side is entirely overlooked and those running small businesses lack the basic knowledge to take advantage of the teaching dispensed.

There are two possible solutions to these problems: to make the courses more realistic, which would entail extra costs, or to reduce them to the strict minimum so as to be able to devote the available resources to improving the programme.

Some of these 'minimalist' programmes, such as those run by PROGRESO in Peru and by ADEMI in the Dominican Republic (cf. Tendler, 1987; and Reichmann, 1988), grant more than a thousand loans a year whereas the 'maximalists' do not grant more than a few hundred.

The training becomes more like tailor-made technical assistance, uses a more informal approach and places the emphasis on problems of marketing.

It is difficult to assess the impact of these strategies on women because some of the 'minimalist' programmes are operated for individual loan applicants and others for solidarity groups.

This approach appears open to even more discrimination than the type of training itself since it must also take the initial level of the persons concerned into account. The members of solidarity groups generally have a lower level of education than the recipients of individual loans.

One of the principles on which the training in administration is based is the separation of the accounts of the enterprise from those of the household. This operation is often difficult and sometimes even absurd in the case of enterprises run by women. Their knowledge of mathematics and bookkeeping is rudimentary and in addition it is practically impossible for them to keep full control over income and expenditure in each case. Any profit made is used to increase consumption, to make improvements to the home or to buy something extra, while any loss has to be borne by cutting down on consumption or obtaining a loan from the family. They have to maintain a precarious balance that clearly does not lend itself to building up capital but is unavoidable in an informal economy completely devoid of social security, systems of insurance and the possibility of making provision for various unexpected outlays.

In a programme of assistance for small businesses in Peru an attempt was made to find out why fewer women attended the courses that had been organized. The most common reason given by the women was lack of time owing to the housework that had to be done in addition to any remunerated work (Arias, 1985, cited by MacKean, 1988).

It is certainly not through lack of interest that women do not come to the training courses. In a survey of all the inhabitants of the Comuneros district, conducted by ENDA and the Community in 1985, 80 per cent of the women replied to a series of questions on training. The questions focused on occupations traditionally engaged in by women that offered the possibility of generating income, such as making clothes, knitting, craftwork, and so on. Of their own accord the women placed the emphasis on training and further training in the occupation itself rather than on the management of the enterprise, and on product quality rather than on marketing outlets. Marketing usually became a subject of interest to small entrepreneurs only after they had acquired some experience.

Training courses for women from working-class districts are offered by many institutions such as SENA (National Apprenticeship Scheme), numerous NGOs, foundations, charities and religious groups, etc. One woman interviewed in 1987 told us that she had attended a large number of courses and obtained eight diplomas (in bread-making, first aid, group leadership, etc.) but that her husband, a taxi-driver working nights, would not let her work!

Some of these courses lead to the establishment of productive groups, such as those in Jerusalen and Patio Bonito, but most of them end up in frustrated hopes, either because the subject studied offered no job opportunities or because the course was not anchored in reality and did not help them to establish or consolidate a business.

The efforts made by certain bodies to support the creation of new businesses based on the training courses come up against many obstacles. These businesses are usually enterprises set up as associations or cooperatives, like the two examples mentioned earlier, but many of them fail. They need knowledge of the commercial field and markets but also of problems relating to group cohesion, the division of labour, remuneration, contracts, profit-sharing, and investment. It often takes at least three years for the enterprise to reach a viable level of profit, which means three years of underremuneration or of subsidies.

As Cressida MacKean observes, 'there is no doubt that the women who attend these courses profit from them as individuals and as active members of the local community but they do not obtain significant dividends from the income generated by the enterprise'.

This difficult and ambitious path is nevertheless worth exploring. If the programmes continue to do no more than support existing enterprises run by individuals or solidarity groups, there will be a serious risk of confining women to activities that are barely profitable despite their initial contribution to raising their income.

Training is a potential instrument of progress which should enable women to develop their personal qualities and acquire greater individual and collective self-confidence by opening up new possibilities and activities.

A study carried out by the University of the Andes on occupational mobility (Rey de Marulanda and Ayala, 1981) showed that women had profited much less than men from a higher level of education over the last ten years in terms of higher remuneration and level of post occupied. In other words, it is not enough to train women, one must at the same time draw attention to the kind of battles that will have to be waged in order to change their role and place in society. Such a transformation should be based on education and training, whose powerful potential as a lever should be recognized. If larger projects neglect this aspect they are doomed to failure.

The task then is to foster social participation at various levels, ranging from trade union associations by branch of activity (itinerant vendors, persons running small businesses, domestic staff, etc.) to local associations and committees and grass-roots housing organizations. We shall develop these points, with a few examples, in the sub-section on recommendations.

The next sub-section is devoted to the problem of housing, since for working-class people a home is not only the principal investment made by a family but is also the base for a possible economic activity. Even temporary accommodation constitutes the beginning of economic stability for the family and for women in particular because it gives them the opportunity to open a small shop or workshop or even to rent out a room.

In view of the importance of housing and its connection with economic activities and the rearing of children, with individual and group undertakings, with monetary and non-monetary relations and with the worlds of men and women respectively, we have considered it helpful to devote a few pages to the subject.

Women and self-help housing

We have already stressed the importance of housing and of the local district in the informal strategies of low-income families for the improvement of their standard of living. This is especially true for women, for whom housing is the linchpin of their particular strategy.

The precarious conditions in the cheapest housing, in which there is so little space that families are crammed into one or two rooms and have to share kitchens and toilets with others (especially in the older houses in which everything lettable is rented out). The 'inquilinatos' (rented homes) make daily life and housework unbearable for women.

This explains the struggle of women to obtain a home, whether or not of a temporary nature and even on land without any facilities, where they know they will have to fetch water by hand and cook and wash in the open air for a long time. But at least they no longer run the risk of being expelled for not having paid their rent. They know that this will enable them to lay the foundations for greater economic stability and will facilitate their social integration.

In all the community organizations involved in the struggle for housing, which take forms ranging from collective 'invasions' to legalized groups of self-help builders, women are the driving force. In most cases their role consists in giving massive support to demonstrations, petitions, complaints, and in endlessly making representations to and negotiating with the authorities while coping with the organization of daily life. When the organization loses confidence or gives up it is they who take up the torch and see things through to the end.

It can therefore be stated that the stability of the family is based on the women. It is they who are behind the strategies aimed at achieving stability and at putting down roots whereas the men are more concerned with mobility. What the men want are better opportunities for work or for doing business, and they are ready to abandon their families if they feel too encumbered by them.

Women are less equipped than men to obtain a job with reasonable wages or to carry off a deal that produces an unexpected income but they are tirelessly energetic in consolidating the services, basic facilities and social organization of their local district while criticizing the individualism, opportunism and irresponsibility of the men. Their comments on the reactions of men and women, including community leaders, to the difficulties of collective survival are severe:

'The men are soft. Here, even when ditches have to be dug, it is the women who do the work'; 'The women are the pillars of all work for the community; the men are macho and arrogant; if a woman starts working they feel ashamed and bustle about. If there were only men around they would simply sit down and drink beer'; 'I could act as president of the district because I have already had to do the job but the man who is president now would be incapable of replacing me as treasurer'; 'The participation of women is essential; it is we women who provide the money, the toil and the determination, who make an effort to go and work on the worksite'. (Comments gathered during research on women and the urban crisis, Suremain, Cardona and Dalmazzo, 1988.)

The women work and end up by being dispossessed of their property, but what do they actually do where housing and landed property is concerned?

The survey already referred to suggests that their strategy helps some of them to become homeowners.

Out of the 1,870 women surveyed, 30 per cent were living in rented accommodation, 30 per cent were the owners of their homes, 22 per cent were in housing officially owned by their spouses, 15 per cent in housing owned by the couple and 3 per cent in housing owned by a close relative.

In other words, 67 per cent of all the families owned their homes, a percentage that is naturally higher than in the city centres or when all urban dwellers are considered. Of the families owning their homes, women are mentioned in the title deeds (with or without legal status) in 67 per cent of cases (44 per cent on their own, 23 per cent with their spouses) while men appear in only 56 per cent of cases (33 per cent on their own and 23 per cent with their spouses).

Here the expected correlation between material goods/property and men is not borne out.

The patriarchal model of male ownership, normal in rural areas and probably among the middle and more wealthy classes in the towns and cities, is not seen in the working-class districts.

Generally speaking, women become property-owners after the breakdown of their marriages but sometimes this is also the case in stable households. The following table shows that although a smaller proportion of married women live in rented accommodation than in the case of women living with a companion or alone, the proportion of them who are outright homeowners is also smaller.

TABLE 24

HOMEOWNERS, BY SEX AND CIVIL STATUS

Owner Civil Status	Women %	Men %	Both %	Relative %	In rented acc. %	Total %
Married	22	31	22	2	23	100
Cohabitating	26	22	12	4	36	100
Separated	55	4	6	5	30	100
Widow	54	6	1	11	28	100
Unmarried	42	2	6	12	38	100
Overall	29	22	15	4	30	100

Source: Suremain, Cardona and Dalmazzo, 1988.

The family's access to home ownership is greater when the marriage is stable; it is therefore more common for married women to become homeowners. Women without a companion, women living in cohabitation or unmarried women are more likely to live in rented accommodation than those who are married (separated or widowed).

When we turn to homeowners, however, it is much more common for women without a companion to have their name alone on the deeds than it is for those living with a spouse.

This statement needs to be qualified since, in the case of women, home ownership is more a consequence of their being the sole economic and moral support of their families than recognition for their efforts to

This is confirmed when we look at the different types of housing: the homes owned by women without a companion are smaller and flimsier than those owned by men. Their property is not worthless but it has a lower market value than that owned by men.

When we look more closely at self-help housing efforts in the working-class districts we find a clear division of labour between men and women. The men who have received some training, even incomplete, as builders direct and take an active part in the construction. The women and children act as assistants, performing unskilled tasks such as carrying bricks, cement and water, bringing what is needed, helping to mix the mortar, preparing the food and bringing it to the worksite, etc.

The building plan is usually worked out by the father. The building operations take years and work goes on a good part of the time. Improvements are made to the inside (floors, paintwork, tiling, etc.) once the basic construction is virtually complete. Kitchens and bathrooms are the last to be given the finishing touches because they are the most expensive parts, but also because, being areas reserved for housework, they are considered the least important.

For women who are heads of the family, self-help housing presents considerable difficulties, not only because of their limited income and shortage of free time but also because it is essentially a male preserve. Even those who are always ready to wield a spade or pick are usually forced, through lack of time or the necessary skills, to hire a builder, which increases the cost. They then have a lot of trouble finding a person who sticks to his estimate, calculates a fair price and finishes on time. They are often unable to supervise the work and the builders tend to cheat them and disappear with the money paid in advance.

Apart from the problem of income, the source of these difficulties is the social and sex-based division of labour. The homes directly owned by women tend to be less sturdy than those owned by men or by couples.

For women, access to home ownership and head of household status may paradoxically be regarded as a sign of poverty! The crisis and the increase in poverty may also be said to be responsible for destroying the patriarchal family model and obliging women to take on new responsibilities which are leading them to change their traditional roles.

Both these statements are probably true since poverty and crisis alike bring out new qualities in women and offer them new opportunities for collective action when they find it quite impossible to resolve individually the growing contradictions that weigh upon them.

Certain examples come to light when we examine the numerous experiments conducted by local organizations in which women, sometimes behind the scenes, work and follow training courses or participate in women's organizations which help them find answers to the problems of housing and food, the economic crisis and systems of protection for their children.

We have studied their participation in a self-help housing organization in Bogotá, with particular attention to their opportunities for loans, the number of days they work and their access to home ownership (cf. Suremain, Cardona and Dalmazzo, 1988).

The number of collective self-help housing organizations in Colombia increased considerably during the 1980s. Some were created by the communities themselves while others were promoted by NGOs or by public institutions. By way of example we shall describe below the activities of a self-help housing organization in Bogotá run by an NGO called the Asociación de Vivienda Popular Simón Bolivar or AVP (Simón Bolivar Association for People's Housing).

The project in question is quite original for Colombia, and even for Latin America, for it is focused on collective housing built on self-help principles and not on pre-equipped building plots (with basic facilities already in place) or on individual housing. The site is a plot of 30 hectares in the north-west outskirts of Bogotá.

One of the aims of the project is to discover how the State or private builders can take advantage of existing resources in building land, workers and on-site prefabrication possibilities to build a quality environment for working-class people that includes socio-cultural amenities and all at a cost 30 to 50 per cent below the market price.

AVP has so far built about 1,000 of the 3,000 homes planned altogether. The first stage, comprising 2,000 homes, has been divided into four subprojects of 500 units each in order to comply with the legislation in force.

At present the number of people who have joined the scheme is as follows:

Project No. 1	167 men (49%)	172 women (51%)
Project No. 2	185 men (49%)	192 women (51%)
Project No. 3	150 men (45%)	183 women (55%)
Project No. 4	198 men (48%)	216 women (52%)
Total	695 men (47%)	763 women (53%)

It is striking that the majority of those involved in the scheme are women. Some 75 per cent of the women, and 83 per cent of the men, state that they are the head of the family. We have studied a sample represented by those involved in Project No. 1 to find out the situation and characteristics of women acting as head of the family:

Seventy-five per cent of these women are between 30 and 40 years old; in other words, they are young (average age 34.4 years) but slightly older than the male heads of family (average age 30.5 years).

Seventy-five per cent of the men live with their spouses, 49 per cent of whom contribute an income, whereas 40 per cent of the women calling themselves head of the family have a spouse (stable or not) and 86 per cent earn an income. In other words, there exists at least a second income in 37 per cent of the families headed by a man and in 34 per cent of those headed by a woman.

According to the application forms (in 1981–1982), the families headed by a woman had an average income of 28,000 pesos, as against 44,000 pesos (57 per cent more) for those headed by a man. Taken individually, the female heads of family contributed 44 per cent of the family income and the male heads 70 per cent, equivalent to an income two and a half times higher. As a result there is a marked difference in the monetary resources of the two types of family.

The construction work is shared between two specialized brigades which the members join according to the amount of free time they have. Both men and women must contribute, in person or through a member of their family, 150 days of work. There are 22 types of task and in principle no discrimination between men and women; according to a 1987 survey, however, the women have specialized in six particular areas: office work: 58 per cent of the women; carpentry: 63 per cent of the women; finishing of formed concrete: 58 per cent of the women; paintwork: 75 per cent of the women; positioning of iron reinforcements: 80 per cent of the women; electricity: 20 per cent of the women.

Out of about 100 persons working on the site each day in 1987, some 30 on average would be women. In 1988 spot checks made over several months indicated that the proportion had risen to 45 per cent.

Examination of a sample of 143 'owners' (70 men and 73 women) showed that 62 per cent of the women (heads of family or not) had had to find someone else to do all the work and 23 per cent of them someone to do part of it; 15 per cent of the women performed the set number of days work themselves. Out of a total of 5,755 days of work covered by the study, 26 per cent were performed by a woman 'owner', 15 per cent by a woman acting as substitute (making 41 per cent in all) and 51 per cent by a male substitute (usually a son or the spouse).

Where male owners were concerned, only 8 per cent did all the days themselves; 33 per cent worked some of the days and 59 per cent used a male or female substitute for the whole period. Out of the 6,116 male owner/days studied, 16 per cent were worked by the owner himself, 62 per cent by a male and 22 per cent by a female substitute. All in all, 78 per cent of the days were worked by men and 22 per cent by women. The figures are summed up in Table 25.

The men make greater use of substitutes because the cost of leaving their own jobs is too high. Since they earn more money they prefer having other members of their family do their share of the work and are even prepared to pay substitutes; the women who act as substitutes are usually wives and the men sons (but few of them are of working age) or a relation who is paid.

TABLE 25
DAYS WORKED BY SEX OF OWNER

Person doing the work	Male owner %	Female owner %
The owner	16.5	26
Male substitute	62	59
Female substitute	22	15
Total	100	100

Source: Ibid.

Where the women 'owners' are concerned, their substitutes are usually their children, brothers or close relations. A smaller proportion of the latter are paid for their work.

These figures illustrate how men and women are able to choose between monetary and non-monetary resources.

Even in a system in which the resources are not meant to be of the monetary type (unpaid days of work that help to lower building costs and create a sense of belonging to the home and of quality), the men reintroduce a monetary element and are more inclined to opt for a solution that costs them less. The women on the other hand have less choice and a detailed analysis of their activities shows that most of those who worked all the necessary days without using substitutes had a full-time wage-earning job (i.e. 8 hours a day plus travel time) as well as their housework. They therefore had to use their holidays, ask for unpaid leave of absence or work every weekend over a long period.

These difficulties appear to present a considerable obstacle to women's obtaining access to housing.

Paradoxically, however, an examination of loan applications and title deeds suggests the opposite. Persons joining the scheme have to satisfy several conditions before they receive their deeds: an initial down payment representing 20 per cent of the cost of the housing within 36 months, the requisite number of days of work, and the submission of evidence to the Home-Loan Funds of an income 2.5 times the minimum wage in order to have their loan approved. The steps to be taken and the forms to be filled in are quite complicated and it is necessary to ask employers for time off repeatedly. These formalities are naturally easier for families in which the husband is able to leave the task to his wife than it is for single-parent families.

According to the norms fixed by the Loan Funds financing AVP, the family's resources must be 3.3 times the amount to be repaid each month on an indexed 15-year loan. AVP prepares the personal files and helps its members, especially the women heads of family, to provide the necessary documents since it often happens that their actual resources are less than the amount they initially declared at the time they joined the scheme, a situation which can often be used as grounds for rejection of the application by the Loan Funds. In such cases the women must, in order to show a sufficient income, seek the financial support (real or simply on paper) of a relation or friend or sometimes of their ex-husband.

Occasionally a guarantor is required.[8] This is somewhat risky for the women who are obliged to use this expedient because the person who co-guarantees repayment of the loan appears as co-owner of the dwelling. In certain cases the deed-holder may succeed in convincing her guarantors to accept her name alone on the title deeds, particularly in the case of a couple living in a consensual union.

When the loan is granted to the head of the family (man or woman), AVP encourages the two spouses, whether or not they are married, to put the deeds in both their names. This solution can cause problems when the husband works for a firm which has given him a personal loan or made a separation payment ('cesantia') in advance[9] because the firm is reluctant to accept the name of any other person on the deeds apart from its employee.

To become a homeowner a person has had to overcome all these obstacles. Out of the first 44 homes handed over to the various heads of family in Project No. 1 in January 1987, 25 per cent of the women received their title deeds as against 8 per cent of the men. This shows the determination and ingenuity displayed by the women, who quickly succeeded in fulfilling the necessary conditions in spite of their handicaps.

The results in other less sophisticated self-help housing organizations are much the same. The women are more determined and disciplined than the men in doing their quota of days, attending meetings, gathering the necessary documents and undergoing the countless formalities. So long as the organization is attentive to their needs in terms of working hours, evidence of income, documents relating to unconventional family situations, the provision of child-minding facilities on the worksite, flexible forms of participation, the non-segregation of worksite tasks and opportunities to specialize according to their skills, the women quickly overcome all the obstacles in their path.

The access of women to low-cost housing in the public sector is clearly selective, depending on the level of their income and on the ways in which certain formal self-help housing schemes are organized. Spontaneous informal self-help housing produces just as much discrimination whereas self-help schemes run as associations make it possible to find more appropriate solutions through which the women from working-class districts can more easily obtain a home. This type of approach needs to be developed in the numerous community organizations concerned with self-help housing so that the enormous effort made by women to obtain housing will not be thwarted by the inflexibility of the internal procedures of the organization itself or of the financing institutions.

A fuller account would require us to speak in greater detail of the women employed by small businesses as distinct from the owners and of those living from prostitution, a taboo subject. However, the lack of qualitative information in the first case and of both qualitative and quantitative information in the second would confine us making general comments of little interest. Both subjects need to be explored in greater detail. With regard to prostitution, an action-oriented research programme in several NGOs in Bogotá and Cali is under way and will yield interesting information within a year or two.

Some lines of actions and proposals

As we have indicated in regard to the problems of housing, small businesses and domestic service, the question of women's role in development involves all aspects of economic activity in urban working-class areas. Taking 'economy' in its broad sense, we shall examine 'the role of women in the informal urban economy' within the context of a more comprehensive approach.

In our view this approach, outlined in the course of the foregoing analyses, is the only possible basis for alternative proposals to resolve the economic, social, cultural and political crisis currently affecting Latin America and even more acutely, Colombia.

In this section we shall try to formulate some alternative policies based on certain philosophical ideas that should underlie all development of the 'alternative' type, facilitating the active participation of women and boosting the country's economy by increasing the contribution and material prosperity of the female population.

We shall then turn to some more concrete proposals concerning, for example, the type of dialogue that needs to be engaged between the national and local planning system and the various agents of economic and social development.

Lastly, we shall suggest some strategies for the implementation of alternative policies that are based on already existing factors of dynamism in which women are the driving force.

From reproduction to production: towards development on a human scale

There can be no solution to the present crisis in Colombia that does not take account of the country's social and political environment, marked by violence and by the clash of disparate and highly complex forces.

The foreign debt is not as high as in certain neighbouring countries but Colombia's internal problems have never been as worrying as they are now. The moral crisis is so serious that the drug barons have no difficulty in recruiting young people from working-class districts to serve as hired killers for the murder of peasants suspected of helping the guerillas or for the assassination of politicians, judges, journalists and civil servants who oppose them.

The democratization and modernization of the country have been impeded by the privileges of and dubious alliances between large landowners, industrialists and drug barons, who are afraid of losing control or giving ground.

The social conflicts, the citizens' movements in the towns and cities and the marches by peasants have vainly protested against the fall in purchasing power, the high cost of living, the absence of urban services and land-grabbing.

The two traditional parties, the liberals and the conservatives, are unable to pluck up the courage to broaden the political debate and involve other potential social forces, preferring to count the dead than to put forward viable alternatives.

The situation is gloomy and might seem largely irrelevant to our particular concern. But this is not so for knowledge of the background is essential to greater understanding of the problems that can arise in the elaboration of serious and realistic proposals to improve the living conditions of women.

Colombia is living in a state of war. In a situation in which the whole population is faced with questions of life or death, the problems of women become of secondary importance.

As Manfred Max Neef states in his 'Desarrollo a Escala Humana' (Development on a Human Scale) (Max Neef, 1986), the crisis in Latin America results from the convergence of various factors: economic, social and political crises; the ineffectiveness of the State and of representative institutions; the arms race; the absence of a democratic culture in the society; the fragmentation of socio-cultural identities; and the impoverishment of a large number of people. All these factors combine and reinforce each other.

One after the other, the neo-liberal and populist 'developmentalist' (desarrollistas) responses to the situation end up by opting for short-term reductionist programmes. Max Neef also speaks of a 'Utopia crisis', which is the most serious crisis of all, since it makes Colombians incapable of tackling their problems by harnassing their own imagination, their own values, their own skills and especially their own reality.

The development policies employed in Latin America have in the past wavered between the 'developmentalism' of ECLAC or IDB (which, despite some nationalist goal-orientation, has resulted in a model of concentrated industrialization that has generated debt and monetary, financial and social imbalances) and neo-liberal monetarism with its desire to impose policies of adjustment aimed at reducing monetary disorder without taking into account the social consequences or even the country's structure of production.

Blocked as it is, the situation requires a radical change of perspective. 'A new approach is needed, directed first and foremost towards the real satisfaction of human needs... Development on a human scale must be concentrated on and rooted in the satisfaction of basic human needs, must strive towards ever-increasing self-reliance and must respect the organic links between human beings and nature and technology, between macro-processes and local patterns of behaviour, between private lives and society in general, between planning and autonomy, and between civil society and the State' (Max Neef, 1986). We might add 'and between one sex and the other'.

Each society and each culture has its own way of responding to basic needs. Its responses may be facile or not genuine, inhibiting or destructive, or they may be synergetic. Responses must be distinguished from needs which, according to Max Neef, are subsistence, protection, affection, understanding, participation, rest, creativity, identity and freedom. This theoretical view is extremely fruitful because it frees us from a narrowly economistic and monetarist idea of development. In a world hitherto ruled by economics, production has dominated reproduction, the monetary aspects of life have dominated the non-monetary aspects and men have dominated women. Like Max Neef, we think that any development centred solely on the indicators of economic growth leads to a dead end; this is especially true in the case of women since such an approach seriously distorts reality not only by overlooking the enormous non-monetary contribution of women to improving the well-being of their families (through an ever-increasing work-load) but in addition by daring to suggest that they should work more in order to achieve equality with or even replace men in the production of monetary resources.

Such a proposal is far from liberating for Latin American women. We must find another way of recognizing and enhancing the value of those non-monetary activities that take place essentially in the sphere of social reproduction, of promoting their redistribution and of creating monetary and non-monetary activities which satisfy in a dynamic (or synergetic, as Max Neef would say) fashion the basic human needs of men and women of all ages.

Achieving a new independence and shaking off the ties of subordination does not mean that women must reject the world of reproduction but it does imply recognition of what they have achieved in terms of identity, self-affirmation, creativity and even of calling into question the division of labour by sex, so that those achievements may be extended to the field of production. A further implication is the need to propose money-earning production activities in tune with the needs of human reproduction, i.e. the basic needs of all people.

The crisis, which has obliged women to group together and come up with new ideas, should help them to develop new forms of solidarity within the production process that are keyed to their own needs and the needs of their families and are rooted in the opportunities and organizations they have created.

It is not enough to improve the credit system for small businesses run by women; we must also question whether their employment in a particular branch of industry is not intended solely to produce cheap goods for export (cheaper than if male workers were used), for in that case any genuine improvement in the incomes and qualifications of women would by definition be rendered impossible.

This leads us to take another look at certain objections raised by various authors concerning the promotion and creation of new enterprises organized as associations. The authors concerned claim that the costs of technical assistance are too high. In our view, on the contrary, it is important to continue since their function lies more in solving a problem of subsistence than in the production of marketable goods. The creation and promotion of new enterprises is one way of regenerating solidarity and creating ancillary services aimed at strengthening ties among people both in day-to-day life and at work. It would also contribute to the building of a civil society and give more opportunities for social participation.

Women have, in the words of Caroline Moser, 'practical gender needs', that is to say specific needs related to their traditional functions. These needs are 'satisfied' in particular by the social services that are indispensable for the 'normal' performance of their work in the home and human reproduction.

They also have 'strategic gender needs', that is to say specific needs relating to their changing role in society and the division of labour by sex. For most women these strategic needs relate to the majority of basic needs that are not satisfied, such as understanding of the world, participation in society, rest, creativity, identity and freedom.

Finding ways to respond to these needs in terms of both monetary and non-monetary concerns and then interrelating the ties so that one is not subordinated to the other calls for creative vision as to open up new perspectives. This is what we shall endeavour to do in the following pages through a number of practical recommendations.

The place of women in the planning of development

We are under no illusions. We do not think that our proposals will one day be integrated into a development plan of the conventional type. When attempts are made to assess the unseen work of women it is sometimes boldly proposed that their work in the home be given an economic value. To be more complete, however, it would be necessary to include the work they do in the community, the extra work they have to do to make up for the complete or partial lack of urban services as well, of course, as a precise evaluation (by means of appropriate statistics) of all paid work done by women, children and other forgotten groups in the male-centred economy.

Experience shows that this exercise is both difficult and controversial owing to the diversity of the criteria to be adopted. For example, should we give housework the same economic value as the work done by a female domestic employee who is herself underpaid because she performs a function that is not esteemed? Should we include all the immaterial functions such as love, affection, play or rest?

If, moreover, it proves impossible to measure their contribution in economic terms, how can we assess it in the context of systems founded on econometric measurement?

It is possible that there exists another way of upgrading the work done by women, based not on a system of measurement but on recognizing that it exists. It would no longer be seen as an obstacle to production ('the heavy family responsibilities of women') but as a basic human activity which therefore merits to be shared and performed by all human beings.

As regards the work done by women for pay, it needs to be more effectively understood and recognized by means of changes in the terms of reference of household surveys and censuses. This could be done, for example, by extending the period of reference so as to include discontinuous activities or by changing the way in which questions are asked so that of all monetary income earned can be taken into account by the woman concerned and mentioned to the man or woman conducting the survey.

To initiate in-depth thinking on this theme and to ensure that the results of the various initiatives are taken into consideration and integrated into the instruments and machinery of the planning system, it is essential to establish a participatory study group within the national planning department.

There already exists (or used to exist) a body designed to bring together women specialists in rural and agricultural questions with the purpose of improving development plans. The task of these specialists is to draw attention to the concerns of women in agricultural occupations and to see that those concerns find a place in development plans.

Unfortunately, there is no such mechanism for women in urban working-class districts. One important measure would be to create at the highest level an instrument for reflection similar to the one for rural women. This would draw attention to the viewpoint of urban women and make it possible to work out a number of proposals and alternatives based on their particular experience.

These bodies should by no means replace other forms of consultation. Women should be able to participate to a greater extent at all levels (we shall return to this later). Some machinery of this kind would contribute to the debate and might even influence some decisions taken within the State apparatus.

Despite the collapse of the welfare state myth, the remaining fragments of which are being eroded more and more each day, it is undeniable that the State is still in a position to play a fundamental role in favour of women through the provision of collective facilities. If it fails or ceases to do this women will be obliged to take action themselves. They should become involved in the joint management of such services in order to ensure that their practical and strategic needs are met. If such services, which facilitate socialization and ease the burden of motherhood, are not provided, the participation of women will always be limited and their access to paid productive work impossible or possible only in conditions of subordination and inferiority.

It is therefore vital that the debate on this issue be activated in many State departments, and especially in the institution responsible for development plans.

In the following section we shall suggest a few basic points on which development policies conducive to the economic participation of women could be founded.

Seven proposals designed to improve the situation of women in the informal urban economy

Some of the following proposals are strategic in nature and designed to ensure that the specific needs of women are taken into account, while others constitute a more practical response to the concerns discussed earlier.

ACTION SHOULD BE BASED ON THE COMMUNITY ACTIVITIES OF WOMEN

Experience with the Patio Bonito co-operative and many other ventures in the cities of Colombia have shown that for large numbers of women the training they receive in the course of community work constitutes their first step in their escape from isolation and total submission to a future with no prospect of improvement.

The fact of joining forces with other women in order to solve a problem, of making representations to public institutions, of speaking in public, of giving their views, of making mistakes and starting again, of resolving their conflicts with other people, of receiving a course of training, and of being able to share their worries and personal problems with others provides a range of experiences that create a new mood among the women involved in community groups. They develop self-esteem and a more open-minded attitude towards the outside world and public life which help them to take initiatives, to have confidence in themselves and to change many aspects of their daily lives. In this process they come up against opposition of many types, including the opposition of their husbands who, in the case of voluntary work, say that they are wasting their time or, if the work is done for a wage, complain that they want to cut free from or take the place of their husbands; whatever they do, the women are always suspected of wishing to abandon their duties in the home and as mothers and wives and even of having an affair.

The women who succeed in overcoming such initial conflicts begin to gain in self-confidence, to acquire a new image of themselves and a new independence.

For these women work is much more important than earning an income. In our view it is through working for the community that they experience profound changes in their perceptions of their own roles and discover their deeper potential.

The women most actively engaged in the community are sometimes those with work experience (paid or unpaid) but the majority of them are mothers working in a group for the first time. They often speak of their activities in terms such as: 'Before, I was stupid; I talked of nothing except washing my children and preparing meals. Now I speak to important people and I am not afraid'.

Some of these women earn an income for their families through intermittent activities such as a grocer's shop, a little sewing work, housework, washing clothes, giving injections, minding children, but in many cases they devote more time to the community organization than to paid work.

Certain projects have become so firmly established that they provide some women with full-time paid work: among them are certain community kindergartens in Bogotá or some of the self-help housing organizations. In most cases, however, the work is voluntary with the result that women with a full-time paid job are able to take very little part in it owing to their almost total lack of free time.

Many projects aimed at the creation of remunerated activities become the starting-point for longer-term projects which develop initiative and perseverance, qualities we regard as at least as important as technical and administrative training.

This strategy is in fact practised by numerous NGOs, which are well aware that the existence of a community organization facilitates the creation or consolidation of productive activities.

In the case of self-help housing associations or fund-raising to provide mains water, sewage systems or other services, the community leaders may have to administer large sums of money. They must therefore be able to organize the work and report to the community.

Mastering a productive process is of course quite different from competing in the market or paying employees but it is found that women with some experience of community work tend to be more serious and disciplined in their approach to the organization of production and to have a more long-term view of the problems. In other words the value of community networks is not limited to the more open attitudes they foster among the women involved but is also bound up with the type, operation and scope of future activities.

Here is an example: a district in south-west Bogotá which has a series of seven community kindergartens each involving between ten and 35 women. They were established between two and 11 years ago in response to the need of mothers to have someone look after their children under 6 in a safe place while they went out to work. These day nurseries were set up by women who, partly in a spirit of altruism and social solidarity, began to form groups with the purpose of minding children in temporary premises. After a while they put their work on a firmer and more professional footing and obtained support from the State as well as from some NGOs. For a few years they were paid by international development agencies, which greatly contributed to the stability of the groups, the recognition of their work and the improvement of their standard of living. When this funding came to an end there arose the question of creating small businesses capable of financing all or part of this social work.

However, the various attempts that were made encountered all the obstacles with which we are now familiar: small scale of production, insufficient credit, marketing problems, lack of training in business management, etc. The women tried to set up shops, bakeries or clothing workshops on a part-time basis but then decided to change their approach: instead of adapting their communal activities to the market they chose, with the help of an NGO, to take advantage of the solidarity that existed between them to establish productive activities aimed at strengthening their organization.

An economic, social and cultural diagnosis of the quality of life in the district was carried out, based on the findings of a survey of 2,000 persons and on various meetings and seminars. Food turned out to be the principal item of expenditure (50 to 70 per cent) for families averaging between one and two minimum wages. Rather than set up a communal grocery store that would have quickly succumbed owing to lack of capital and a host of other problems, it was decided to organize a consumer network initially based on the kindergarten mistresses and parents. Some 29 staple products were selected after a study of selling prices in local shops and in the city centre. The scheme started with a membership of 400 families which later grew to 1,750. The volume of purchases made it possible to negotiate with wholesalers and producers (e.g. 30 tonnes of dried vegetables per month). The resulting network presented a number of advantages: a comparison of wholesale and retail prices (even when the cheapest retail prices were used) showed that a profit could be made that could then be used to strengthen the group and establish alternative economic circuits which would in turn provide outlets for the small businesses and make possible a savings and loans system among members of the network.

The system worked as follows: the wholesale price of an egg, for example, which retails for between 25 and 30 pesos depending on the district, is 19 pesos. The difference between the lowest retail price and the wholesale price is therefore 6 pesos. This sum will be put to several uses: 1 peso for the consumer (the egg is sold at 24 pesos) in order to retain his loyalty to the scheme and 1 peso to cover the overheads of the scheme. The remaining 4 pesos are distributed in the form of coupons to persons recruiting new members and thus helping to expand the network. These coupons may be cashed every two months but are preferably exchanged against other products, services (kindergarten, health care, medicines, etc.) or objects manufactured by small businesses belonging to the scheme, or simply saved in a solidarity fund set up to meet urgent needs in the event of some temporary problem.

The district of Bogotá, which provides a market for the community kindergartens through its social assistance service, is currently thinking of using the system to supply and strengthen its network of families by affiliating about 100 extra consumer groups (the day nurseries). If the contract is confirmed the State (actually the Municipality of Bogotá) will be supporting a grass-roots initiative brought into being by groups of women. The scheme will promote economic redistribution on a large scale by making use of both formal and informal networks.

Other associations are holding discussions with a view to joining, including a group of women that prepare dried vegetables obtained from peasant co-operatives, a small business making soap, wax and shoe-polish, a transport association and a carpentry firm. The latter has begun making educational toys for the kindergartens out of leftover pieces of wood.

This example is too recent to serve as a model but it strikes us as a promising initiative rich in ideas that could be applied elsewhere. It relates the world of reproduction to the world of production in a most interesting way in that it seeks simultaneously to solve concrete problems, to create new forms of synergy and chains of solidarity and to regain cultural and economic control over entire processes rather than just parts of them.

Difficulties will certainly arise and have already done so when certain middlemen realize that they are faced with a competitor. Nevertheless, we feel that this network is a good example of a 'creative Utopia', of an idea which opens up new horizons.

The community kindergartens in Bogotá represent an experiment with women's organizations that is comprehensive and firmly established, but numerous other groups exist throughout the country, such as health groups and community restaurants, who have similarly consolidated their organizations.

Mention should also be made of a new undertaking by the Instituto Colombiano de Bienestar Familiar (ICBF) with a view to providing greater social coverage for pre-school-age children, namely the 'homes' run by 'community mothers'. The idea is to pay mothers in working-class districts half the minimum monthly wage in return for looking after, in their own homes, about 15 children up to 6 years of age. They are supplied with the necessary food, which they have to cook, and are given a small loan for improving their accommodation.

The number of these 'homes' has grown rapidly throughout the country; there are now several thousand of them and they are to be found even in districts with community kindergartens. The wage offered, though very low, has proved to be a powerful incentive. Training a maximum of two weeks has been reduced to a minimum.

In contrast, the experienced kindergarten mistresses in the community kindergartens have never managed to obtain such advantages from the State. In response to their demands they were told that all they had to do was to each take 15 children home and then they would be given the same 'advantages' as the others.

When this programme was first introduced people expected disaster owing to the lack of experience of the 'community mothers', the poor physical conditions (15 young children in unsuitable and in many cases unhealthy premises) and the difficult relations between these 'mothers' and ICBF officials, who were primarily concerned with reaching quantitative targets. Today a protest movement is taking shape with the aim of improving the food (very inadequate) and the remuneration. An increasing number of the 'homes' are being amalgamated to form collective day nurseries whose staff are trying to learn the basics of pedagogy. A new large-scale network is coming into being despite the hostility of the State towards new initiatives of any type. Started without thought as a purely economic device of limited scope, the scheme may give birth to a social movement that offers solutions to social and economic problems. We must keep an eye on developments.

RECOGNITION AND GREATER RESPECT FOR THE WORK OF WOMEN

This subject has been explored directly or indirectly in the course of our study. It covers such matters as the remuneration of community kindergarten mistresses (when the State creates or makes use of such a service) and their right or the right of domestic employees to social security.

It appears that more women than men benefit from some form of social security cover 87 per cent of them in the formal sector and 19 per cent in the informal one. It is one of the rare cases where they are at a slight advantage even though social security cover is minimal in the informal sector.

In the informal sector, the standards of social security and the various benefits are of course difficult to apply in practice. They are aimed more at preventive than at curative medicine. They can therefore have a decisive impact of the state of health of the population, especially women. State support could take a wide variety of forms without detriment to its role, including the provision of equipment, the training of temporary staff and the delegation to these bodies of most work in the field of prevention. The present Minister of Health has recently put forward certain proposals of this type.

STUDIES BY BRANCH OF ACTIVITY

A detailed economic study of each branch of activity could bring out existing interrelationships between large and small businesses and the role played by each sex within those relationships. However, it is scarcely conceivable that the balance of power between the informal and formal sectors can be improved where incomes, contractual relations, market sharing, capital accumulation and value added are concerned. Higher incomes and greater productivity in the informal sector will only be achieved by improving the individual skills of those running small businesses and by changing the structure of the market.

We could take as an example one of the programmes on which we are at present working. This programme is concerned with innovatory systems for the processing of household refuse. Several NGOs are basing their current aid programmes on 'scrap-hunters' who derive their income from recovering scrap from the large waste dumps or from the refuse bins of rich districts, offices and factories. On closer examination it emerges that the more organized these scrap-dealers are, the more technical and efficient the recovery process becomes. The small traders are then driven out and the business is taken over by two or three large companies specializing in glass and cardboard. Peldar, a multinational corporation making glass, now derives 70 per cent of its raw material from recycled glass and supports all the campaigns to encourage recycling and the pre-sorting of waste. As a result the scrap-hunters even those possessing large storage hangars are as poor as ever.

This makes it necessary to create a linked series of activities that will tap the value added at the point where it is really worthwhile, i.e. in the transformation process itself, in the small-scale recycling industry and in the manufacture of everyday products. A women's co-operative supported by ENDA is planning to manufacture toilet paper and plastic articles such as buckets and pipes from urban waste and to use organic waste to make fertilizers for the cultivation of plants and shrubs to embellish their district.

Though of undoubted merit in its present form, the Patio Bonito co-operative should follow the same path in order to achieve greater independence than at present.

The methodology of 'employment basins' makes it possible to supplement this study with an analysis of the local impact of employment policies in terms of local supply and demand with a view to finding ways of gearing training to the experience of the workforce.

TRAINING: POWERFUL LEVER OR SIMPLY A MIRAGE?

Vocational training is not enough in itself to improve the productivity of small businesses, particularly those run by women. This is especially true when such training merely reinforces their traditional role. Even though it opens doors for them, its impact may be purely theoretical unless it has the explicit aim of profoundly transforming the respective roles of men and women.

Improvements in the education of women have not been reflected in employment. To use a quick simplification, we now have domestic employees who have degrees rather than being illiterate!

It is essential to think out new types of vocational training for women so that they may engage in the more highly regarded and better paid occupations traditionally reserved for men.

There are few young women in the technical institutes for construction and mechanical engineering and these few have to overcome numerous obstacles to complete their training. On the other hand those who obtain their diplomas are generally appreciated on the labour market for their professional conscience and for their high standards.

If the technical and vocational training of women is to serve as a genuine lever for their social advancement, it should cover topics such as the roles of men and women as well as the needs and aspirations of women in regard to the division of labour. In its programmes on Appropriate Technologies for Women, ENDA discovered that despite the training seminars and workshops organized to teach women how to make slow sand-filters (for the provision of drinking-water in the community kindergartens) the women concerned reproduced the gender-based division of labour when it came to actually making the filters: they delegated the skilled work to their husbands (plumbing and making of the actual filters) while they themselves for hours engaged in the long, fastidious and unskilled task of washing the sand to be used. As a result they ended up by feeling frustrated and claimed to be unable to cope with any problem related to the functioning of the filter. A special teaching module had to be introduced, focused on male and female roles and the aspirations of women, before they would dare to tackle the crux of the technological problem other than in theory and thus master the practical side.

Another aspect of training not to be overlooked is what could be called 'civic' or 'citizenship' education, which encourages the participation of women in society. We have already seen how women with a greater understanding of local problems regarding relations with the State and their community transformed the image presented of themselves, acquired self-confidence and developed a more objective attitude to setbacks, misfortunes and difficulties in their community work. This new outlook is obtained by extending the range of their daily lives and making them feel a part of the social life of their country.

The State should encourage progress in this direction among the women with leading roles in their districts and associations instead of frightening them away and impeding their personal development. By encouraging such women the State would find new interlocutors more interested in the solution of their problems than in political wheeling and dealing.

ENCOURAGEMENT FOR WOMEN'S ORGANIZATIONS

Our proposals in regard to training should form part of a broader objective concerning the social organization or structuring of civil society. Colombia, a country torn by political and social conflicts, does not have enough fora for dialogue, negotiation and exchange between the various segments of its society. The weakness of civil society is recognized as one of the main causes of violence and poverty.

Under the administration of the previous government, SENA made great efforts and provided financial support to several organizations for small businesses with the aim of strengthening the unions. It also encouraged and supported the organization of 15 meetings at which women from working-class districts throughout the nation or in a particular region discussed topics in the news such as the foreign debt or municipal reform. Each of these meetings attracted over 100 women, including many artisans and heads of small businesses (see our earlier discussion of the survey).

Unfortunately these efforts have been interrupted under the present administration. This is a pity because all the programmes aimed at helping the informal sector and small businesses lay considerable emphasis on the organization of unions. The itinerant vendors and shoemakers in various cities have had some success in this respect and have managed to negotiate improvements to their respective regulations with the municipalities concerned. More support, encouragement and publicity should be given to the participation of women in these organizations and to the establishment of organizations for women.

LOW-COST HOUSING

Housing is a key issue in the informal economy and of particular importance to women. The large numbers of women who participate in self-help housing associations throughout the country are testimony to the enthusiasm with which they perform all the tasks generally regarded as men's work in the hope of finding a solution to their biggest problems and achieving economic and domestic stability. The more precarious their economic situation, the more pains they take to resolve this type of problem.

In several countries the gradual introduction into State-subsidized housing plans of schemes in which work on the site takes the place of monetary payments (homes that are self-built little by little rather than delivered complete by professional builders) has enabled more women to become directly involved.

The existence of non-discriminatory regulations facilitates the access of women to housing whereas 'spontaneous' self-help construction maintains them in a position of inferiority subject to the man-dominated 'law of the jungle'.

These experiments have also shown that women are able to find a skilled job after practical training on the worksite. Some production units for breeze-blocks are run by women while other women have become housepainters, masons, plumbers or carpenters with a reputation for well-finished work.

This seems to us a promising approach exemplified in several programmes in Mexico, Jamaica, Bolivia and Peru. Where Colombia is concerned, the idea needs further promotion in order to obtain official support for existing proposals.

A BROADER SYSTEM OF LOANS

We have left this subject to the end because it is often the main or even the only question covered by studies on the informal sector. This fact is worth emphasizing because, in our view, loans cannot be regarded as the only means of improving the conditions governing gainful employment in small businesses run by women.

One important measure would be to make general use of the 'solidarity groups' method which, as we have seen, has a number of advantages for the women who take part. This approach should not be the preserve of NGOs and private foundations alone but should be developed into a much broader system that will help women to make greater use of their non-monetary resources, namely their sense of solidarity and responsibility.

This type of credit could also be used to strengthen informal revolving funds. Such funds, set up on the initiative of the local inhabitants of working-class districts, could be strengthened or refinanced through recognized institutions or NGOs which would guarantee the genuineness and seriousness of the projects. This approach has been tried out with success by various NGOs, which have placed money in co-operative banks as security for loans to persons running small businesses or for home improvement. Such guarantees are usually backed up by technical assistance to make sure that the money is properly used.

Our proposal is that the system should be applied to all co-operatives and associations of enterprises since this sector is currently the poor relation of the financing system. The State could assume part of the cost of technical assistance if it employed to different ends a part of its resources which are at present hard to mobilize, being directed towards the formal sector. Here we are referring to SENA.

As the informal sector makes no contribution to the financing of the apprenticeship system it has practically no access to the benefits of that scheme. It should be possible, however, as a measure of social redistribution, to exert a significant multiplier effect by means of relatively minor adjustments.

Conclusion

We must discard the numerous clichés and prejudices and imagine fresh solutions for all the economic, social and emotional problems which the women from the poorest segments of Colombian society have to face. Much remains to be done if we wish to assess the real contributions of women and reveal the limitations of what has been proposed so far.

Though we hope that we have cleared the ground we are well aware that what we have done is a mere drop in the ocean.

Perhaps our major contribution has been the attempt to convey the importance of the invisible and intangible 'non-work' of women on behalf of the community as a source of creativity, solidarity and vitality in a society dominated by threats to life itself and crushed by the power of money.

This vitality must be regarded as an asset and not as a burden or as a mere bandage for a sick society. Numerous women are working in this spirit and fortunately they are still hopeful.

Notes

1. Mission established in 1985 to examine employment problems in Colombia and formulate recommendations.
2. It should be recalled that this survey covered 1,870 housewives in the outlying working-class districts. The term 'housewife' signified that the person concerned was responsible for the housework and/or a mother.
3. Pages 63 and 64 of the report. See bibliographical reference No. 8.
4. The author was one of the organizers and discussion leaders for these meetings. The report for UNICEF was drafted by two members of the team of organizers.
5. A State vocational training organization.
6. In 1987 130,000 pesos was equivalent to US$505.
7. Since 1983: CIDES, Bogotá; Banco Mundial de la Mujer, Cali; FUNDESCOM, Cali; CDV, Cartagena. Since 1985: ACTUAR, Medellin; CORFAS, Bucaramanga; Cruzada Social, Manizales. Since 1986: Banco Mundial de la Mujer, Medellin; ACTUAR, Tolima; CORFAS, Bogotá; Banco Mundial de la Mujer, Puerto Tejada.
8. In one case, the loan was contracted by a group of six persons!
9. The 'cesantías' are a form of unemployment benefit which the employee receives on leaving the firm and the amount is in proportion to his years of service. It is possible to request part of the sum due for the purchase of a dwelling even without leaving the firm.

SELECTED REFERENCES

Out of about 120 documents consulted we have selected the most relevant ones.

1. Aguiar, Neuma. 'La Mujer en la fuerza de trabajo en América Latina, un resumen introductorio', in: *Desarrollo y Sociedad,* No. 13, CEDE UNIANDES, Bogotá, 1984.
2. Berger, Marguerite, Mayra Buvinic et al. *La Mujer en el sector informal,* ILDIS Quito Ed. Nueva Sociedad, Caracas, 1988.
3. Bonilla, Elsy, Coordinator, Plaza y Janés, Bogotá, 1985.
4. Bourguignon, François. 'Pobreza y dualismo en el sector urbano de las economías en desarrollo: el caso de Colombia', in: *Desarrollo y Sociedad,* No. 1, CEDE UNIANDES, Bogotá, 1979.
5. Chenery (Chenery Mission or Employment Mission). *El problema Laboral Colombiano.* 2 vols. Ed. José Antonio Ocampo and Manuel Ramirez. Published with the support of the Contraloría General de la República, Departamento Nacional de Planeación, Servicio Nacional de Aprendizaje, Bogotá, 1987. Articles referred to:

• Flores, Carmen Elisa, Echeverri, Rafael, Mendez, Regina. 'Caracterización de la transición demográfica en Colombia.' London-O, Juan Luis. 'La dinámica laboral y el ritmo de la actividad económica.'

• Lopez, Hugo, Sierra, Oliva and Henao, Martha Luz. 'Sector Informal:

entronque económico y desconexión jurídico política con la sociedad moderna.'

- Maldonado, Héctor and Guerrero, Bernardo. 'Evolución de las Tasas de participación en Colombia.'
- Reyes, Alvaro. 'Ingresos laborales y empleo.'

6. Comision de Estudios Sobre la Violencia, several authors. *Colombia Violencia y Democracia.* National University of Colombia, Colciencias, Bogotá, 1988.

7. Eljach, Sonia. Final evaluation report on the project 'Acciones para transformar las condiciones socio-laborales del servicio doméstico en Colombia'. Mimeo., Bogotá, June 1988.

8. National Federation of Shopkeepers. *El comercio informal: un tratamiento nacional para un problema nacional,* paper presented at the National Congress of Shopkeepers, Cali, November 1982, Mimeo., Bogotá, 1982.

9. Garcia, Castro Mary. 'Ser Mujer, ser pobre y ser jefe de hogar en Bogotá, Eh Ave María!', paper presented to the IV Congreso de Sociología, Cali, 1982.

10. Lautier, Bruno. 'La Jirafa y el Unicornio', paper for a forum on employment, held in Bogotá in February 1989. GRIEDT, Paris, 1989.

11. Leon, Magdalena. Preparatory document for a seminar on: 'Las estrategias de intervención comunitaria', for a master's degree in community psychology, Javeriana University, Mimeo., Bogotá, 1988.

12. Lopez, Hugo, Henao, Martha Luz, Sierra, Oliva. *El Sector Informal Urbano, estructura, dinámica y políticas.* Centro de Investigaciones Económicas, University of Antioquia, Medellin, 1986.

13. Lopez, Hugo. 'Racionalidad y políticas para el sector informal, el caso del comercio callejero en Colombia', in: *Sector Informal y Organización Popular,* Instituto de Estudios Liberales, Bogotá, 1988.

14. Mac Ewen Scott, Alison. 'Desarrollo Dependiente y segregación ocupacional por sexo', in: *Desarrollo y Sociedad,* No. 13, CEDE UNIANDES, Bogotá, 1984.

15. Max Neef, Manfred. 'Desarrollo a Escala Humana', in: *Development Dialogue,* Special Issue 1986, CEPAUR and Dag Hammarskjöld Foundation, Sweden, 1986.

16. Patin-O, Carlos, Arturo et al. UNICEF. *Pobreza y Desarrollo en Colombia, su impacto sobre la infancia y la mujer.* UNICEF/Departamento Nacional de Planeación, Instituto Colombiano de Bienestar Familiar, Bogotá, 1988.

17. *Plan Nacional para el Desarrollo de la Microempresa,* 1988–1990, Document DNP, Mimeo., Bogotá, May 1988.

18. Several authors. *La actualidad del sector informal urbano en Colombia,* Memorias del taller sobre trabajos de investigación, Cali, September 1983. CIID (Centro Internacional de Investigaciones para el Desarrollo), Department of Political Science, University of the Andes, Bogotá, 1984.

19. Several authors. *Pobreza absoluta, críticas y expectativas del Modelo de Desarrollo.* Co-published by Editorial Oveja Negra, Nikos, Instituto de Estudios Liberales, Fundación Friedrich Naumann, Bogotá, 1986.

20. Quintero, Víctor Manuel, et al. *Mercado y Microempresas,* FESCOL University of San Buenaventura, Cali, 1987.

21. Ramirez, Socorro and Gomez, Ofelia. *Informe de Análisis de los Resultados*

del Trabajo de la Investigación - Acción - Capacitación de los Encuentros con Organizaciones de Mujeres pertenecientes a los Sectores Populares, report for SENA and UNICEF. Mimeo., Bogotá, 1987.

22. Ramirez, Gómez Fernando. 'Algunas consideraciones sobre el trabajo independiente en Colombia', in: *la Transición Demográfica y la oferta de empleo en Colombia,* Vol. II, ILO/SENALDE, Bogotá, 1986.

23. Rey de Marulanda, Nohra and Ayala, Ulpiano. 'La reproducción de la fuerza de trabajo en las grandes ciudades Colombianas', in: *Desarrollo y Sociedad,* No. 1, CEDE UNIANDES, Bogotá, 1979.

24. _____. 'La Mujer y la Familia en la economía Colombiana', in: *Foros interdisciplinarios, Sexualidad, Familia y Economía,* CEDE UNIANDES, Bogotá, 1982.

25. Rey de Marulanda, Nohra. *La Mujer jefe de Hogar.* Document CEDE No. 068. Mimeo., Bogotá, 1982.

26. _____. 'La unidad producción reproducción en las mujeres del sector urbano en Colombia', in: *La realidad Colombiana, Debates sobre la Mujer en América Latina y el Caribe,* Vol. I, Editora Magdalena León, ACEP, Bogotá, 1982.

27. Rico de Alonso, Ana. 'Características de la Oferta de Fuerza de Trabajo en Colombia, Bogotá, Medellín, Cali, Barranquilla. Conclusiones y Recomendaciones', in:*Transición Demográfica y Oferta de Fuerza de Trabajo en Colombia,* Vol. I. SENALDE, ILO and UNFPA, Bogotá, 1986.

28. Rico de Alonso, Ana. *La Feminización de la Pobreza en Colombia. Aproximación a un Diagnóstico y Recomendaciones para la Acción.* Fundación para la Educación Superior, FES Mimeo., Bogotá, 1987.

29. Schmink, Marianne. 'La Mujer en la economía urbana en América Latina', in: *Debate sobre la mujer en América Latina y el Caribe,* Vol. III, 'Sociedad, Subordinación y Feminismo'. Magdalena León Editora, Bogotá, 1982.

30. Segundo Encuentro O de investigadores sobre la microempresa, Cali, 1985. University of San Buenaventura, ICFES, Bogotá, 1987.

31. Servicio Nacional de Aprendizaje. *Proyecto de Planificación de Recursos Humanos,* SENA HOLANDA. 'Bases de conceptualización del "Sector Informal"', Bogotá, no date.

32. Suremain, Marie Dominique, Cardona, Lucy, Dalmazzo, Marisol. *Las Mujeres y la Crisis Urbana,* research supported by the National University of Medellín, CEBEMO and UNCHS-HABITAT, Bogotá, 1988.

33. Uribe, Echevarría and Forero, Edgar. *El sector informal en las ciudades intermedias,* CIDER-CEREC, Bogotá, 1986.

34. Vandelac, Louise, Belisle, Diane, Gauthier, Anne, Pinard, Yolande. *Du Travail et de l'amour,* Saint Martin, Montreal, Quebec, 1985.

Chapter V

Integrating women in development planning: the role of traditional wisdom

M. A. Singamma Sreenivasan Foundation

Planning for women

The Indian experience of planning for women from the 1950s to the late 1980s, closely mirrors the changing perceptions of policy-makers and administrators, on the location and role of women in development. The era of community development and decentralized planning passed by without any serious effort at stimulating the active participation of women in critical sectors in the economy. However, this period did see the emergence of many new features, such as the creation of a vast army of women extension workers at the village, block and district levels, an increasing emphasis on training rural women in skills relevant to their household and motherhood roles, e.g. nutrition, health care, food processing, storage, kitchen gardening, sewing, knitting, tailoring etc., and a rising awareness of the yawning gaps in literacy, both in absolute terms as well as in terms of gender differentials in education. This approach was severely limited however by the very widely prevalent view of woman as essentially a maintainer, a nurturer of the household, whose economic contribution, if perceived at all, was a supplementary one.

The Green Revolution years also passed by with no more than a marginal heightening of interest in women's contribution to agriculture — confined to teaching women modern methods of storing, conserving and saving. Agricultural universities set up in various parts of India disseminated knowledge of different agricultural technologies — a large number of these universities catered to women students almost exclusively through domestic science. Most women students either turned to teaching or laboratory research after graduation. An infinitely small number opted for field placements in extension. While the preoccupation of the programme formulators and implementers was on raising incomes through viable economic activities and creation of durable economic assets, the prevalent attitudes and perceptions of women's economic and social 'roles' in the household severely restricted and handicapped efforts to include women in these programmes in a meaningful way. Since simultaneously quantitative targets for men and women were programmed, this led to a crisis situation where a few activities relevant to women such as embroidery, knitting, tailoring, etc. began to be monopolized by the beneficiaries of these programmes.

The International Decade for Women was preceded by the publication of a major survey on women by the Committee on the Status of Women in India entitled, appropriately, 'Towards Equality'. The most important contributions of these two events were the results of research investigations into the condition, characteristics and concerns of women. The volume, scope and methodology of the research undertaken not only widened the knowledge base for planners and implementors and identified macro and micro issues and their linkages for organization and action by women themselves, but challenged the very principles and concepts of social science theory. Research on working women redefined the concept of gainful activity, identifying sub-occupational tasks and ensuring that they enter the NOC (National Occupational Classification), opening the door of the household and listing the characteristics (especially economic) of individual members, etc. This paid off directly by influencing policy, the statistical system and, thereby, programmes. It identified not only the hitherto invisible women workers through refining work/economic activity and using the methodology of time allocation studies, but also the characteristics of their employment and unemployment. As a result, the Planning Commission of India issued a directive in the 1980s that all data gathered for the evaluation and monitoring of anti-poverty programmes should be disaggregated by gender. A technical panel has been set up for this purpose.

The International Decade for Women also succeeded in bringing about a perceptible increase of new women's organizations at the grassroots level. The growth of these autonomous women's groups is predicated by occupational work clusters or common occupational/work distribution. Economic activities have been seen to be the most effective entry point for organization.

About this time, the hitherto unquestioned acceptance of the beneficial impact of planned development on women began to give way to a more critical questioning of development models, theories of growth etc. The large quantities of data and information thrown up during the decade showed considerable displacement of women workers through new technologies, including Green Revolution technologies. Women's occupational patterns were affected by macropolicies and movements, especially in traditional strongholds of women's work such as textiles. Changes in land ownership and population led to migration, both seasonal and permanent, from the countryside. It also led to a rise in the number of women looking for work on public sites under the various employment guarantee programmes. The emphasis on women's productive role as an economic contributor in her own right, led to a new perception of her reproductive role and the need to both functions. Services such as child care, fuel, fodder, water, sanitation etc., were seen as crucial inputs to ensure this meshing. These services and inputs began to be viewed as basic or minimum needs for women.

The Sixth Five Year Plan document of the Government of India for the first time devoted a whole chapter to women's development. It spoke of the need to inspire women with self-confidence and to increase their managerial and supervisory skills. The Seventh Plan document had a similar chapter, while the end of the Women's Decade saw the setting up of a Department exclusively for the development of women and children by the Government of India. The Department was appropriately placed under the Ministry of Human Resources Development.

Operational issues

Looking back over the past three decades from the vantage point of the late 1980s and the challenges of the present-day situation of women, the crucial issues seem to revolve around making policies and programmes more gender-aware. In India, women workers are predominantly found in the unorganized or informal sector (89 per cent). The unorganized sector is characterized by lack of supportive labour legislation in the matter of wages, maternity benefits, child care, illness compensation etc. It is also characterized by long hours of work at comparatively unskilled levels and unremunerative wages. Women workers in the unorganized sector are mainly found in the following eight sectors: agriculture and allied occupations, dairying, small animal husbandry, fisheries, sericulture, handicrafts, handlooms, khadi and village industries.

These sectors are looked after by large departmental agencies with an extensive field infrastructure, R&D facilities and infrastructure. However, as a historical consequence of the perceptions of women's work, these agencies are not geared to serve the production roles of women by either enhancing their capabilities or bringing large numbers of women workers into the workplace. The integration of women in mainstream sectors, therefore, has to take into account the following parameters:

1. The nature of women's work in the above eight sectors is very different from that of men workers. Women's work is discontinuous, sporadic and does not correspond to the normal peak periods of labour demand and supply which are formulated on the basis of male labour.

Women, for example, have far less access to agricultural labour than men (50–120 days per year on average, as against 150–200 days per year for men).

2. Since women workers in the unorganized sector are more akin to self-employed workers, they have no contract or terms of appointment from employers and they tend to be isolated. Therefore, the priority programme is to group them into homogeneous producer groups such as co-operatives, trade unions, societies, associations and so on.

3. The existing Government programmes in these eight sectors are mainly focused on men, through women supply the major labour input in many activities. The meshing of women's programmes in these sectors cannot therefore be done without keeping the total sectoral context in view.

4. Women are at their weakest in managerial and supervisory skills. Traditionally, they supply the labour input but the decisions are taken by the men. For building up managerial and supervisory skills, women need the space and the time to be alone together so that they can build up self-confidence. This, however, does not mean a regression to the 'women only' programmes of previous years where the total sectoral context was not kept in view. The operational challenge here is to build up cadres and groups of women producers within the overall work sector. This would involve greater emphasis being placed on training and reorientation in the extension and research fields as well as at middle and higher policy-making levels. It is important to ensure that women are not seen as an isolated group of workers in any of these sectors and that 'special programmes' are not prepared for them at lower levels of skill, information, training research, etc., than those available to men.

5. The above shows that greater attention needs to be focused on designing sectoral programmes for women in the eight areas outlined. Gender analysis appears to be a useful tool in this context and could be of immense use to planners, policy-makers as well as to practitioners and implementors. The basic ingredient in gender analysis is a quantification of the differential roles of men and women in productive activities in any sector as well as the differential impacts of a development programme on men and women in the catchment area. This methodology could be usefully applied before preparing major investments in any of the eight sectors. At present, what appears to be happening is that investment decisions in these sectors are taken without assessing their impact on women or quantifying these contributions.

The operational problems of integrating women into existing programmes are:

• Should all-women co-operative societies be started at the village level?

• Should women's membership in the existing, predominantly male societies, be increased?

- How is one to ensure, through elections, that women in adequate number are represented in the district unions?
- How is one to ensure that male societies are not being duplicated by forming all-women societies in the villages?
- How is one to ensure that the process does not lead to mere co-option of women in large numbers without corresponding involvement in the process of decision-making?
- How is one to ensure that large numbers of women get involved in extension services, e.g. in the dairying sector, while at the same time ensuring that they form a cohesive part of the total field machinery in the district?

Other operational problems are even more difficult to define and tackle, Thus, while it is universally accepted that women field workers are needed to bring home the fruits of technology to the women producers of the villages, there remains a lurking apprehension that an all-female field extension cadre may create problems of lack of upward mobility, placement, co-ordination with male staff etc., which may interfere with efficiency. These problems have already arisen in field situations where pilot programmes of integrating women in dairying have been tried out. Leaving women's co-operative societies to women extension workers only appears to be a sound initiative. The male extension machinery, on the other hand, is not fully convinced of this. A great deal of healthy intro-spection within co-operative federations and their constituent units appears to be called for.

The problems of dealing with large numbers of women inevitably arises when government initiates programmes on an area basis. Voluntary organizations deal with a micro-situation consisting of, say one to five villages at a time. The need to learn from the micro-situations for the purpose of area planning has to be operationalized in terms of more frequent feedbacks and interactions between government and non-government agencies dealing with women in the same sector. Most important, given the basic illiteracy and cultural shyness of women, large-scale government programmes should take care that women's co-operative societies are not reduced to men operating through women, and managing the affairs of the society. Co-operative education for women has to precede the setting up of formal organizations. In India, these problems are further compounded by class and caste divisions within the village.

The need to mesh women's productive and reproductive roles has already been referred to. The added responsibilities falling on women members of the co-operative societies have to be balanced with mechanisms to successfully manage their workload at home. Earlier references to child care, fuel, fodder and water, etc. as basic needs must be translated from policy concepts to operational strategies. One possibility is to use the co-operative society as the focus for these basic needs programmes. This would require a major policy shift at the highest national level. There should, however, be a willingness to look at the co-operative society not merely as a collection and dissemination centre for knowledge about certain kinds of economic activity, but also a vibrant focal point in the village which could evolve into an organization and take on responsibilities for other inputs as well.

Tradition and education

If one accepts the argument that the planning will improve through the inclusion of existing survival strategies as practised by women then it would be useful to evolve a loose format or guideline to help development and policy-makers (International Conference on Checklist and Guidelines, Helsinki 1986). At Helsinki, during the workshop convened jointly by INSTRAW, FAO and the Institute of Development Studies, it was recognized that pre-project surveys usually determine the nature of the project and further influence not only the size of involvement but choice of technology as well as the monitoring and evaluation module of indices.

Information on the value and applicability of traditional wisdoms is a critical input in pre-project field surveys. If sufficient record of documented experiences can be made available and if it is found to be enhancing effective utilization of development benefits and programmes, it would be appropriate to redesign the curricula of education and training at all levels from primary school through universities and technical institutions to include this kind of knowledge. Several promising starts have already been made. At the Round Table on Survival Strategies of the Poor and Traditional Wisdom held during May 1987, an agenda of action was determined by the group which included Nobel Prize Winners, political leaders, diplomats and grass-root organizers. It was suggested that traditional knowledge be collected in book-form. In November of the same year, forty-two women from twenty-one countries came together at Mount Holyoke College for a three-day conference on 'Worldwide Education of Women'. The conference raised a broad range of issues about the nature and purpose of women's education. There was general agreement that development as it has been designed and practised in the Third World has been a disaster for the poorest people and for women, and that information and ideas which are important to the survival of these people are not considered in development plans. The fact is that violence against women is commonplace and often the cause of teenage pregnancy. Women's education does not address this problem, nor the fact that there is a connection between violence against women, ignorance about women, and violence against the earth and its resources.

One of our primary concerns was the issue of redesigning curriculum to include awareness of tradition, cultural history and women as gleaned from oral sources. This was recognized as one of the more important needs of those engaged in development education. Mount Holyoke College proposes to undertake an integrated, a five-year programme of curriculum development, research, apprenticeship, conference and material exchange that will have a significant impact on undergraduate education and the nature of scholarship about women while contributing to the formal and informal educational development of women from around the world. It will be entitled 'Reconstructing Women's Education from Grass Roots Knowledge'. Our approach is unique at several levels:

1. It values traditional systems of knowledge as repositories of information that enable societies to live in harmony with nature;

2. It recognizes that such traditional knowledge is now primarily the preserve of women in Third World countries since men are increasingly living and working in cities outside their local environment;

3. It directly addresses the conflict between dominant modes of knowledge (that marginalize women, their traditional knowledge and their contribution to life and labour) and indigenous, local knowledge systems and cosmologies which encode sustainable forms of livelihood;

4. It responds to the pressing need of women involved in educational, labour, conservation, peace and other organizations from around the world to learn from each other's experiences and to develop alternative modes of economic growth and livelihood;

5. It acknowledges the value of including traditional systems of knowledge in Western formal education so that future generations of leaders in the developed world have a better understanding of the needs of women, appreciate their values and practices, and design programmes that do not marginalize women and destroy the environmental base in the Third World.

Successful traditional survival strategies in India

In what follows, we have selected three traditional survival strategies particular to women — traditional savings and thrift practices; menstruation, pre- and post-natal practices; women's informal social networks — and two survival strategies which pertain to India rural society as a whole, namely, rural markets and traditional agricultural practices. The thrust of our argument is to show the appropriateness of these practices in rural India and that rather than sweeping them away in an excess of modernization, they should be built on and used intelligently in the work of development.

Traditional savings and thrift practices

In traditional societies savings were of the informal kind, such as hoarding money or buying gold, jewellery and other valuables; holdings of livestock or stores of commodities like grain; rotating savings groups in which each member deposits a small amount of money regularly into a central fund, the whole of which is given to each member in turn, perhaps by drawing lots. In such societies, individuals or families were seemingly content with having procured their basic requirements of water, agricultural, forest produce, firewood and fodder for a given day. They did not have to worry about the next day's needs, since these could be obtained in exchange for some other goods of corresponding value. On the other hand, in today's context, especially in the Third World where tribal and rural communities lead a hand-to-mouth existence, it is certainly no exaggeration to state that formal savings are practically non-existent.

Therefore, if a rural household wants or needs to make expenditures which are, within any period of time, larger than its income for the same period, then it will need either to draw upon its savings or to make use of credit. Informal credit sources available include owners of capital assets, relatives and friends, shopkeepers or other suppliers, produce buyers, moneylenders, landlords and other wealthy individuals. The intervention of formal credit institutions in recent times has somewhat reduced the importance of informal credit institutions but the latter, nevertheless, still play an influential role in advancing credit. Beside, they have contributed to a steady increase in rural cash savings as well.

The women in the primary fishing village communities around Cuddalore in South Arcot District of Tamil Nadu have followed a variety of traditional thrift practices which are continued to this day. The rationale of these practices can be best understood when one views them in the context of the existing patriarchal society in which men were the main breadwinners. The women were expected to manage the household within limited earnings and hence any amount saved secretly in cash or in kind assumed particular significance.

One practice which is common in many households is what is called in Tamil the 'padi arisi' (a handful of rice). Each day, before cooking, women take out a handful of uncooked rice from the amount kept aside for the days meal and put it into a separate pot. This accumulated rice is then used when stocks of rice are depleted, or the money thus saved was used to meet emergency medical or other expenses or used to buy material for a blouse or a trinket. These savings were also an important source of the dowry many families paid for their daughters marriages. Others succeed in saving for their children's (especially their son's) education.

Other traditional savings practices such as the *hundi* and the rotating savings group could also be cited but one basic lacuna of informal credit is that the turnover is small, which means that it can be used only for decentralized micro-level initiatives. Yet, despite several disadvantages in terms of high interest rates charged and dangers of exploitation, the continued use of informal credit mechanisms is proof of their usefulness. Their main advantage is accessibility. By contrast with formal credit schemes, informal borrowing requires neither literacy nor costly and time-consuming journeys away from the villages nor adherence to specific office opening hours. Transactions are mostly carried out with familiar faces in familiar surroundings.

In addition to these general advantages of simplicity and convenience, informal borrowing has the specific advantage of not requiring formal security, rather it is based on the lender's understanding of specific borrowers needs and their likely ability to repay. Loans can be monitored in the normal course of village life. In practice, informal credit plays a crucial role for those who cannot otherwise obtain formal credit and allows women to retain their self-respect and participate in development.

It is important to note that a formal credit scheme may not be necessary if existing mechanisms were used or adapted. Also, care should be taken to see that a formal credit scheme should not disrupt existing community practices. Rather, both could co-exist harmoniously. Instead, indigenous systems of saving can sometimes be adapted to meet needs other than those for which they were originally devised. Where no such mechanisms exist or where schemes are not readily adaptable, it may be appropriate to encourage the formation of a locally-based savings and credit society affiliated to a wider network of credit unions. In this context, the Self Employed Women's Association (SEWA) under the leadership of Ms. Ela Bhatt in Ahmedabad has proved a great source of inspiration to many women's groups in India and elsewhere.

In a changing social environment, the traditional thrift and savings systems have a vital role to play in knitting together and preserving human relationships. At the same time, modern credit systems have helped to create self-reliance and leadership initiatives among women. On the other hand, with monetization, many modern chit systems have led to bitter quarrels and estranged human relationships. However, it is evident from the survey that credit intervention has led to the breakdown of existing caste and class barriers and to a far greater degree of intermingling than even before.

Menstruation, pre- and post-natal practices

Menstruation practices are often elaborate with seemingly no *raison d'être* except that they have been observed for generations. However, certain dietary and bathing rituals during the period appear meaningful when viewed in a rural context where a bath a day is considered a luxury and two square meals is the most a villager can hope for. Thus traditions and customs have to intervene in order to ensure that the menstruating girl maintains a certain standard of hygiene and is not denied the essential dietary intake.

Traditional pre-natal practices have fewer rituals attached to them but have sought to ensure an adequate diet for the expectant mother. Delivery practices differ widely and sometimes include negative aspects such as the traditional bias in favour of male children and a lack of attention to dirt and infection. Despite these dangers, it is important not to attempt to suppress abruptly traditional practices as most mothers in India still give birth within their own homes and villages. Better to support and train the traditional *dai* (midwife) to be a maternal health informant for the local community and to act as a more capable instrument for mother and child, especially during childbirth.

Women's informal social networks

A *sine qua non* for development everywhere is a vast improvement in the condition of women. Throughout the developing world, they are the group most prone to poverty, discrimination and illiteracy — a fate reinforced by the extensive gender separation characteristic of many traditional rural societies. Yet strong, if informal, women's networks exist, whether in the spheres of collective work, cultural roles or leisure activities. The division of labour in traditional society has ensured that women frequently work in groups together. Traditional culture normally leaves women their own space for expression and they retain a privileged role where community and folk traditions are concerned. Again, leisure activities, where they do exist, are traditionally gender-based. Examples of such interaction among Indian rural women abound, e.g. in the Malnad area, most agricultural activities are done on a community basis. therefore, women from a given village generally walk to the next village and collect the other women and this group then moves on to third and so on, before finally reaching the work place. At the end of the day the reverse process occurs. The quality and quantity of interactions that take place here is beyond one's imagination. Women from different castes are involved here again. The same hold good for fuel and water collection.

Women's informal networks are therefore very extensive and closely knit in rural societies. Though education for girls, provided by the State, is evidently a goal for all developing societies, the difficulties involved ensure that education for adult women must likewise increase. In this task existing informal networks should not be ignored and can be used to communicate essential survival information and support basic literacy programmes.

The rural market

Markets known as *haats* or *shandies* are to be found throughout southern India. These are markets held either weekly or monthly or during festivals. They usually occupy an established place on the pavement or in a square or on the street. Although mostly general, they are occasionally specific to a commodity such as cattle or wool. These markets are popular because their prices are often lower than in built-up markets. This is possible because of low overheads in terms of building space and also because the producers themselves are often the traders. Most of those who sell in these markets have other occupations and therefore the income on 'market day' is supplementary income.

It ought to be stressed at this juncture that many rural women have resisted programme and policy attacks on the rural markets. They see the built-up market not only as a threat to their daily bread but also as a replacement of their place in the 'job market' by men. Thus it is resisted by them both on grounds of class and gender.

Negative 'formal' hierarchical aspects of traditional markets do, of course, exist. They are not as innocent as they look. Vendors are often 'held' by larger suppliers, moneylenders and so on. But in spite of the prevalence of these shortcomings, they offer a larger space for the population to make a living.

The Hosur *shandy* held on Wednesdays draws an average of 10,000 customers from about 10 neighbouring villages. The *shandy* is held on government land spanning an area of 4.5 acres. The *shandy* plot is auctioned every year to bidders who then recover the money by charging a levy on all those who wish to operate within it. The range of products at the *shandy* caters to the villager's every need.

Fortunately, poor women especially those with no land holdings or other definite means of livelihood seem to have done well in the modern *shandies*. *Shandy* day implies a shade more money than other days. For some women, it is the *shandy* day that has to see them through the rest of the week. Others make a living by selling at four to five different shandies a week. One comes across also the occasional women who finds the *shandy* an ideal outlet for her home made products. Of a total of 117 women vendors at the Wednesday *shandy* at Hosur on 1 Feburary 1989, there were only eight women who were selling wares that they had prepared themselves. Some of the items they prepared were rather innovative but are yet to find favour with a wider market. For instance, Mirabai sells little balls made from a mixture of crushed onions, garlic, mustard, urud dal, curry leaves and oil. These are essential ingredients used in the seasoning of Indian curries. These pre-prepared balls could save the Indian housewife a great deal of time. Another young girl, hardly 20, deserted and with a 2-year-old baby makes beautiful pot holders from ropes. She also makes intricate designs on coloured ropes. This is used to tie up calves. She learnt the art as part of the family trade but at present is the only female exponent in her family. Another woman comes all the way from Bangalore to sell masala, curry, dhanaya and turmeric powder. She prepares these powders at the local mill. She also sells kumkum powder which is prepared by her uncle in Madras. She visits four shandies a week and prepares her powders on Mondays and Fridays. Vijaya makes wooden combs with her husband. They are easy to make even at the shandy itself. Her husband claimed that he is sure of earning Rs. 200 if he makes an initial investment of Rs. 100 on wood.

The *shandy* also helps to perpetuate individual arts and crafts. For example, the Kumbharas are traditional pot-makers. This art is now mechanized, leaving the Kumbharas frantically looking for other means of livelihood. Thus at the Hosur *shandy* we came across one woman selling pots made by members of her family. There were other women who sold pots but these were purchased from merchants. They sold pots rather than other items, because they belong to the Kumbhara community and hence were not permitted to dabble in other commodities.

Of the half a dozen people who sold bambooware, only one was a woman whose family trade it was. Her role was again confined to making only small items like fans and moroms (used in cleaning grains, cereals, etc.). Other women who had some role in producing the commodities they sold were vegetable sellers, but there were only three or so of them. Of these, two owned small holdings. The third woman, together with members of her family, have taken a lease on a plot of land for one season at a cost of Rs. 4000. None of the eight women mentioned was aware of any schemes nor have they availed of any loans (i.e. Governments, banks, etc.). A majority of the other women are vegetable vendors.

Some of the women sell the same item in shops in towns but on *shandy* day they either close shop or leave one of their family members in charge of it and settle down with their wares on some plot in the *shandy*. The volume of transaction on *shandy* day definitely compensates the lower prices at which they may have to sell (vegetables are 50 ps. to 1 Re. cheaper in the *shandy* than in the local market). Other women, who do not have any such established shops in town, conduct business only on *shandy* days and probably the day after that, if they are left with any unsold goods. They have no money to start with but local merchants lend them a certain amount either on a daily (*shandy* days) or on a weekly basis. This money has to be returned in the evening, once the day's transaction are over or when next she approaches the merchant to buy goods. They claim that the money they make (ranging from Rs. 35 per day) is a pittance but this is the maximum they will earn during the week.

Though the Tamil Nadu Government has set a minimum wage for labour (Rs. 12), they earn only Rs. 6–7 if they are hired by private contractors, whereas men's wages are much higher. This may be one of the reasons why the *shandy* attracts a number of women. Also, there are many women who are too old or weak for hard labour and the *shandy* is their only chance to make a few rupees. Most of these women sell at least at two *shandies* a week.

Applying marketplace experience to development projects: the challenge for DWCRA

The information gained during the course of various surveys of *shandies* and *haats* in Karnataka and Uttar Pradesh villages provide insights into the survival strategies adopted by poor women, faced with innumerable problems ranging from scarcity of working capital, dependence on traders and merchants who sell goods on their behalf, poor marketing outlets, discrimination in the labour wage market, replacement of traditional wares by modern substitutes, old age and consequent loss of energy and initiative, lack of storage space, processing facilities, raw material, equipment, transport, and information about existing support-schemes which could be used by them to get a better return from their work. In each case, the women cope with their problem at a suboptimal level. The scope of outside intervention, through development planning, should encompass micro-project levels, taking occupational clusters of production, trading and marketing as the schematic parameters.

The women who use the *shandies* and *haats* are, as we have seen, producers selling on their own account, traders selling on their own account and agents of traders, merchants, or middlemen selling on others' behalf. There are many promising possibilities of designing an interface between activities in the *haats* and *shandies* with programmes being implemented by Government development agencies for women in poor households, to the mutual benefit of both.

Development of Women and Children in Rural Area, or DWCRA as it is popularly known, is the largest national programme for poor women in the country. Aimed at women in poor households, with a focus on female-headed households, it is a sub-scheme of the Integrated Rural Development Programme, and seeks to form viable groups of women workers and support their economic activities with bank finance, subsidies, marketing support through working capital grants, backed with social inputs in child care. In the six to seven years of its existence, the programme has been able to form about 25,000 groups of women workers and finance a large number of them.

One of the biggest challenges facing DWCRA is the choice of economic activity, keeping commercial viability and local relevance or needs in view. The trade-off between centralized supervision and micro-planning is crucial in a geographically extensive programme. The produce or the activity chosen by the women has to have local relevance by way of existing or potential demand in the shape of a market. Owing to a variety of factors, not least a preoccupation with middle-class perceptions of what constitutes 'suitable' income-generating activities for women, the choices made by DWCRA functionaries have not satisfied the tests of commercial viability or local needs. The result has very often been that women have made products which do not sell locally. They also have been unable to link up with markets situated at a distance, where there might be a demand. Some of the products do not have any market at all, being the result of undoubtedly wrong choices.

A look at the activities undertaken by women in the traditional markets could easily suggest ideas for DWCRA groups. In fact, DWCRA programme design does include provision for a village survey as a pre-group formation activity. One such survey revealed that only 8 out of 117 women using the weekly traditional market are 'own account' producers, the rest being traders or agents of merchants or middlemen. The trend appears to be the gradual replacement of producers by traders and agents of middlemen. We also see that the latter are faced with problems of working capital and are exploited by middlemen. Thus, two problems have to be tackled simultaneously: a shrinking resource base that is decimating the producers; inadequacy of cheap and timely credit for marketing.

DWCRA finances the purchase of capital assets for production as well as working capital. Products sold in *shandies* such as food items, pot holders, condiments, pottery, bambooware etc., could either be made by the women or bought from the producers by the women, with DWCRA financing the capital goods and the working capital. Wherever the margins are higher and the risks lower, the women could buy from bulk producers, as for example, ready-made clothes, using the DWCRA revolving funds to finance the purchases. Successful retailing in the *shandies* by the women depends on cheap capital and availability of transport. For landless women, for instance, retail vending of vegetables could prove viable on the basis of cheap credit, along with other items such as dry fish, tobacco and betel leaves, toiletry articles, etc.

The DWCRA insistence that a group be the basic unit does not postulate a common activity being carried out by all members of the group — the cohesion and unity of the group is to be ensured by a process of training and consciousness-raising, and not necessarily by following a common activity. One survey shows a mixed pattern of visits to the *shandies* by the women — some once a week, some more often and a few daily. The existence of a coherent DWCRA group, with a sense of unity and self-identity, could help in reducing these visits, which involve a lot of hard physical labour by each woman.

Two traditional items, bamboo and pottery, are sold by women in the Hosur *shandy*. With the mechanization of pottery their livelihood is endangered. Similarly, though this is less clear, bamboo availability could also be decreasing. The DWCRA functionaries could keep a check on such declining sectors of activity and replace them with new activities. DWCRA is closely linked to a training programme termed TYRSEM — Training of Rural Youth for Self-Employment — which could be utilized for the diversification of skills.

The Uttar Pradesh survey shows a slightly different pattern of village fairs — instead of markets — taking place at different places throughout the year. The women, besides visiting these fairs to sell their products, also visit the villages with their wares. The terrain being hilly and inhospitable, with great distances between villages, the women find it very difficult to manage the hazardous journeys. In almost all the villages where the survey has been conducted the demand has been either for a shop to be set up in the village and/or for cheap transport arrangements, so that visits to local fairs could be facilitated. The IRDP (of which DWCRA is a sub-scheme) is entitled to grant infrastructure subvention up to of a certain percentage of the total project cost. They could be utilized for subsidizing transport and for setting up village shops to sell woollen products, ringaal items, grass mats, etc.

Depletion of raw materials such as wool, bamboo, grass and diminishing inputs such as fodder for milk cattle are major problems in the Uttar Pradesh villages. Women are able to cope with these ecological crises by walking further and further into the jungle or buying more expensive wool or by accepting lower yields of milk. The solution lies, however, in linking up with sources of bulk supply, e.g. the Khadi Village Industries Commission for wools. This linkage could be forged by DWCRA.

The lack of storage or working space, equipment, processing facilities etc. can be addressed either under the infrastructure provision of IRDP/DWCRA or by having a common production unit or facility centre. Where a common facility is needed, such as dyeing, carding, storage, working space, etc., it would be cost-effective to have a common facility centre. Since the activities of the Uttar Pradesh village groups are more homogeneous, the DWCRA has a provision for the construction of community development centres to be located at the district level.

The DWCRA revolving fund could help the women workers in Kausani and Gwaldam to make bulk purchase of wool from the Khadi Village Industries Commission as well as to make seasonal inventories of finished products. Rs. 10,000 is admissible as a revolving fund per group. If the amount should be too small, it could be used as a margin with banks in order to borrow a greater amount.

The lack of fodder in villages around Almora in Uttar Pradesh appears to restrict the scope of dairying by the hill women. However, information on the inputs available from major programmes of dairy development could improve the perspective. A special programme known as Operation Flood II operates as a national programme in all milk shed areas of the country. Linking the microsituation of these villages with Operation Flood II could help in upgrading the cattle stock, improving the feed situation (through feed concentrates) increasing fodder cultivation, and providing health care facilities at village level, including artificial insemination, etc. However, the economics of converting fresh milk into *khoya* has then to be evaluated against the returns obtained from the sale of fresh milk. Though Operation Flood II does not particularly encourage decentralized production of milk products at village level (the choices of products to be manufactured are generally made at district level) the difficulties of transport over rough terrain, especially in inclement weather, indicate that renewed importance be given to the traditional activity of *khoya* making and preparation of sweets with a long shed life.

With Operation Flood II's insistence on the formation of dairy co-operatives at village level, the lack of access of women to income through the sale of milk, khoya products, sweets, etc. would no longer remain a major constraint if a decision were taken to enrol women, and not men, as members of the co-operative society on the Operation Flood II/Anand model.

This, however, still does not solve the problems posed by the drudgery the women are subjected to in making *khoya*. Since fuel is perennially in short supply in the hills, the convergence of ecological interests with women's interests in this situation appear to warrant a programme for fuel-efficient stoves. This would reduce drudgery, health hazards from inhaling wood smoke from open stoves and reduce the rate of deforestation through saving fuel. A national programme on improved stoves is in operation in India.

Post-harvest technologies in agriculture and horticulture also constitute an important extension sector. Extension workers in the field are mostly male agricultural graduates. They, in turn, build up face to face contact with the farmers. It is predominantly the male farmer who is the target for extension messages, who absorbs the new knowledge and who gets trained in the Farmers' Training Centres.

Women in agricultural extension have traditionally been from the home science disciplines. Their entry into agricultural graduate courses is a comparatively recent development. Unfortunately, home science colleges and agricultural universities tend to lean heavily on non-indigenous knowledge. 'Modern' practices of food preservation, storage of grain, pest control, etc. constitute the conventional wisdom with which these young graduates arm themselves during their college days. Use of chemicals for rodent and pest control, use of chemical fertilisers and modern storage bins for food grains have all become part of this conventional wisdom.

There have, however, been several new approaches to programming for women in agriculture in India. Many states have experimented with extension programmes in agriculture, directly focused on women, where women having qualifications either in agriculture or home science are trained to work at village and block level as extension workers. The face to face interaction with women farmers is thus facilitated.

These local practices and models need to be documented so that their major advantages could be quantified, and improvements suggested. A more flexible approach by extension workers, both male and female, will considerably help in avoiding conflicts. To a certain extent, graduates in agricultural sciences and home economics will have to 'unlearn' and 'deschool' themselves, in order to convince themselves that local relevance can ensure functional value and viability, and that use of local materials can repel rodents and mice as effectively as chemical alternatives.

Feedback on these traditional models should be directed not only towards male and female extension workers, but also towards those charged with the designing of extension programmes as well as towards the academic circles responsible for designing the curricula in domestic science colleges and universities.

Traditional agriculture practice

Can traditional agriculture and its modern renewal, known as organic or natural farming, save the Indian farmer? If the first task of efficient farming is that of reducing the costs, it can do so by re-orienting farmers away from industrial inputs: by increasing the natural resource base, using organic manure, recycling agriculture waste, increasing common property resources through inter-cropping or companion cropping and by using indigenous methods of pest control to reduce the use of pesticide. A case study, the experience of a successful farmer, is presented to illustrate the cost efficiency of traditional agriculture.

Case study

'A farm should be a self-contained body, nothing should come from outside. If anything at all has to come, it should be a new seed or plant variety.' (Rudolf Steiner, pioneer of bio-dynamic farming)

N. Reddy, a farmer from Sorahunase Village, Bangalore District, practises organic farming on his 8 acres of irrigated land. After successfully trying his hand at various occupations, he returned to his farm at the age of 35 and started farming on his 1.5 acres of land, which was allotted to him as his share. He started by using chemical fertilizers and was possessed with the idea of producing more and more. In five years he became one of the successful farmers of Karnataka. He was able to produce 23 quintals of Ragi per acre, a record in Karnataka and still not broken. But Reddy increasingly realized that in spite of his high yields and recognition from Government and fertilizer companies, his income was only sufficient to buy chemical fertilizer, pesticide and fodder. Then accidently, he contacted a European who introduced him to organic farming.

Reddy started his 'experiments' in organic farming, initially reducing the quantum of fertilizer in a phased way. During the first year his returns went down to one-third of what he was able to produce earlier. The second year also there was not a substantial improvement. Reddy says that he even thought of giving up agriculture and returning to his old profession. Somehow, he decided to continue for one more year; that year, he was encouraged by an improvement in the yields and he continued the practice. At present he does not use fertilizer or pesticides.

Reddy practises optimum utilization of land, water and other natural resources on a sustainable basis, and re-cycles all agricultural wastes. Organic manure is a main emphasis of his farming, and he spreads as much agricultural waste as possible into the field. Though it takes time to decompose, the organic material increases the microbial activity of the soil and promotes soil and moisture conservation.

Reddy is critical of some of the practices of farmers who expose organic matter to the sun and wind, thus eroding its nutritional content. Similarly, he says, farmers unnecessarily plough their land five or six times. He advocates single and shallow ploughing across the slope, not along. Ploughing with the tractor makes the soil prone to heavy erosion and decreases its fertility. The fertility of soil and its maintenance and improvement over a period of time is the most important aspect of organic farming and Reddy rigourously follows this principle. Fukoaka (1984) distinguishes farming according to its impact on the soil. She argues that in the traditional method soil remains the same while in chemical farming it becomes depleted and lifeless over a short period of time, whereas in 'organic natural farming' fertility of the soil steadily improves.

In Reddy's farm one could observe a series of complex interrelationships, each reinforcing and sustaining one another. Reddy practises the three tier system in one portion of his farm — the purpose is maximum utilization of sunlight. He cultivates coconuts, bananas and creeper respectively in first, second and third tiers. The sustainability of any system is determined by its complexity and diversity. Reddy cultivates different food grains, vegetables, fruits, etc. (Ragi, groundnut, beans, coconuts, fodder crops, bananas, etc.). There is an intricate relationship between live-stock, silk worm, chicken (droppings) and the fish in the water tank. Chickens feed on ticks from cows, dropped grains etc., the residual eating of silkworms is fed to the cows, fish in the pond makes more fertile the soil in the pond which is transferred once a year to the field. To meet the fodder needs of his 10–12 livestock, he cultivates fodder crops along the bunds and also grows multi-purpose trees which supplement the fodder needs. He has even gradually changed the dietary habits of the livestock (for example habituated the livestock with a shift to bitter leaves etc.). Reddy's fertilizer needs are met from his farm itself. He takes care to rotate different crop combinations to enhance soil fertility and check pests. The nutrient flow in this farm is cyclical and soil is enriched and protected through various methods such as building of stable bunds, recycling of organic wastes, using organic manure that increase the microbial activity, protecting the soil from direct inflows of rain, sun or wind.

Damages incurred by farmers through pests in this part of India are enormous. Reddy practises a variety of methods of pest control, in particular, proper conservation and improvement of the soil; careful selection of seeds; crop rotation; growing natural pest repellants such as marigolds; spraying with natural pest repellants such as pulverized chilly or salt powders, cattle urine etc.; encouraging natural predators such as birds, frogs, snakes, ladybirds, spiders and praying mantis. While Reddy does not claim complete success for any of these methods, they do nevertheless work and are worth comparing with chemical means of pest control in terms of energy inputs, soil depletion and the like.

Conclusion

Rural women have a considerable knowledge of their own capacity for critical analysis of new information. However, the dominant ideology of the élite and the powerful has submerged and devalued this traditional knowledge, even in the eyes of women themselves. Consequently, women have tended to consider their own knowledge as worthless and themselves as ignorant. For example, the knowledge of herbal medicine among tribal women was viewed as mumbo-jumbo or at best as second-class medicine. If empowerment of women is a national goal, then validating and legitimizing women's own traditional knowledge and skills is vital. The immediate need is dissemination of women's knowledge for their own empowerment.

Much of women's folk wisdom survives in the oral tradition and remains uncollected and uncodified. Attempts to collect and understand popular knowledge will sensitize all concerned, including women themselves, to the value and legitimacy of this knowledge. This could be done at two levels: research and mass media.

Given the fact that research generates the social data and insights on which planning is based, it assumes great relevance in the context of women. Yet a considerable part of today's research is based on wrong assumptions about women and on incorrect priorities. Consequently many plans and programmes targetted at women continue to miss the mark. In order to correct this trend and generate more meaningful and relevant plans, policies and programmes for women, some fresh approaches for research need to be taken. Fundamentally, this means a more two-way approach, learning to listen to women, valuing and understanding the considerable knowledge they already have, and making research and information more participatory. Thus women's traditional knowledge should be collected, codified and ecologically integrated into women's development programmes.

Dissemination of information could be carried out by organizing workshops, exhibitions, *melas,* folk theatre etc., through which women's popular knowledge might be validated and reflected back to them. These fora should also be used for women to discuss and express their own perceptions of and priorities for development.

The process of looking anew with respect at their own knowledge would also enable women to look more critically at other knowledge and information rather than automatically accept them as superior, more scientific or more modern. In this way, they would begin questioning the planning process and gradually make themselves heard.

SELECT BIBLIOGRAPHY

1. Alvers, Claude. Subsistence vs Development. Evangelsche Akadamic bad boll. Materialien.
2. Balasubramanian, A.V., and Radhika, 1989. Local Health Introduction, *ISPSS Monograph,* No. 1, Madras.
3. Christensen, Cycle, and Litvinoff, Miles (eds.). The Greening of Aid-Sustainable Livelihood in Practice.
4. Dankelman, Irene, and Davidson, Joan. Women and Environment in the Third World.
5. Devereux, Stephen, Pares, Henry, and Best, John. 1987. A Manual of Credit and Saving for the Poor of Developing Countries. *Development Guideline* No. 1 and OXFAM, United States.
6. Dharmapal. 1971. Science and Technology in the 18th Century.
7. Data on discussion on traditional tank irrigation indebted to Somesekhara Reddy.
8. Foods and Food Production Encyclopaedia.
9. Fukuoka, Masenobu. 1984. One Straw Revolutions: An Introduction to Natural Farming. Friends Rural Centre, Rasulia.
10. Gopalan, C., Rama Sastri, B.V., and Balasubramanian, S.C. 1986. Nutritive Value of Indian Foods. NIN Publication.
11. Greenwald, Douglass (ed.). Encyclopedia of Economics.
12. Jain, L.C. 1988. Violence of Green Revolution.
13. Korschi, Johanness. 1989. Eco-Farming in Agricultural Development.
14. McNeely, Jeffrey, and Pitt, David (eds.). Culture and Conservation: The Human Dimension in Environment Planning.
15. Nadkarni, M.V. 1985. Socio-Economic Conditions of Drought Prone Areas Concept. Delhi.
16. Nadkarni, M.V. 1988. The Crisis of Increasing Cost in Agriculture: Is there a way out? *Econ. and Pol. Weekly,* 23–24 Sept. 1988.
17. Sacred Plants. Karnataka Forest Department publication.

18. Stoll, Gaby. 1986. Natural Crop Protection in the Tropics. Scientific Publisher. F.R. Germany.
19. Swaminathan, M., and Bhagawann, K.K. 1966. Our Food. Ganesh & Co Pvt Ltd. Madras.
20. Swaminathan, M. 1985. Essentials of Foods and Nutrition: Ed 2. Vol. I. Bangalore Printing and Publishing, Bangalore.
21. Theodore De Bary, N.M. 1972. Source of Indian Tradition. Motilal Banarsids, New Delhi.
22. Vatsyayan, Kapila. Ecology and Indian Myth.
23. Vandanashiva. 1989. Violence of Green Revolution.
24. Vijayai Pillai. 1982. Where There Is No doctor: A Village Health Care Handbook. The Hesperian Foundation, USA.
25. Women and Economic Development: Local, Regional and National Planning Strategies. Berg/UNESCO publication.
26. Women in Food Processing Industry. A Survey in Gujarat. Industrial Development Bank of India publication.
27. Women and the Food Cycle — UNDP Publication.